THE
PSYCHODYNAMICS
OF
ORGANIZATIONS

In the series Labor and Social Change,
edited by Paula Rayman and Carmen Sirianni

EDITED BY

Larry Hirschhorn and Carole K. Barnett

Temple University Press

Philadelphia

THE
PSYCHODYNAMICS
OF
ORGANIZATIONS

Temple University Press, Philadelphia 19122
Copyright © 1993 by Temple University. All rights reserved
Published 1993
Printed in the United States of America

The paper used in this publication meets the minimum requirements of American
National Standard for Information Sciences—Permanence of Paper for Printed Library
Materials, ANSI Z39.48-1984
Library of Congress Cataloging-in-Publication Data
The Psychodynamics of organizations / edited by Larry Hirschhorn and
   Carole K. Barnett.
      p.   cm. — (Labor and social change)
   Includes bibliographical references and index.
   ISBN 1-56639-020-6 (cloth : alk. paper). — ISBN 1-56639-021-4
(pbk. : alk. paper)
   1. Psychology, Industrial.   2. Industrial sociology.
3. Organizational behavior.   I. Hirschhorn, Larry.   II. Barnett,
Carole K.   III. Series
HF5548.8.P755   1993
158.7—dc20   92-21061

To the next generation
of organizational inhabitants,
our children:

Aaron and Daniel
Elizabeth and Andrew

CONTENTS

PART III: CULTURE, POLITICS, AND RACE:
ORGANIZATIONAL PSYCHODYNAMICS IN CONTEXT

x

ACKNOWLEDGMENTS

A work of this kind can be accomplished only by the collaboration of many creative individuals past and present. It has grown out of our earlier efforts to produce a special issue of *Human Resource Management* on organizational psychodynamics during 1988–89. Noel Tichy, in his role as editor of the journal at that time, deserves thanks for his faith in the importance of scholarly work that links organization theory and management practice to psychoanalytic and psychodynamic thinking. With his encouragement, the articles that appeared in the summer 1989 issue of *HRM* became the foundation and inspiration for this book.

The members of the International Society for the Psychoanalytic Study of Organizations provided an important forum for the authors represented in this volume. The society, approaching its tenth anniversary, has grown to include scholars and practitioners from the United States, Europe, and Israel. Under the chairmanship of Donald Levine and later Michael Diamond, it has offered an exciting venue for the development of a psychoanalytically based understanding of work and organizations.

Several of its members provided us with particular help and guidance. Howard Schwartz has been unfailing in his commitment and creativity, and Laurence Gould has been generous with his time, support, and leadership.

Barbara Feinberg has, as she always does, provided us with extraordinary editorial assistance.

We also wish to thank Larry Hirschhorn's colleagues at the Center for Applied Research and are particularly grateful to its president, Vinnie

Carroll, who has been most generous with his time and his encouragement. In addition, we wish to thank our clients, who provided us with opportunities to help them and have in turn helped us bridge the worlds of research and practice.

Finally, our deepest thanks must go to the first generation of scholars and practitioners at both the Tavistock Institute in London and here in the United States who established the core ideas and pragmatics of a psychoanalytically oriented theory of organizational functioning and a consultation practice based on this framework. Wilfred Bion, Harold Bridger, Harry Levinson, Eric Miller, A. Kenneth Rice, Eric Trist, and Abraham Zaleznik built the conceptual and practical world that the second generation now inherits and hopes to develop. There are signs that a psychoanalytic approach to organizations is indeed taking root. The growth of the International Society for the Psychoanalytic Study of Organizations, the establishment of the training program in psychoanalytic consulting at the William Alanson White Institute in New York, and the growing links between the A. K. Rice Institutes and the International Society point to an increasingly vigorous research and practice enterprise. We are hopeful and excited about these developments.

INTRODUCTION

Imagine the following.

Believing that his company needs technical breakthroughs to beat its competitors, a charismatic president of an engineering company builds a powerful coalition of engineers and scientists to launch a new technologies program. But as he focuses increasingly on these new technologies, he becomes enthralled by their power and soon ignores prices, costs, and customer needs. Marketing managers complain and grumble, but he and the engineers and scientists dismiss them as technical neophytes unable to appreciate the technology's potential. After several years the company's technical breakthroughs still cannot be built into salable products and the company almost goes bankrupt. The board replaces the president, and a new coalition based in marketing and sales emerges with a program to reposition the company.

What happened here? As Steven Feldman shows in his compelling case study in Chapter 6, a leader can idealize technology as an extension of his own narcissism, his own reach for perfection, and may consequently lose touch with marketplace realities. Building a coalition that draws on the power bases of the engineers and the scientists, the company president has succumbed to the irrational process of idealizing himself, the company, and its technology. While ostensibly pursuing his interests, he has defeated himself.

How does this happen: why does this happen? How does social irrationality take hold of an organization's process? How do individual fantasies shape group life? How does a leader's character mold a company's culture?

How does an organization's concrete tasks impress its members' unconscious life? The fifteen essays in this book show how the psychoanalysis of organizations can help answer these questions. This introduction highlights its key assumptions and methodologies, its history, its emerging status, and its prospects for the future.

The Irrational Domain

Psychoanalysis is one of several approaches that provides us with insights into the essentially irrational character of organizational life. To be sure, scholars have long sought alternatives to the conception of the organization as a rational enterprise. Thus, for example, some political scientists have argued that the organization is best seen as a political entity in which coalitions struggle for the control of resources and jockey for power. Division heads fight the corporate center for control over their budgets; scientists don't want line managers to oversee their work; and the controller ferrets out expenditures hidden in vague line items in a division's budget. Similarly, sociologists have focused on ideologies, informal structures, and co-optation as mechanisms that deal in irregular ways with unmet needs to shape an organization's processes. Workers exert influence to have their friends and relatives hired and then informally supervise their performances; different ethnic groups monopolize different jobs in a factory; and a work group penalizes members who work too zealously. A wide variety of approaches that guide investigation of organizational life have openly and strongly challenged the assumption that organizations behave as rational systems.

The psychoanalytic perspective adds depth to these and other perspectives in two ways. As our brief example of the engineering company president suggests, it highlights how unconscious processes contribute to social irrationality. A leader idealizes his company's engineers and scientists, they are gratified by the status he confers on them, and then they all devalue and scapegoat the marketing managers. The resulting process is both irrational and unconscious: people engage in self-defeating activity and are unaware of the character of their motives. In such situations, people are driven by unconscious fantasies, not by rational calculations or political interest. In other words, unacknowledged fantasies and wishes shape behavior.

While explicating the irrational, psychoanalysis also highlights its links to the rational domain. Building on the concept of an organization's "primary task"—the task an organization must accomplish to survive—it traces how the gravity of this task itself may lead people and groups to act irrationally. Thus, in the example above, we might hypothesize that the president, feeling anxious in the face of tenacious competitors, invented a comforting fantasy that he and his engineers could create beautiful and unassailable products. This illusion helped him deny that his competitors were indeed formidable, and so he ignored their encroachment. *Psychoanalysis thus highlights the links between the rational, the political, and the irrational.* By integrating these domains of experience, psychoanalysis provides a comprehensive explanation of organizational life.

Methodologies

The psychoanalysis of organizations as an academic and clinical discipline is based on both qualitative research methods and consulting encounters. Social scientists grounded in the positivist tradition of research try to isolate a cause and its effect while controlling for extraneous factors. By contrast, researchers in organizational psychoanalysis use methods closer to the canons of historical research. A proposition linking a cause to an effect gains credibility and plausibility only when it is tied to a broader *story* of events. Such a story links causes, effects, observed actions, and unexpressed feelings in a psychologically coherent *narrative*. To be sure, other traditions of qualitative research also use case studies and stories to illuminate the causal texture of an event or situation. But while relying on narratives, the psychoanalysis of organizations highlights in particular the frequently paradoxical quality of group life. It shows how and why in the realm of human affairs we often choose what we (consciously) hoped to avoid, or accomplish what we could not or did not expect. It takes the concept of "contradiction" for granted. For example, consider the following. A manager who believes that he empowers line workers berates his factory team for coming to him for help. "I want you to solve this on your own," he commands them, but then finds that the more he pushes them to be independent the less competent they become. Why does this happen? The manager, berating his subordinates for being dependent, may be afraid of the consequences of being authentically aggressive. He uses empowerment unconsciously as a cover for pushing people away to protect both them and himself from his own aggression. Sensing his anger and anxiety, his followers feel less empowered and, paradoxically, come back to him for guidance and reassurance. He is defeated. This is a story of contradiction and paradox, in which cause and effect are linked obliquely by the manager's personal narrative. His conscious wish to empower makes others feel vulnerable; his unconscious attempt to avoid feeling angry makes him feel angrier.

When practiced as a clinical discipline as a form of organizational consulting, the psychoanalysis of organizations uses interpretation as the vehicle for learning and dialogue and as the medium for clarifying the paradoxes of group life. For example, consider the following. A charismatic leader with great powers of imagination launches a product that fails dismally in the marketplace. The postmortem suggests that his direct reports, eager to please him, could not think critically about his ideas and plans. But why did they have to protect their boss in this way? This manager wants to know why his people didn't tell him what they are really thinking. We offer an interpretation. "People want to please you. Perhaps you evoke that in them. If that is the case, how might this be happening, why might it be happening?" The interpretation is a vehicle for putting the manager back into *his* story, for making him less the object of his unacknowledged fantasies and more the subject of his actions and conscious intentions. If our interpretation "feels" right, it stimulates a process of learning and reflection, so that the manager clarifies not only one experience but a set of experiences. Through the consulting process the executive expands his own story so that the puzzles of his experience that he has hidden from his own view are now clarified.

History

The history of the application of psychoanalysis to organizations has yet to be written. Scholars and practitioners who worked at the Tavistock Institute in London from World War II until the mid-1960s, such as Wilfred Bion, Eric Trist, Harold Bridger, Elliot Jaques, A. Kenneth Rice, and Eric Miller, were the great pioneers. Drawing on the work of Melanie Klein, they showed how people internalized the feel or character of the groups in which they worked, while projecting their unconscious hopes and anxieties into the group. They provided a psychodynamic model of the "social individual" at work.

This work, however, developed only a limited following in both England and the United States. Organizational theorists, T-Group practitioners, and consultants in the United States were influenced primarily by Kurt Lewin's field theory, traditions of church and missionary work, behaviorism, and Abraham Maslow's seminal work on the psychology of health, and therefore ignored the role of unconscious processes in group life. Instead, they focused on a person's conscious aims, modes of reasoning, and observed preferences. Moreover, the decline of psychoanalysis as a cultural discipline in the sixties limited its impact throughout the academic world, including in the field of organizational behavior. Original thinkers and theorists such as Abraham Zaleznik at Harvard and Harry Levinson at the Menninger Institute were left to think, write, and practice in relative isolation.

Similarly, Eric Trist, a member of the Tavistock Institute and a pioneer in the application of psychoanalysis to groups, was drawn increasingly to the study of "sociotechnical systems" (that is, self-regulating or self-managing groups at work) and progressively deemphasized his psychoanalytic roots. Ironically, the theory of the self-regulating group had deep roots in Wilfred Bion's group-psychoanalytic work. Bion showed how a patient group in a mental hospital could regulate its own affairs and thereby facilitate its members' healing, and he later demonstrated how small self-study groups could effectively regulate their own processes of self-study. But as Trist and his highly original colleague, Fred Emery, were drawn into the challenge of redesigning work systems to facilitate self-management, they emphasized social rather than group psychodynamic processes. Emery, as well, was deeply influenced by the prospects of a new form of industrial democracy that seemed to be emerging throughout the Western world in the sixties, and he believed that psychoanalysis distracted theorists and practitioners from the practical task of building new social and power-sharing arrangements.

The Current Prospect

We believe that the psychoanalysis of organizations is reemerging as an important academic and clinical discipline. Stimulated by the founding of the International Society for the Psychoanalytic Study of Organizations, a new group of scholars, many of whom are represented in this book, have begun to deepen and extend the work done by the early pioneers. Drawing on both American Ego Psychology and the Tavistock's Kleinian traditions, this group is examining the dynamics of leadership, the vicissitudes of personal authority, the links between individual psychodynamics and organization culture, the impact of risk and uncertainty on group process, and the political culture of the modern corporation.

Collaborating with others, these theorists and practitioners are also deepening the practice of consulting to organizations from a psychodynamic point of view. Under the direction of Laurence Gould, several psychoanalytically oriented consultants have established a program on organization consultation at the William Alanson White Institute, the psychoanalytic institute founded by Karen Horney and Eric Fromm. This is, to our knowledge, the first time that a psychoanalytic institute has sponsored such a program anywhere in the world. In addition, the A. K. Rice Institutes throughout the United States continue to provide opportunities for "experiential learning" and training through their group relations conference.

The authors represented in this book have participated in these recent developments, and their work represents the diversity and richness of the psychoanalytic tradition. For example, Gould, Krantz, Lapierre, Hirschhorn, and Gilmore draw extensively on psychoanalytic "object relations" theory; Baum creatively links Erikson to the problems of power and psychology; while Diamond draws on Sullivan's work to explore bureaucracy. Thomas extends psychoanalytic thinking to the problem of racial taboos; Zaleznik links anthropology and psychoanalysis by highlighting the connections between corporate myths and irrational process; and Feldman joins the problem of innovation to psychological idealization.

Drawing on his highly original concept of the "organizational ideal," Schwartz shows how social irrationality shapes a political culture, while Kets de Vries focuses on the links between individual neurotic styles and an organization's climate and feel. Finally, Gilmore, Hirschhorn, Young, Swogger, and, in a classical essay, Trist highlight the power and relevance of psychoanalysis to organizational intervention.

Organizational psychoanalysis is reemerging as a vital discipline because the character of organizational life in the postindustrial world is changing. People confront novel sources of anxiety as modern technologies and the global economy create ever greater risks. Increasingly, they must work in teams to meet the challenge of product development in a fast-changing economy. People at every level of the organization are being asked to assume more authority and accountability, they expect more from their interpersonal relations, and they work in increasingly diverse and heterogeneous settings. The character and culture of group life is becoming ever more crucial to the success of private and public organizations operating domestically or worldwide.

We face particular dangers here. Leaders may hope to change the culture of organizations by relying on their charisma or by idealizing the company and its achievements. But as Schwartz makes clear in Chapter 15, these attempts can suppress critical thinking, cut off leaders from discomforting information, and create organizational cynicism. To strengthen groups and teams, people in organizations must build a culture from the bottom up. As Laurence Gould shows in Chapter 4, they must learn to talk directly with one another, take up their roles in more sophisticated ways, acknowledge their interdependence, and be vulnerable to one another.

They cannot accomplish this task by participating in simple training programs, nor can their leaders "engineer" a company culture that will magically support them. Instead, as psychoanalysts have long emphasized, people will develop as they "work through" the anxieties, doubts, and conflicts that plague their organizations and teams. People can get help from consultants, trainers, teachers, and mentors, but ultimately they must learn from one another and from their own experience.

There is a new dialectic emerging here. People must deepen their ability to work in groups if they are to master the new challenges to organizational life. But these same challenges can make people anxious, rigid, and vulnerable to simple nostrums, slogans, and fads. They may turn away from the work group just when they need to work more deeply in it. Organizational development hangs in the balance. We feel confident that the psychoanalysis of organizations as a clinical and academic discipline can help shape the outcome and are greatly encouraged that it is once again flourishing.

PART I

The Person and the Organization

CHAPTER 1

The Managerial Couple:

Superior-Subordinate Relationships

as a Unit of Analysis

James Krantz

Introduction

The superior-subordinate relationship (called the *managerial couple* in this chapter) is pervasive in hierarchical organizations and essential to their effectiveness. Through this primary interpersonal link, the delegation of work, the division of labor, and accountability are all realized. Together, both members of the managerial couple must accomplish a job, but neither can control that job individually. Therefore, each must trust the other while coping with feelings of dependence on the other. The extent to which each relies on the other and can be let down by the other often touches upon deep-seated anxieties.

Managerial couples in work organizations take on a life of their own,

Reprinted from *Human Resource Management*, vol. 28, number 2 (Summer 1989), pp. 161–175. © 1989 by John Wiley & Sons, Inc. Reprinted by permission of John Wiley & Sons, Inc.

replete with shared fantasies, hopes and disappointments, collaborative dialogue, and collusive, defensive patterns. On one end of a continuum is the productive, creative, evolving, and mutually stimulating couple. On the other is the rigid, stalemated, sometimes mutually punishing relationship characterized by excessive conflict, numbing detachment, or debilitating dependency.

The managerial couple is a unit of analysis that, I believe, organization theorists have generally underrepresented. This two-person field has its own systemic properties, and like other elements of a system, such as divisions or individuals, is in reciprocal relationship with its system and its parts. The couple is influenced by and influences its context.[1]

Consider the following managerial couple. Sarah, the president of a for-profit urban medical center, has been widely recognized for the innovative programs she initiated in the hospital. Al, a new vice-president for community-based programs, oversaw two major units. One unit had been actively involved in the restructuring and refocusing programs that received so much recognition; the other unit had been largely outside this new strategic orientation. Al's predecessor had felt unable to intervene deeply in this second unit. Part of Al's new assignment, then, was to bring this unit into the hospital-wide change agenda. Sarah was eager to have this work begun and realized, along with Al, that he needed to develop a vision that would both embody the hospital's strategic orientation and serve as a blueprint for the unit's development.

The following incident typifies the difficulties this managerial couple experienced. The hospital management was accustomed to developing strategic plans collectively, believing that it had produced good results. Sarah thus encouraged Al to benefit from the other top managers and to build on their experiences in planning and implementing programs appropriate to the hospital's mission. She also realized the others could contribute an understanding to Al's unit over time.

While Al agreed that he needed a "vision" for the unit, he responded to her suggestions and prodding in a way that made Sarah feel dismissed and unwanted. She encouraged him to set up a meeting with the senior management group and offered to help him design the meeting so that it would be effective and lively. She felt Al's reluctance, so she suggested several times that he call a consultant the hospital used to help in designing working meetings. Again, though he didn't say so to her, Al conveyed through his actions that he did not want to call the consultant.

Sarah and Al were heading toward a stalemate. Al claimed he felt increasingly pressured while Sarah reported she felt increasingly angry, dismissed, and agressive toward him. Finally, Al scheduled a meeting in a deeply ambivalent way. He tried to line up others' schedules on very short notice for a busy executive group, selecting a day when the vice-president of the large nursing unit, someone with an invaluable contribution to make, was typically out of the hospital. Moreover, the executive team's consultant was also unavailable.

The importance of the event, however, was generally recognized and the meeting was arranged. Sarah sensed that because Al had "not taken in" her supervision and direction, he did not really "own" the meeting. Instead, sullen and resentful, he appeared to be doing it out of obligation to Sarah, rather than in a spirit of collaboration and shared development. His inability to own his task was clearly illustrated by his scheduling the meeting in Sarah's office, as if it were her meeting rather than his.

As the date approached, there was no briefing or preparation for the group's work, and Sarah sensed that Al wasn't ready. She was anxious about the meeting failing, not only for the project itself, but for what it signaled about their relationship and Al's entry into the executive team. At this point, direct communication seemed impossible, so she indirectly suggested to Al, through another member on the team, that if he wasn't ready, perhaps he should postpone the meeting. Al decided to go ahead, knowing, by his own recounting, that he wasn't ready and that he would "get his behind kicked." Exactly this happened. As the meeting unfolded, Al was painfully unprepared and the meeting lacked a design or focus, leaving the other team members with no effective way to participate. This, in turn, enraged Sarah, who became quite punitive and critical.

What is happening here? The working relationship between Sarah and Al is unsatisfying for both, and the work they are producing is of low quality. The two have developed a relationship characterized by certain patterns, anxieties, and defenses that give it a recurrent, systemic quality. Each had some enduring tendencies, traits, and ways of taking up their roles that were observable across settings. Yet together they seemed to bring out the worst in each other and to create a pairing that continually elicited Al's passive, sullen ineptitude and Sarah's overbearing, punitive dissatisfaction. They were each depending on the other—Sarah on Al to accomplish an important job she had delegated to him and Al on Sarah for leadership and authorization. The experience of this interdependency was frightening because it entailed a mutual vulnerability to the other, including a susceptibility to the other's irrationality and fears.

This chapter attempts to unravel some of the strands that go into shaping this important relationship. First, I explore the central characteristics of the managerial couple, as distinct from other pairwise relationships either inside or outside organizations. Then I consider three psychodynamic frames of analysis useful for understanding the forces that shape the managerial couple: the interpersonal relationship, the pair embedded in the work group, and the pair as a function of intergroup relations. The impact of structure on the managerial couple is then considered.

5

Characteristics of the Managerial Couple

Every managerial couple shares two features that distinguish it from other kinds of couples. First, every managerial couple contains a hierarchical boundary. Work in hierarchical organizations is divided into discrete segments to allow for the management of subtasks. Each successive structural differentiation creates a level of authority, with a manager retaining responsibility for the original sphere, and the subordinate being delegated a more delimited area to handle. The manager and subordinate meet, therefore, at a juncture in the organization where an internal boundary has been created, and each couple must manage the transactions across this boundary.

6   A superior's accountability for a subordinate's performance—the second feature of the managerial couple—is simultaneously the curse and blessing of the arrangement. On one hand, it enables organizations to adhere to a primary mission and to multiply effort efficiently through successive levels of delegation and accountability. On the other, it ties the subordinate and manager together in an emotionally charged, interdependent bond: they need each other to succeed. While the levels of influence obviously differ, each can damage or empower the other. What gives each couple its distinctive character is the way accountability, authority, and dependence coalesce within this human relationship and define its internal process as an element of the larger organization.

The subordinate has been delegated tasks, and the superordinate manager has responsibilities. These responsibilities include those delegated to the subordinate, but not vice versa. This is the sine qua non of the managerial couple—the superior is accountable to his or her own superior, in turn for what the subordinate does. Superiors can be held accountable only if they have authorized their subordinates to be responsible for some subpart of their own responsibilities and have sufficient authority to hold the subordinate accountable. Thus, the boundary between the two is an authority boundary as well as a task boundary, and the two must handle the issues of authority between them. Equally, this is why the superior is vulnerable to and dependent upon the subordinate; inadequate work by the subordinate threatens the superior's position with respect to his or her own boss.

The impact of this task/authority boundary on the human relationships involved is enormous and differentiates it from other pair relationships in the organization, such as lateral or collegial ones. This boundary, and the need for the individuals in the couple to transact across it to accomplish work, elicits powerful emotions within the pair. Dependency, in both directions, is established, and each individual's emotional response to authority is activated. The managerial couple, as a result, becomes a vehicle for expressing deep archetypal processes.

The Interpersonal World of the Managerial Couple

Each individual in the managerial couple must tolerate the irrational substrata of complex authority relations if the pair is to be creative and productive. Those involved must confront inner conflicts associated with issues of independence and dependence, rivalry, giving and getting, controlling and being controlled, competing and cooperating, success, failure, evaluation, trust and accountability, sharing, mutual recognition of differences, and so on (Gould, 1985; Levinson, 1959; Zaleznik, 1966). And such dilemmas face not only the individuals in the couple but the pair itself, which establishes enduring patterns and propensities that define the two-person field as a unit of analysis with its own properties.

7

While the impact of interpersonal influence is pervasive, the means by which couples establish and maintain recurring patterns is enigmatic and elusive, precisely because the most profound influence is unconscious and not known by either party (Stern, 1989). An important clue, however, can be found in the research in group and organizational life, which shows that the anxieties and defenses elicited in such settings are of a powerful, early, and primitive sort (e.g., Bion, 1959; Jaques, 1955; Menzies, 1961; Kernberg, 1980).

Group life resonates with some of the earliest, most troubling conflicts of group members, including those that are reawakened when authority figures are symbolically equated with parents. Subordinates often relive and attempt to rework emotional experiences with their superiors that they had with their parents as young children. As these and other important very early feelings are revived, the resulting anxieties often lead members of the couple to engage in psychological maneuvers designed to reduce the painful feelings, maneuvers that often subject the pair to difficulty in working together.

The way these defensive maneuvers bind members of working couples to one another in a sort of joint enactment process has been conceptualized as "projective identification" by psychoanalytic writers (Horwitz, 1983; Ogden, 1979). Painful doubts and anxieties lead one or both of the pair to disavow some important but troubling aspect of their own selves and project it into the other. The recipient, also more susceptible under stressful conditions, actually enacts this projected part as if it were him- or herself, absorbing the feelings and behaviors associated with the rejected parts. As a consequence, each party relates to some bothersome part of him- or herself, which has been split off and projected into the other, as if it were actually a trait of the other, who then begins to enact that behavior. Thus one may despise or fear or even love some part of oneself that has been lodged in another, as if it actually were an attribute of the other.

Sarah and Al exhibited the kind of mutually reinforcing pattern of projective identification that results in a stable yet rigid pairing. Sarah was embarrassed by the failure of one hospital unit to align with the widely recognized changes, feeling this reflected unfavorably on her performance and reputation. Further, as is typical in such situations, she was anxious about her appointment of Al—would he be as competent and productive as she hoped? Al shared complementary feelings of worry about his becoming a fully respected member of this executive team and performing well at this new and higher level.

Sarah, as was her bent, tended to deny her own sense of uncertainty and doubts, a trait that heightened her confidence and enhanced her considerable leadership capacities in many situations. In this instance, however, she projected her doubts onto Al, whose already existing worries were amplified; he now felt especially doubtful and incompetent in relation to Sarah not only because of his own makeup but because of Sarah's disowned feelings, which he was taking on as well. She distanced herself from Al, and her contact with him took on a tense and slightly suspicious texture, partly because she was relating not only to Al but to certain unwanted parts of herself that were now lodged in him.

As Al became less able and more frightened, he grew more passive, splitting off his own aggressiveness and sense of mastery. The idea of acting authoritatively and risking possible failure under these conditions made him feel extremely vulnerable and exposed. As a consequence, he disowned these parts of himself and projected them into Sarah, who now had to manage not only her own aggressiveness, competence, and dominating aspects, but her subordinate's as well. Feeling as if she had to be aggressive for both of them, Sarah then felt and behaved in an overly responsible manner. In relating to Sarah, Al now had to face not only her frightening assertiveness but the frightening parts of himself that he had projected into her. Sarah became increasingly aggressive and critical while Al became more passive, self-protective, and incompetent. A stable but dysfunctional relationship is thus established.

In mild form, projective identification in managerial couples, as in any pair, can promote sensitivity, empathy, and understanding as partners are able to put themselves "into the others' shoes" (Gilmore and Krantz, 1985). But when it shapes the relationship with greater intensity and rigidity, the effects can be crippling to the collaboration. Not only is the interaction disabled by anxious withdrawal or excessive conflict and contempt, but the individuals are left depleted. The manager who disowns and projects away his or her aggressiveness, for example, will be unable to act decisively in managerial situations calling for action. Alternatively, if the superior's dependency and vulnerability has been split off and projected into the subordinate, as with Sarah, the boss will likely have trouble receiving bad news from the subordinate, and the subordinate is likely to be helpless and submissive. The resulting collaboration will be flawed as a result of the shared, two-person pattern created.

Thus, managerial couples create unconscious agreements in order to maintain mutual misperceptions as a defense against recognizing the underlying problems, conflicts, or differences (Alderfer, 1986) inherent in achieving and maintaining collaboration across lines of authority. While the degree to which these misperceptions are used and maintained depends partly upon each member's individual development (Gould, 1988), there are also a variety of organizational or systemic influences on managerial couples.

9

The Couple in the Group

Managerial couples work and interact within a group context and are therefore profoundly influenced by the group's dynamics. A variety of systemic and group-level dynamics can cause managers and subordinates to regress (Kernberg, 1980), rendering the individuals of the managerial couple even more vulnerable to disabling forces. Particular individuals, as members of groups, are induced into roles (Redl, 1963; Rioch, 1970) on behalf of the entire group. Thus every couple not only contends with its own internal dynamics and interrelations, but must carry some degree of emotional freight for the group.

An important contribution to understanding the couple in the group is Bion's (1959) description of how groups tend to elicit pairings among their members and use them as projective targets for unconscious group emotion. What he calls the Basic Assumption Pairing Group will invest its hope and creative excitement in a group. In a sophisticated work organization, this emotional background can support many creative pairings, as leadership shifts around the group (Gould, 1985).

Managerial couples must often bear the weight of group fantasy. In a higher functioning group, this may support the couple and foster welcomed, stimulated collaboration between pairs within the group. Under the impact of intensified anxiety, however, its more primitive manifestation appears, in which the "pairing group" invests wildly grandiose hopes in one of its couples, who then become the repository for all possibility in the group. The managerial couple can easily then become burdened by these projections and overwhelmed with such high expectations, while the others passively await the pair's magical creation. The group's idealization of its messianic couple will, for example, create strong pressures for the pair to deny its aggressive and conflictual dimensions, rendering the couple less capable of achieving sophisticated collaboration. And of course, it will be doomed to disappoint the expectant others. Finally, a creative pair may elicit jealousy and destructive envy from other group members, in part because of the measure of exclusivity inherent in any true interpersonal joining.

A good example of both dynamics can be seen in *Powerplay* by Mary Cunningham (1984), her story about the events at Bendix surrounding her meteoric rise and pairing with the chairman, William Agee. Agee was regarded as a wunderkind who would save the endangered company. Both loved and despised, he went about changing the culture of managerial work in the company. He hired Cunningham, a bright young Harvard MBA whose analytical ability consistently outshone that of the older executives, as his executive assistant.

10

She and Agee grew increasingly closer, while the deep changes Agee pursued in a turbulent environment created enormous anxiety. From her description (p. 98), it seemed as if, over time, the two of them could trust only each other. The pair, according to this book and other sources, became an object of enormous interest and concern within (and outside) the company, representing both hope and danger at different times. From a group-as-a-whole perspective, certain factions invested the couple with great hope; it would produce the Bendix of the future, a firm making high-tech electronics rather than used auto parts. Yet the envy, hatred, and resentment grew fiercely, until finally the board forced Agee to fire Cunningham.

While the strong connection between the two may have been partly independent of the powerful emotional forces within Bendix at the time, the couple was unconsciously used by the group to contain, or enact, the hope for a magical renewal of the company. This, and the attendant envy and resentfulness toward them, clearly had a disastrous impact on their ability to collaborate effectively. Both the hope and the envy drove them together; they progressively became isolated from other resentful senior executives and simultaneously responded to the board's expectation that they would accomplish wildly grandiose results. As they came to enact these irrational dynamics, they progressively lost touch with the company and became increasingly disabled.

Thus to the extent the managerial couple is "containing," or enacting, some aspect of the whole group's emotional life, it is subject to forces that can amplify powerful emotions. When the work group is in the grip of a too-powerful unconscious process, the managerial couple will have to contend with the underlying fantasies being used defensively to evade task-based anxieties, and the corresponding emotional states will suffuse the collaboration.

The Couple and the Intergroup Relationship

Not only are managerial couples embedded within groups; they may also constitute the interface between two organizational groups—for example, structurally based hierarchical and task groups such as headquarters and field units or marketing and sales, as well as "identity" groups such as women and men or blacks and whites. The superior and subordinate, while being members of the same group from one perspective, from another are members of two different groups, which in turn subjects them to another set of powerful dynamics.

The superior and subordinate each have their own peer-level groups, which are brought together by the managerial couple. By representing their work roles, each becomes imbued with the outlook and unconscious orientations of its group memberships and, equally, each symbolizes its group to the other. Inevitably, the historic intergroup relationship between the two units the couple represents will be enacted within its own relationship.

11

A vertical chain of three managers in a human service organization providing a range of services to an adolescent population is a good illustration. The commissioner, who oversaw the entire operation, had a tense relationship with the director, who headed up the long-stay center treating the most disturbed children in the agency. The director, in turn, had an equally tense working relationship with the heads of the dormitories.

These managerial couples were having difficulty in working effectively. According to the director, the commissioner-director couple was characterized by mistrust; communication and dialogue were poor, and as a result, the commissioner doubted his director's ability. Ultimately, the two discovered that their relationship was, in part, enacting a historic mistrust and suspicion between the field institutions and headquarters.

Hierarchical group as well as identity group relations were shaping relations between the pair. Historically, the central office was run by white managers identified with governmental affairs, while the field institutions were run by black managers, who identified more with the children and their plight. The task of forcibly institutionalizing poor black children, even if they were trying to help those in their control, was anxiety-provoking for socially concerned managers, black and white alike. Elements of social oppression and racism were inevitably manifested in the work of the organization; the feelings they engendered had to be managed by all segments of the enterprise.

The anxiety and pain were often culturally simplified through a process in which the field units attributed all the racism and oppression to headquarters staff, who were mostly white, came largely from a higher social class, and of course were more closely linked to the larger issues of political governance. Through such attribution, the field units were able to exonerate themselves psychologically from confronting the complexities of belonging to the enterprise. Senior headquarters staff managed their mixed feelings differently. They disavowed the part of themselves that was ill at ease with the agency's work and projected it onto the field managers, believing the latter weren't invested in the agency's overall well-being but instead were parochially concerned with their own narrow interests. Field-headquarters relations were tense and adversarial, as one might expect. The commissioner and the director recreated this intergroup dynamic inside their own relationship, with each feeling both misunderstood and mistrusted. Only when they saw the link between their experience as a pair and the dynamics of headquarters-field relationships did they understand the chronic and seemingly obscure roots of their own strained working relationship.

12

The Couple and the Formal Organization

All human relationships involve irrational, unconscious dynamic processes, deeper connections in which the meaning of the relationship, for each, is rooted. The irrational, unconscious background to the managerial couple can be the wellspring of creativity, zest, and excitement or the source of destructiveness and detachment.

Traditional organization theory has excluded recognizing the irrational, affective dimensions of role relations. The legacy of Weber's (1947) theory of bureaucracy is a normative orientation toward an impersonal, rational conception of organizational life, based on a foundation of rationally derived structures. In this scheme, furthered by Taylorist approaches and the "scientific management" tradition, rationally derived structures allow for the elimination of irrationality and unwanted emotion from role performance (Levinson, 1959).

Yet we also know that people inevitably bring more to their work roles than only those capacities required by their tasks (Rice, 1965). People use their work roles to manage their anxieties and meet other socioemotional needs as well as to satisfy their needs to accomplish work alone. Thus the irrational dimensions of life are brought into the workplace and find expression in social relations. Indeed, by emphasizing impersonality, an organization may drive emotional needs underground, thereby increasing people's irrational responses to work. In such an environment, a subordinate, for example, feeling punished by a superior's evaluation, may sullenly withdraw from work or punish his or her own subordinate in turn. The "repressed returns."

While rationally derived structures cannot eliminate the uncontrollable realm of human feeling and irrationality from organizational life, they can shape and channel it. The presence of the irrational bond between the managerial couple is shaped by the formal structure in which the couple is embedded and by the bit of the structure that is embedded within the couple—the boundary of authority and delegation between them. Structure can help link the irrational bonds to the managerial couple's work, and thereby facilitate it, or it can enhance the potential disturbance within the working pair.

When role definitions are confused, vague, or inappropriate to an organization's tasks, the result is regression on the group level to dysfunctional, antitask cultures (Kernberg, 1980; Menzies, 1979; Hirschhorn, 1988). Unclear role definitions create significant conflicts between members of the managerial couple as well: people can easily arrogate authority to themselves, on the one hand, or deny accountability on the other, resulting in distorted internal boundaries.

The case of David, who managed a section of an R&D lab for a pharmaceutical company, illustrates how an inadequately structured situation can stir deep and disruptive interpersonal dynamics. As section manager, he was responsible for the unit's performance, though he had no authority to remove subordinates from their positions. He was in a particularly difficult situation with Mary, who worked below standards but not with such glaring incompetence that David's own superior would fire her. Yet the unit operated under very tight performance standards, and Mary could undermine David's performance without his being able to respond effectively, leaving David vulnerable and exposed for his own performance in relation to his boss.

Consequently, David felt persecuted by Mary and expressed his helplessness and rage by becoming suspicious and punitive. The situation touched on some of his very deep anxieties about control and dependence. The couple's interaction developed into a rigid pattern of suspicion and concealment; both were locked into dealing with each other's personal defense because the formal structure failed to enable David to manage his dependence on her productively. With the requisite authority he might have removed her or, alternatively, been able to shape her performance through the process of genuine accountability.

Finally, the managerial couple is not only affected by the organization's structure, but affects it as well. When the couple is regressive, pressures will arise to blur or obfuscate the formal role relations even more. This leads to an increased avoidance of anxiety and confronting issues of dependability, accountability, and trust, which are inevitably painful in a failing collaboration.

The case of Sarah and Al illustrates this nicely. Sarah wanted Al to take more initiative with the strategic planning process. Over time, a considerable amount of anxiety had built up over this event. As both sides tended to engage in mutual projective processes and got locked into the

13

stalemate described earlier, lines of accountability tended to blur. Sarah did not feel she could trust Al to carry out her wishes, so she pushed him to do a task without really delegating it to him. Al then felt demeaned; he wasn't being given an authentic delegation but rather was performing in a rote fashion, leading him to blur the lines of accountability from his side. This led to an odd set of actions conveying the confusion over whose meeting it was. For example, the invitation to the meeting from Al was: "Sarah wants me to have a meeting . . ." Thus, in this instance, the formal structure that lodged accountability and responsibility clearly within the supervisory structure gave way to a vague, fused sense of responsibility as the couple defended against confronting the painful realities of the collaboration at that moment.

Not only does investment in formal structure create the conditions in which people can work productively; it also provides an ongoing way to understand a working relationship. A considered formal structure provides a model against which the managerial couple's actual collaboration can be assessed. Though she had developed a difficult pattern with Al, Sarah was an exceptionally capable manager and supervisor. She was able to understand how off-track her relationship with Al had become, in part because she saw how cloudy the lines of accountability had gotten. The model of organizing and the clearly delineated boundaries to which their management group aspired and often reached stood in sharp contrast to the confused, blurred pattern of accountability she had with Al. This difference provided the essential diagnostic information. Her investment in formal structure provided a set of principles to help guide her in the relationship and thereby understand the defensive processes, which in turn enabled her to establish fuller, productive collaboration with Al.

Managerial Implications

All members of any organization are involved in managerial couples and are inevitably affected by the forces discussed in this chapter. The two-person relationship can become very loaded, both because of what is inside it and because of what is projected into it by others. Managers trying to improve organizational functioning are likely to benefit from considering the managerial couple as a unit of analysis—both as a source of invaluable information as well as a locus for development.

This requires appreciating the many forces that are finding expression through and shaping the pair's working relationship. Unbundling these various influences can be confusing and difficult. As the case of Sarah and Al illustrates, managerial structure and boundaries provide a point of departure for sorting out different influences. One of the key functions of managerial leadership is to provide conditions that support accountability.

Accountability, and its capacity to harness social dynamics to task, occurs only in conjunction with certain patterns of authority and can be achieved only when the formal boundary across which the members of a managerial couple transact has certain characteristics (Jaques, 1976). Clearly defined roles and well-negotiated distribution of shared responsibility enable members of the working couple to understand their interpersonal relationship in the context of the larger, shared task and its human meaning. An enabling formal organization and rationally derived structure allows members to bring their irrational, feeling-full aspects into productive relation to the task. Defensively derived structures and boundaries pit the inevitable irrational connection between the couple against the demands of task, and are thus disabling.

While inadequate structures are often the source of difficulties in the managerial couple, enabling structures can be undermined as the result of other regressive pressures that are rooted in interpersonal, group, and intergroup dynamics. These are more difficult to ferret out and understand, although managers often enhance their own competence by developing the reflective capacity to see how these wider systemic forces are enacted by working pairs. Outside consultation is often helpful in exploring these elements because of the unconscious nature of these powerful emotional undercurrents, or worse, because the pair has gotten locked into patterns dominated by projective identification.

15

Conclusion

As with all social realities, understanding the managerial couple requires taking multiple levels of analysis into account. The individual, interpersonal, group, and intergroup perspectives all help to untangle the many determinants of the managerial couple's life. Similarly, to appreciate the managerial couple in context as a systemic process, an understanding of the impact of the social and technical subsystems is necessary to explore the couple's experience.

The changing social, economic, and political situation is naturally represented microcosmically in the evolution of working couples, putting them under greater stress. Vastly greater diversity in the workforce means that many more couples will have to manage the tendency toward projection and splitting that racial, ethnic, and gender differences promote. Increasingly complex and unpredictable settings render ritualized, unexamined pair arrangements maladaptive (Hirschhorn, 1988). Turbulent environments make demands on both organizations as a whole and their constituent managerial couples to achieve an ongoing, active adaptation and learning.

Every boundary in the midst of managerial couples contains the seeds of conflict; these are inherent in an organization's needs to make decisions based on function and efficiency rather than in the personal interests of people. Nonetheless, in deep and genuine collaboration there is also the possibility of creativity and mutual growth (Hirshhorn, 1988; Gould, 1988). Achieving this is the challenge for the pair and for the group in which it is situated.

NOTE

1. This chapter looks at the managerial couple relationship in its organizational context and examines its major components from a sociotechnical perspective. By sociotechnical perspective I am referring to a frame of reference first developed by Trist and his colleagues at the Tavistock Institute (e.g., Trist and Bramforth, 1951; Trist et al., 1963), which emphasizes the interrelatedness of the functioning of the social and technological subsystems of an enterprise.

16

The social system refers to the people in the work situation and the relationships among them, including their particular physical and psychological characteristics and requirements. The social system includes the cultural mechanisms that govern social relations. The technological, technical system refers to aspects of formal organization such as procedures, policies, techniques, tools, and structures that are used by the social system to accomplish work. Sociotechnical studies show that the two subsystems are related to each other, serve as constraints on each other, and must be effectively fit to each other to achieve optimal functioning.

Typically used to describe manufacturing systems (Cummings, 1978), the design of jobs (Davis, 1978), methods of organizing overall enterprises, and a philosophy of work organization (Emery, 1982), sociotechnical systems theory is a frame of reference that can be used to study the relationship between and within any level of a system. Although efforts have been made to explore the interpersonal dimensions of work relations (e.g., Bennis et al., 1979; Argyris, 1962; Baird and Kram, 1983; Gabarro, 1979) and the interpersonal aspects of authority relations (e.g., Rioch, 1970; Kernberg, 1980; Levinson, 1959; Kets de Vries, 1979), this is the first time I am aware of sociotechnical systems theory being specifically used to shed light on the managerial couple.

REFERENCES

Alderfer, C. 1986. "An Intergroup Perspective on Group Dynamics." In J. Lorsch (ed.), *Handbook of Organizational Behavior*. Englewood Cliffs, N.J.: Prentice-Hall.

Argyris, C. 1962. *Interpersonal Competence and Organizational Effectiveness*. London: Tavistock.

Baird, L., and K. Kram. 1983. "Career Dynamics: Managing the Superior/Subordinate Relationship." *Organizational Dynamics*, 11(4), 46–64.

Bennis, W., J. Van Maanen, E. Schein, and F. Steele. 1979. *Essays in Interpersonal Dynamics*. Homewood, Ill.: Dorsey Press.

Bion, W. R. 1959. *Experiences in Groups*. London: Tavistock.

Cummings, T. 1978. "Sociotechnical Experimentation: A Review of Sixteen Studies." In W. Pasmore and J. Sherwood (eds.), *Sociotechnical Systems: A Sourcebook*. La Jolla, Calif.: University Associates Press.

Cunningham, M. 1984. *Powerplay*. New York: Simon and Schuster.

Davis, L. 1978. "Sociotechnical Systems: The Design of Work and Quality of Working

Life." In W. Pasmore and J. Sherwood (eds.), *Sociotechnical Systems: A Sourcebook*. La Jolla, Calif.: University Associates Press.

Emery, F. 1982. "New Perspectives on the World of Work: Sociotechnical Foundations for a New Social Order?" *Human Relations*, 35(12), 1095–1122.

Gabarro, J. J. 1979. "Socialization at the Top: How CEO's and Their Subordinates Evolve Interpersonal Contracts." *Organizational Dynamics*, 7(3), 3–23.

Gilmore, T., and J. Krantz. 1985. "Projective Identification in the Consulting Relationship: Exploring the Unconscious Dimensions of a Client System." *Human Relations*, 38(12), 1159–1177.

Gould, L. J. 1985. "Derivations of Bion's Basic Assumption Theory in Klein's Developmental Positions." Presented at the 7th Scientific Meetings, the A. K. Rice Institute, Arlington, Va., April.

———. 1988. "The Capacity to Work: Developmental Origins of Mature Collaboration." Prepared for the First International Symposium on Group Relations Contributions to Social and Political Issues, Oxford, England, May.

Hirschhorn, L. 1988. *The Workplace Within: Psychodynamics of Organizational Life*. Cambridge, Mass.: MIT Press.

Horwitz, L. 1983. "Projective Identification in Dyads and Groups." *International Journal of Group Psychotherapy*, 33, 259–279.

Jacques, E. 1955. "Social Systems as a Defense Against Persecutory and Depressive Anxiety." In M. Klein, P. Heimann, and R. E. Money-Kryle (eds.), *New Directions in Psychoanalysis*. London: Tavistock.

———. 1976. *A General Theory of Bureaucracy*. London: Heinemann.

Kernberg, O. 1980. *Internal World and External Reality: Object Relations Theory Applied*. New York: Jason Aronson.

Kets de Vries, Manfred F. R. 1979. "Managers Can Drive Their Subordinates Mad." *Harvard Business Review* (July–August).

Levinson, D. 1959. "Role, Personality, and Social Structure in the Organizational Setting." *Journal of Abnormal and Social Psychology*, 58, 170–180.

Menzies, I. 1961. "The Functioning of Social Systems as a Defense Against Anxiety." *Human Relations*, 13, 95–121.

———. 1979. "Staff Support Systems: Task and Anti-Task in Adolescent Institutions." In R. Hinshelwood and N. Manning (eds.), *Therapeutic Communities*. London: Routledge and Kegan Paul.

Newton, P., and D. Levinson. 1973. "The Work Group within the Organization: A Sociopsychological Approach." *Psychiatry*, 36, 115–132.

Ogden, T. 1979. "On Projective Identification." *International Journal of Psychoanalysis*, 60, 357–373.

Redl, F. 1963. "Psychoanalysis and Group Therapy: A Developmental Point of View." *American Journal of Orthopsychiatry*, 33, 135–142.

Rice, A. K. 1965. "Individual, Group and Intergroup Processes." *Human Relations*, 22(6), 565–584.

Rioch, M. 1970. "All we like sheep . . . [Isaiah 53:6]: Followers and Leaders." *Psychiatry*, 33, 56–66.

Stern, D. B. 1989. "The Analyst's Unformulated Experience of the Patient." *Contemporary Psychoanalysis*, 25(1), 1–33.

Trist, E., and K. Bramforth. 1951. "Some Social and Psychological Consequences of the Longwall Method of Coal-Getting." *Human Relations*, 4, 3–38.

Trist, E., G. Higgin, H. Murray, and A. Pollock. 1963. *Organizational Choice: Capabilities of Groups at the Coal Face under Changing Technologies*. London: Tavistock.

Weber, M. 1947. *The Protestant Ethic and the Spirit of Capitalism*. London: Oxford University Press.

Zaleznik, A. 1966. *Human Dilemmas of Leadership*. New York: Harper and Row.

17

CHAPTER 2

Mourning, Potency, and

Power in Management

Laurent Lapierre

Managing, directing, realizing one's visions, creating systems, and leading human beings in pursuit of a goal: all of these activities require that
a leader have a certain feeling of potency. This chapter discusses the difficulties such people face developing and drawing on these feelings of
potency. For to do so, we will argue, a leader must cope with feelings
of both impotence and omnipotence that accompany and may derail the
attempt to excercise power. Such feelings, we will argue, are remnants of
the leader's early development. One's capacity for mature action, based
on *relative potency*, is always exercised in their shadow. One can neither
deny feelings of impotence or omnipotence nor escape them; rather, one
faces the challenge of integrating them so that neither dominates the way
in which leadership is assumed.

The chapter begins by presenting cases of leaders that illustrate this
conception of leadership practice. Next are traced the broad outlines of a

Reprinted from *Human Resource Management*, vol. 28, number 2 (Summer 1989), pp.
177–189. © 1989 by John Wiley & Sons, Inc. Reprinted by permission of John Wiley &
Sons, Inc.

model of individual development that explains our concept of leadership based on feelings of relative potency. Finally, some implications of our model are presented; these touch upon notions of responsibility in liberty and leadership.

Feelings of Potency: Some Definitions

Potency is defined here as the state of the individual that makes him or her capable of actions having a relatively far-reaching impact on people and things. By leadership, we mean the actual practice of the person who has the responsibility of mobilizing human resources in order to attain specific results efficiently. We distinguish between the manager and the leader: the *manager* gives an organization direction by reacting to a situation that is outside (opportunities or threats in a given environment, strengths and weaknesses of available resources), while the *leader* initiates or directs a firm by being more centered on a personal vision (internal universe). The exercise of both leadership and management necessarily implies the use of power. The notion of *power* is used here in a psychological sense to signify the actualization of feelings of potency in leadership practice. In practice, the leader calls upon various sources of power: hierarchical authority, technical and professional competence, conceptual skills, capacity for vision and imagination, aptitude for developing constructive (consensual or confronting) interpersonal relationships, personal charm, and so on. Looking at power this way raises the idea of the psyche. By the *psyche* or *psychic* we mean all that concerns an individual's internal reality, and in particular the images or representations that we hold of our first love objects and the first authority figures who marked our life, and the first people we loved. This psychic or internal reality largely determines the nature of our feelings and how we interpret them, as well as the types of interpersonal relationships that each of us maintains.

Feelings of Potency: A Vignette

To act, to take charge and take risks, leaders must come to believe in their feelings of potency, of their capacity to shape a situation. But as we have argued, in doing so the leader faces the dilemma of integrating feelings of omnipotence and impotence, each of which alone can distort judgment and derail plans. The following vignette shows how one leader fell victim to feelings of omnipotence and impotence that he could not integrate and how another, facing the first in a political conflict, could integrate the two.

20

Career Decline: Splitting Impotence and Omnipotence

Don Bird has been the chief executive officer of Famous Products for over twenty years. He is sixty years old and has directed this firm with the help of a management team consisting of men of about the same age who are totally devoted to him. His management is judged to be conservative, but it has yielded good results.

Famous Products is acquired by Omega Corporation, a conglomerate, despite the opposition of Bird. Omega names Bird chairman of the board of directors (a "promotion!"); Jim Donovan, a young, dynamic, and experienced executive of about forty, who enjoys the confidence of Omega, is transferred from another division to take over as the new CEO. His mandate is to get things really moving at Famous Products.

When Omega had selected him, they had told him that Don Bird, the current president of Famous Products, was close to retirement and would be moved upstairs to chairman of the board. Bird had been president of Famous for 22 years and had done reasonably well, building sales steadily and guarding quality. The top management group was highly experienced, closely knit, very loyal to the company, and had been in their jobs for a long time. As long-term employees they were all reported to be good friends of Don Bird. They were almost all in their early 60s and quite proud of the record of their moderate-sized but successful company. Famous had not, however, grown in profits as rapidly as Omega expected of its operating companies, and Omega's president had told Jim that he wanted Jim to "grab a hold of Famous and make it take off." [Cohen and Merenda, 1979, p. 1]

Since the takeover by Omega, however, Bird has been feeling both helpless and enraged. Though he has been politically defeated in the takeover, he cannot yet accept his loss. Feeling angry, he hopes to still defeat Omega by mobilizing his team of once-loyal managers to oppose Donovan, to draw a line and enlist them in his program of opposition. His rage, stimulated by feelings of impotence, paves the way for feelings of omnipotence, and he comes to believe unrealistically that he can mobilize his managers, who understand the political shifts all too well, to fight his battles.

Jim Donovan, the new CEO, is eager to meet his new challenge. He decides to pay a courtesy visit to Bird and the other top managers at Famous Products on his way to Omega's head office to receive further instructions. He calls Bird one week before his arrival to inform him of his visit. Bird then calls a meeting of the management team, which happens to coincide with the visit of Donovan to Famous Products, and will serve to set the stage for the "entrance" of the new CEO.

As soon as Donovan sets foot on the premises, Bird takes him to the meeting room where all the vice-presidents of the firm are waiting, looking serious and tense. Bird seats Donovan to his right and introduces him as follows:

> "Gentlemen, I want you to meet Mr. Donovan, but before I turn the meeting over to him, I want you to know that I do not believe he should be here; I do not believe he's qualified and I will give him no support. Mr. Donovan. . . ." [Cohen and Merenda, 1979, p. 2]

Bird, who has led up until that moment a very successful career, has acted in an extremely hostile and inelegant manner, one that is doomed to failure. If he succeeds in "getting" Donovan, Omega will have no choice but to get rid of Bird. If Donovan extricates himself from the trap set for him, Bird will be seen as having been very petty; his old colleagues, who despite their previous allegiances recognize that power has shifted hands, will end up blaming him for having subjected them to such tension and will feel guilty for having "welcomed" their new boss in this way. In either case, Bird will have to live with the image of a "botched exit," a failure despite all of his past successes.

In short, feelings of impotence have aroused his rage, and, acting as if he had nothing to lose, he behaves unrealistically, as if he were invulnerable. Unable to cope with his feelings of impotence and his subsequent omnipotent fantasies, he denies reality and acts "as if" Omega Corporation had not taken over.

Donovan himself faces a difficult situation, one that could be very costly for him. It is important for a manager to make a successful "entrance" into an organization. Had he been more sensitive to the dilemmas facing a leader such as Bird, Donovan might not have scheduled the meeting so haphazardly and with so little preparation.

Confronted by Bird's open hostility, he is forced to recognize his interior tumult and his own vulnerability in order not to become a victim himself of a reaction of impotence or omnipotence.

> His mind racing just ahead of his pounding heart, Jim stalled by smiling broadly at Don Bird and looking slowly around the room. "Why don't I smoke a pipe so I could fiddle with it and look wise," he thought ironically to himself. Then, " 'Son of a bitch, I'm going to win; I'm going to make sure that the people in this room know that I'm going to lead.' " [Cohen and Merenda, 1979, p. 3]

Donovan then begins by noting calmly that he is glad to be at the meeting but that others may feel to the contrary. He says that the company has a good reputation but only the future will tell how it will perform under his leadership. He then describes his own past, talks extensively about his family, and turns the meeting over to Bird!

Clearly, there is a maturity and sensitivity in Donovan's response. He deflects his impulse to give play to feelings of omnipotence, to look wise by "fiddling with a pipe," but neither does he succumb to feelings of anger that might lead him to feel trapped by a conspiracy of the old guard. Instead, he affirms Bird's anger, acknowledges his own vulnerability in the face of an unknown future, and underscores his own value as a leader by delineating his background and family life. Overcoming the poles of omnipotent and impotent feelings, he acts with relative potency and takes the risk of turning the meeting back to Bird. (He reported later that the meeting was quite boring since its only agenda was Donovan himself.)

The end of the meeting contained its dramatic moments as well. Walker, one of the vice-presidents of the company, took up Bird's work by asking Donovan why he hadn't stayed in his old position and what made him think that he had something to contribute to Famous Products.

> Smiling once again, while rapidly thinking to himself, "He's attacking me, not my qualifications . . . what kind of person am I? Am I really pure and doing the right thing? What would General Patton, a great leader, have done now? Oh, hell, you have to be a bit Machiavellian if you're going to be powerful!" [Cohen and Merenda, 1979, p. 4]

23

Donovan's thoughts once more move between omnipotence and impotence. Feeling attacked as a person, he berates himself for not being pure, then fantasizes that to act he needs to be like General Patton. Finally, he affirms that he wants to be powerful and decides to act tactically, as Machiavelli would advise. Working with these feelings, he then thanks Walker for being so frank and, acknowledging that the future is still unknown, says to him: "You are a man who says what he thinks."

Again, he has contained aggression without getting angry himself. Able to act with relative potency, he shapes a "tactical" response, that is, one based on a realistic assessment of the power dynamics. He thanks Walker for his frankness, thus reframing an attack as a collaborative gesture.

Indeed, at the end of the meeting Bird approaches Donovan suggesting that he, Donovan, talk with Walker privately. This was a complex interchange. By asking Donovan to talk with Walker, Bird is finally acknowledging Donovan's legitimacy, while also taking some responsibility for shaping and facilitating the change in leadership. Donovan's maturity has enabled Bird to recover his own.

Maturity and the Career Peak

What shapes the capacity for such mature action, for acting without succumbing to fantasies of omnipotence or feelings of impotence? A study of francophone leaders in Quebec at the midpoint in their careers, thirty-five to forty-five years of age, provides some insight (Lapierre and Toulouse, 1984). These were leaders within the business community who were clearly successful (most of them were at the head of their organizations); their elders or peers identified them as having a great deal of potential.

These leaders identified (1) the *motivation factors* they deemed most important: the encouragement they had received from their parents and the importance of challenge and of action in their lives; (2) their *vision of management:* here the importance of action emerged once again, as did the tendency to view competition as a game, and the need to know a particular area of activity as well as the aims, the resources, the strengths, and the weaknesses of the organization itself, in depth; (3) their *concept of leadership,* which included ambition, a huge capacity for work, a belief in one's own competence in the area of activity, and a feeling of confidence in oneself and in others that made teamwork possible. They chose their team members for their autonomy, their self-confidence, their ability to work hard, their flexibility, and their judgment much more than for their intelligence.

24

With these leaders, however, issues of potency, impotence, and omnipotence were always present just below the surface. They stated that in their choice of colleagues, they avoided those who had no self-confidence (the fantasy of impotence) as well as those who had too much, who suffered from a "God-the-Father complex" (the fantasy of omnipotence).

As far as their own confidence and feelings of potency were concerned, the leaders generally used phrases such as "if the world only knew!"— thus revealing that they were conscious of their own vulnerability beneath the external images of confidence and success. Because they were sufficiently conscious of these feelings to master them, to manage them within themselves, they did not fall victim to their feelings of omnipotence or impotence.

It is with the same awareness and prudence that the *quebecois* leaders mentioned a danger that they all wished to avoid: giving in to the intoxicating effects of power; they gave examples of people whose rapid career rise they had witnessed and who had been led to their doom by an exaggerated feeling of potency. These examples revealed that for some, the first moments of success, the first real experiences of power, had reactivated the fantasy of omnipotence, leading them to undertake unduly high-risk adventures that would inevitably fail. Victims of feelings of omnipotence and impotence, these people had brought onto themselves the crises that resulted. The *quebecois* leaders demonstrated prudence in their own actions and did not wish to be caught in the same trap.

Psychic Development and Feelings of Potency

Situations of change or crisis, such as Bird's impending retirement or Donovan's ascendancy to the CEO position, can test a leader's capacity to act with relative potency. But early development, a person's early experience as a child in relationship to parents and other important adults, creates a core of feelings and fantasies that color (though don't determine) adult behavior and responses.

The life of James Riddle Hoffa, the president of the International Brotherhood of Teamsters, is suggestive here. His entire career was marked by reactions of omnipotence and impotence. His links to organized crime were well known, and he personally met a tragic end. Hoffa had an insatiable hunger for personal power, and he acquired his fame as a result of his failures rather than his achievements (Silver, 1968; Selznick and Glickman, 1983). He seized all of the power within his union and refused to share it with anyone; everything fell under his personal and total control. He gave the impression that he owned not only his own union but the entire trucking industry as well. Even though he was sentenced several years before his actual imprisonment in 1967, he acted as if he would always be at the helm, never once referring to his imminent imprisonment. Those surrounding him became his accomplices in this denial of reality.

25

We have some information about Hoffa's parents, the first love objects, and the first authority figures that could have determined in part his feelings of potency and his relative ambition for power. Hoffa himself had rather unhappy memories about his childhood. His father was frequently away, and died when James was seven years old. His mother was extremely demanding, energetic, and industrious. After his father's death, she was reduced to a life of poverty. She raised (controlled) her children very strictly, meting out physical punishment and discipline (the "strap" and castor oil).

It is easy to imagine Hoffa's feelings of helplessness in this situation. Up until the age of seventeen, he was a conformist, socially withdrawn, calm and submissive. But as soon as he felt that he had found a just cause in the union movement, his experience of impotence seems to have transformed itself into a desire for omnipotence. Gifted with a lively intelligence and a prodigious memory, Hoffa apparently had great abilities of concentration. He maintained that he never made a mistake and in fact was unable to deal with any opposition. He would fall into uncontrollable rages if contradicted. He would rage against his associates and would even attack the pride of those whom he most admired. During negotiations, apparently losing control of himself, he would let his anger explode, tear up the written offer and fling it in the faces of the negotiators, or simply walk out of the conference room.

His desire for omnipotent control made him reject all forms of authority. He mocked religion and openly rejected the law. For him, his personal ethic constituted an alternative to the law. He began to feel persecuted quite early on in his career, becoming suspicious of many people in his entourage and demanding absolute loyalty from his colleagues. This persecution anxiety led him to project out his own ever-present feelings of omnipotence; we may suppose that he was referring to himself when he stated that Robert Kennedy was just "a brat that believes that everybody is supposed to surrender and give in to whatever he wants, right or wrong" (Silver, 1968, p. 20).

Hoffa's unhappy childhood as well as his own inner constitution, his biological temperament, made it difficult for him to come to terms with early feelings of persecution and consequent impotence. Instead, these feelings were masked by compensating feelings of omnipotence so that each successive feeling of disappointment, when something did not go his way, triggered feelings of rage and then omnipotence.

26   Melanie Klein's Theoretical Scheme

Through what process does a person mature? How do adults avoid the pitfalls of impotence and omnipotence? Melanie Klein, a psychoanalyst of great depth, argued that such pitfalls were endemic to each person's earliest developmental experiences. *Being* helpless, a child is likely to *feel* helpless, and if its environment is too frustrating or it cannot cope with normal frustration, the child, Klein argued, is likely to create a fantasy life, which it regards of course as very real, in which it has both a good and bad mother, good and bad parents, in its intimate world. Identifying with the good adults, the child develops an omnipotent image of itself; acknowledging the bad adults (for both belong to the child's fantasy, to its inner world), the child develops an image of its helplessness, its impotence. Indeed, this is the psychological basis for the structure of fairy tales, in which wonderful queens and fairies are counterposed to terrible witches.

A child typically outgrows this early position of splitting, but not without difficulty. As the child matures, fantasy is displaced by the emotional reality that it has only one mother, not two. But the child faces two emotional challenges. It must relinquish its fantasy of the ideal adult and its corresponding omnipotent core, and it must acknowledge that the bad mother, which it hated and feared, is also the mother it loves. Mourning the loss of its ideal world, the child first learns to struggle with feelings of *ambivalence*. It realizes that it sometimes hates the very person it loves and depends on. Indeed, if it cannot tolerate the anxiety and guilt that such ambivalence creates ("Will I lose my mother's love if I dislike her?" and "How can I hate the mother I love, how can I hurt her in this way?"), the child will be unable to develop a whole and realistic relationship to her.

Klein suggested that this emotional trajectory, while rooted in childhood experience, is restimulated at times of change and crisis in adult life.

She thus characterized these dilemmas as "positions" rather than "stages," suggesting that while they have their roots in childhood, they can shape feeling and thinking throughout life. For example, in facing Bird's management team, Donovan faced the problem of aligning and collaborating with the people who were potentially his opponents. But being relatively mature, he did not succumb to feelings of persecution ("They are out to get me") or to feelings of self-idealization ("I can be General Patton") and so fashioned a workable connection to Bird and his subordinates.

Indeed, Abraham Zaleznik has argued that such dynamics shape a leader's critical turning points in his or her career (Zaleznik, 1977). Examining Winston Churchill's extraordinary career, he argues that Churchill's capacity to manage the disappointment he felt when failing as navy secretary in World War I set the stage for his more powerful return as prime minister some two decades later. He relinquished his omnipotent hopes, while containing his feelings of persecution so that he developed a more realistic image of both his own powers and the world around him.

27

By contrast, Zaleznik suggests, James Forrestal, the secretary of defense under Truman, committed suicide precisely because he could not cope with his loss of power, his growing distance from Truman, and his growing realization that he would not and could not become president. Zaleznik argued that Forrestal's rigid and complete break with his family when a young man, his rejection of them as "all bad," made it difficult for him to acknowledge his own limits when facing career disappointments.

Calling these moments of disappointment the "depressive position," Klein suggested that at such periods the child and the adult must learn to "mourn." They mourn the loss of their ideal world, and they mourn the damage they have done to those they have depended on in the pursuit of their omnipotent fantasies. The alcoholic's dilemma is an extreme case, which illuminates these links between omnipotence and mourning. Faced with the collapse of his omnipotent fantasy—that he can control his drinking, that he can control his fate while creating an ideal, conflict-free world—the alcoholic who hits bottom faces for the first time the damage he has done to his family and loved ones. He must mourn the damage he has done as well as the loss of his omnipotent core. Indeed, by hitting bottom the alcoholic gives up his illusion of control, acknowledges his own despair, and can finally recognize the despair he has caused others as well. To be sure, the alcoholic presents an extreme case. But alcohol dependence is a symbol for the addictive power of all ambitions that stimulate omnipotent feelings and lead people to damage those they rely on, those they love.

The Capacity of Vision, the Ability to Mourn, and Management

Under "normal" conditions, the developmental process that Klein describes gives rise to a feeling of potency, whereby the person recognizes and accepts his or her own limits, recognizes and accepts external reality (people, natural forces, and created forces) as it is. This feeling of potency presupposes the ability to mourn afresh illusions of omnipotence.

To create or build, to conduct or manage, to change oneself or the world while making sure that one's feet remain on the ground represents neither impotence nor omnipotence, but ordinary human potency. It is an acceptance of individual and organizational realities that are imperfect and limited; it is an acceptance, therefore, of the imperfections and the limitations of one's associates or colleagues and an assumption of one's relative managerial responsibilities. This relative potency leads to a relative confidence in oneself and in others and to a desire to take calculated risks (in work, love, personal development, awareness, knowledge, etc.). One can foresee the pleasure that accompanies success as well as the grief that accompanies failure, yet remain sufficiently sure of oneself to keep a sense of humor, and to learn and recover from failure.

Figure 2.1 summarizes our argument. Leaders must both imagine a future and develop a vision while also remaining vigilant and careful. If they fail in the former task, they cannot develop the organization. If they fail in the latter, they cannot protect it. But each of these abilities is rooted in primitive or primal feelings. The capacity to imagine is linked to the capacity to idealize and thus has its roots in feelings of omnipotence. The capacity for vigilance is linked to feelings of vulnerability and thus has its early roots in feelings of impotence.

But these two feelings will remain split off from each other unless integrated by the ability to mourn. Leaders cannot link their capacity for imagination with their willingness to be vigilant unless they can mourn their failures and losses, whether they be dreams or unrealistic projects they were forced to abandon. Mourning represents an ability to accept one's faults and limitations and to integrate them with one's strengths and assets in practice (some faults may even be transformed into assets). We recognize the need to accept a human reality that is inevitably imperfect and blemished. In so doing, we finally develop the ability to accept ourselves, to abandon ourselves to what we truly are; this acceptance presupposes a capacity for introspection and integration. The ability to mourn thus presupposes an ability to recognize one's psychic reality, to return to and to live in reality after living within the imagination (the capacity for vision and imagination), to develop and to realize one's visions and projections in *works*, in *practice*. This capacity to accept reality, to work in it and not be blinded by one's necessary idealizations or be trapped by the rage one can feel at enemies, is the second pole of leadership.

Figure 2.1   The Leader's Feelings of Omnipotence, Impotence, and Relative Potency

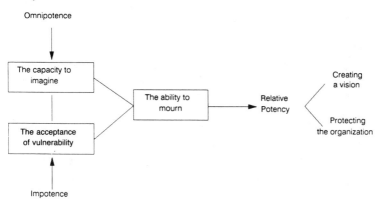

It is mainly in moments of personal or organizational crisis that the psychic foundations referred to above are most likely to be reactivated. Both impotence and omnipotence are profoundly human. The human condition (being mortal, having faults and limitations, and being aware of these to a certain degree) is hard to accept and narcissistically unbearable without a certain wish or desire for perfection, without a quest for absolutes, without a certain illusion of omnipotence, and without a flight into the imagination.

The *quebecois* leaders mentioned earlier demonstrated that they possessed a capacity for vision and vigilance as well as an ability to mourn. They knew themselves sufficiently well to wish to avoid falling into the traps of their own impotent or omnipotent reactions. In the exercise of power and of leadership, knowing onself means being aware of the potential existence of these two poles within oneself.

Implications for the Leader

Situated in the pressures of everday reality, leaders may be unable to explore psychologically their feelings of omnipotence, impotence, and relative potency. The more readily accessible experiences of feeling *responsible* and feeling *free* or at *liberty* can provide a window into the less accessible and unconsious conflicts between omnipotence and impotence.

We have suggested that the capacity for vision and vigilance and the ability to mourn determine leaders' feelings of relative potency and confidence in their ability to take risks and to succeed. In practice, underlying these two aspects of the leader's capabilities are issues of responsibility and liberty.

Like the unconscious, human liberty is a subtle phenomenon. Our liberty is inevitably very limited and restricted, but it is nonetheless real and essential. The distinction, however, between liberty and slavery is not always clear. There is a very large component of slavery in compulsive behavior, for example, even in the compulsive quest for liberty. There is obviously an element of slavery and a yielding to inner conflicts of unconscious origin in the constantly sought-after (and rarely fully exercised) pseudoliberty demanded by those rebels unable to accept any form of authority. We have seen this driven quality in the case of James Hoffa. In contrast, revolutionaries who struggle against corrupt or tyrannical regimes, against illegitimate leadership, or against untruths (even if these happen to be popular) demonstrate an authentic exercise of liberty. The exercise of liberty calls for courage and will. But paradoxically enough, true liberty cannot exist without the acceptance of a degree of inevitably imperfect authority, just as power cannot exist without the acceptance of human weaknesses and limitations.

30

There are two ways to become a victim of one's weaknesses or limitations. In each, omnipotence or impotence are split apart, with one or the other dominating. In the first case, one can view them as an insurmountable obstacle and give up from the start. Impotence dominates omnipotence, so one *fails by anticipation*. It is interesting to note that in Quebec, in French, we use the word "defeat" to mean "excuse" when we justify a refusal to take action. To our knowledge, this is the only francophone country where one says, "He has given himself a defeat." Sociocultural elements may thus contribute to feelings of impotence. In the second case, one does not take one's flaws or limitations seriously enough and then falls victim to them along the way. Omnipotence dominates impotence, and one fails *through oversight*. Each case leads to the inability of acknowledging both his or her responsibility and liberty. In the first, leaders act as if they have no freedom, no liberty to choose and shape their environment, and so avoid responsibility for their failure to act, to take risks. "Fate" precludes success. In the second, leaders act as if destiny magically determines their choices, so that acting irresponsibly, they become reckless and overstep bounds. In the first case pseudofate and in the second pseudodestiny shape awareness and action.

In order to succeed despite one's inevitable faults, one must first of all recognize and acknowledge both responsibility and liberty, "swallow and digest" them, and then manage them. Leaders interested in exploring their feelings of omnipotence, impotence, and relative potency can examine how they manage feelings of responsibility and liberty, being fated or destined. When confronting obstacles, what tendencies or pulls do they experience? Is one pulled in the direction of relinquishing one's right to act, or by contrast, does one act with obstinacy and recklessness, as if nothing is permitted to stand in the way? Finally, if one experiences both pulls, how are these contradictory experiences managed; and if they are, how are they ultimately integrated?

Such self-knowledge is critical, because when one is forewarned, one can be forearmed against one's weaknesses or faults and transform them externally and objectively into strengths. This also is a rational choice, a choice in which the subject accepts his or her responsibility.

Conclusion

In this chapter, we wished to show the relationship between a capacity for vision and vigilance and the ability to mourn on the one hand, and relative potency and humanistic leadership practice on the other. Since a human being's development is a lifelong process, the individual's actions, progress, the crises that must be confronted, can all reactivate the original feelings of persecution and frustration. As a result of this progression, the human being acquires what we call a capacity for vision and vigilance, which forms the basis of creativity and care, and the ability to mourn (specifically, to mourn omnipotence and magic thinking), which forms the basis of realistic action and the courage to express one's visions through concrete projects.

31

The ability to mourn is the bulwark both against the illusion of omnipotence (always landing on one's feet) and against impotence (hopelessness and rage). The constantly renewed awareness that our mortality in fact gives meaning to life should counteract our desire for possession, for domination. We are not referring here to acting "as if" one was immortal or "as if" one was going to die tomorrow, which are both subtle ways to deny death. To be human is to go on despite the awareness of the reality of death. It is the only way to enjoy life fully, powerfully, really to be alive. We could also hypothesize that the ability to mourn can be a remedy against stress, which is none other than the physical tension resulting from vain efforts designed to maintain the illusion of omnipotence (Freudenberger, 1980).

We could finally maintain that the ability to mourn is also the source of knowledge and of love, which would more closely approach the thinking of Melanie Klein. The power that is used to serve the desires of some for domination over others is paranoid in nature. We believe, however, that managing, directing, demonstrating leadership, and proposing a meaning for individual and collective action are not far removed from love.

REFERENCES

Cohen, A. R., and M. Merenda. 1979. "Jim Donovan (A), (B), and (C)." Unpublished case. Whittemore School of Business and Economics, University of New Hampshire.

Freudenberger, H. J. 1980. *Burn-out: The High Cost of High Achievement.* Garden City, N.Y.: Anchor Press.

Lapierre, L., and J.-M. Tolouse. 1984. "La graine à Monseigneur." Research paper. *75th Anniversary, Colloquium Series*, Division of Research, Harvard Business School.

Selznick, D., and J. Glickman. 1983. *Kennedy vs. Hoffa*. Twentieth-Century Fox Corporation (a series of four hours).

Silver, H. 1968. "James Hoffa and the Presidency of the International Brotherhood of Teamsters." Unpubished case. Harvard Business School.

Zaleznik, A. 1977. "Managers and Leaders: Are They Different?" *Harvard Business Review* (May–June), 67–78.

CHAPTER 3

Organizational Politics Against

Organizational Culture:

A Psychoanalytic Perspective

Howell S. Baum

Workers' frequent complaints about organizational "politics" indicate that many prevailing organizational cultures do not "feel right." Hoping to attract workers' loyalty, senior managers frequently promote the image of a conflict-free organization, in which all interests are congruent and politics is unnecessary. Nevertheless, while they promulgate mission statements and implement training programs to create integrated organizations, actual company cultures often demand social relations that conflict with workers' wishes for competence and attachment to the organization. For different reasons, managers and workers may be drawn to the organizational ideal, but both suffer from the absence of a sophisticated politics that permits people to promote their interests, even in conflict with others, without being expelled from the organization. Consider the following case.

Reprinted from *Human Resource Management*, vol. 28, number 2 (Summer 1989), pp. 191–206. © 1989 by John Wiley & Sons, Inc. Reprinted by permission of John Wiley & Sons, Inc.

Michael Anderson has worked for twenty years as a transportation planner with a county planning agency. He began with ambitions of designing an extensive modern transportation system in the county. He received three promotions in his first four years and acquired administrative responsibilities. Nevertheless, there were early signs he was not fitting into the organization.

In explaining his failure to get ahead, he used the following analogy to describe the dangers of acting aggressively or politically at work.

> Among coyotes, males are born into a pack; you have a whole litter. You have men who will never be leaders because of their biology, their genetics. And you have some more aggressive cubs, and they will do whatever they need to do to become leaders. And they have to eat the pack leader. And he never gives up until he can't resist any longer. I think I was born in that other group. When the puppies are born, they do all sorts of things to give the dominant male his rights, and they will do all sorts of growling, and the puppy will turn over. There are linkages back and forth between humans and coyotes. Somehow I must not ever have given my bosses that yelp and stomach up, and they sensed it. And I never got the membership and support I needed.

34

Anderson responded to his anxiety about politics in two ways. When he started out in the agency, he went with his director to present his transportation plans to the county council. He argued vehemently for his ideas, but he realized that elected officials considered him out of touch with local politics, and the director eventually stopped taking him along. Anderson reacted by isolating himself from others. He emphasized his autonomy in perfecting proposals without concern about their use.

At the same time, he turned his attention to renovating a houseboat. In part, this was another retreat from the dangers of acting aggressively: he could plan and develop the houseboat without fear of opposition. In addition, the move was a physical expression of a growing emotional retreat from the organization. Anxiety about power led him to work in isolation, and the more he focused on his autonomy, the less he felt able to identify with the organization as a whole.

Anderson's jungle analogy for bureaucratic politics expresses in exaggeration some common concerns about the nature of politics and the consequences of acting powerfully to get work done. A boss may seem like a father who insists on dominance and whom a subordinate must harm in order to advance. Often even small initiatives seem like vicious attacks on others, and devastating reprisal seems likely. Anderson's career suggests that anxiety about politics may lead workers to retreat from taking initiatives and to fail to identify with an organization.

This chapter examines how conventional organizational politics arouses anxiety that induces workers to withdraw emotionally from organizations, thereby defeating managerial hopes that workers will adhere to an integrative culture. The first section looks at aggression, power, and politics in work organizations. In the second section, the unconscious, developmental meanings of different power orientations and politics are analyzed. The third examines how conventional politics makes it psychologically difficult for workers to feel loyal to an organization. And in the final section, prospects for an integrative organizational culture are considered.

Aggression, Power, and Politics in Work Organizations

Many workers complain that organizational "politics" is something alien and antagonistic to their efforts to work (Baum, 1983, 1986, 1987, 1990). They find themselves in relationships where others treat them calculatingly, and they cannot be open to say what they think and feel. **35**

Yet every organization, at least tacitly, has a politics (i.e., procedures for promoting interests to allocate scarce resources). Some who complain about their organization's politics realistically describe practices interfering with their professional autonomy. Others, however, are expressing their discomfort with becoming involved in politics. Some dislike politics because it demands abilities they lack; they have difficulty conceptualizing issues in terms of interests or are poor strategizers. Others may feel uncomfortable confronting people, especially those who oppose them, and particularly those who seem powerful.

Their unease points to a number of *psychological* problems with politics. The organizational "politics" to which most workers react is a particular type of politics: the win-lose politics of interpersonal conflict. This politics depends on and engenders a specific experience of *power*, and people's largely unconscious reactions to it lead them not simply to complain but to avoid considering conflict productive and to retreat from organizations.

Politics and Aggression

Acting politically means acting *aggressively*—encouraging, persuading, or forcing others to act differently than they otherwise would. Hence people who criticize others for being "political" may be themselves particularly anxious about aggression. They may have legitimate grievances against leaders or managers, but they also hold back from thinking and acting politically in order to isolate themselves from a realm of aggressive activity.

Psychoanalytic theory helps understand people's reactions to politics and power by shedding light on typical patterns of unconscious thoughts and feelings about aggression. People who fear or are ambivalent about aggression often unconsciously associate small aggressive intentions with much larger ones. Then, exaggerating their own aims, they may imagine succeeding in the seeming effort to destroy someone else. In turn, they may feel guilty, fear retribution in kind, or both (Fenichel, 1945). Thus to avoid guilt, anxiety about punishment, or even shame from thinking of themselves as aggressive, they may deny their aggressive wishes and thoughts and attribute them to someone else. By denigrating politics they can even take pleasure in attacking others for what they do not want to accept in themselves (Klein, 1952).

The Fantasy of the Ideal Organization

36

The flight from aggression may be expressed and reinforced by the fantasy of an aggression-free organization, where politics can be avoided because it is not necessary. In an organization without aggression, so the fantasy goes, all would be close; crucially, all would be one and the same. And all, being one, would be omnipotent and omniscient. Further, all would care for one another; the great organization would care infinitely for everyone. This fantasy, which Schwartz (1985, 1987) characterizes as an "organizational ideal," corresponds to an individual's ego ideal: finding in adult life something that represents the power and loving that the self-centeredness of early infancy supplied (Chasseguet-Smirgel, 1985, 1986). Someone who identifies totally with an organizational ideal can feel loved and protected by a powerful entity. He or she can feel powerful without having to act aggressively. Thus some complaints about organizational "politics" register unconscious objections to a world of differences, in which some are larger and others are smaller, in which people are in conflict, and where outcomes are uncertain.

The Need for Aggression

Even though managers may have an easy time with workers who care for the organization and harbor no aggressive wishes against it, they also want subordinates to "work hard" and to "attack problems"—to be aggressive after all. Work requires an individual to act aggressively on materials and people in order to change them and direct them in desired ways. However, it also requires him or her to act with enough care so that materials or people are not physically or psychologically destroyed. Aggression in the task must not be so great that it hinders workers from identifying with one another and the organization.

Thus managers confront a dilemma: to encourage sufficient aggression to get work done, but to elicit enough caring to ensure that workers don't hurt one another and feel loyal to the organization. Unconsciously, workers face the quandary of how aggressively to act to be competent without feeling guilty or anxiously awaiting reprisal.

Yankelovich and Immerwahr's (1983) survey of American workers provides evidence of this dilemma. Eighty-eight percent say they want to work hard and do the best they can on the job, and more than half say they have an inner need to do the best job regardless of pay. Nevertheless, 75 percent say they could be significantly more effective on the job, and half say they work just hard enough to avoid getting fired. In other words, workers say they want to work aggressively but hold back. Some explain that they don't get paid any more for doing so. Others, pointing to the dilemma about aggression, say that managers provide little incentive to work harder.

Complaints about "politics" and workers' conflicts about working hard both express the problem of aggression in organizations: how to incorporate appropriate aggression in work while permitting realistic attachment to the organization. If a corporate culture is to allow workers to care for a realistically perceived organization, it must be supported by political norms that regulate aggression reassuringly.

37

Power Orientations and Alternative Politics

Conventional organizational politics is only one possible politics. In general, politics may be defined as the exercise of power to promote interests (for example, Dahl, 1961; and Lasswell, 1958), but there can be as many types of politics as there are types of power. The most common conception of power portrays independent parties asserting themselves to defeat one another. This is the principle of politics in a world of scarcity and conflicting interests. It is a zero-sum politics: when one party wins, another must lose. Normal organizational politics is an example.

Arendt (1958) has conceptualized power differently: as the ability of different parties to achieve something together they could not accomplish individually. This power governs a politics concerned with creating new possibilities in a world where resources may be scarce but some interests may be joined and new resources created. This is a win-win politics: victory is only collective, and one party's loss defeats all. This politics could offer an alternative to current organizational norms.

Significantly, different persons conceive power differently and practice politics differently in the same situation. McClelland's (1975) study of the experience of power finds that everyone acts through one of four "power orientations," which vary according to two dimensions. The *source* of power may be external (another person or a principle) or internal (oneself). The *object* of power, similarly, may be external (influencing or

TABLE 3.1. **Relations between Power Orientations, Developmental Stages, and Politics**

Type of Power	Stage of Development	Type of Politics
I ("It will strengthen, me")	Trust vs. Mistrust	Subordinacy
II ("I will strengthen myself.")	Autonomy vs. Shame, Doubt	Isolation
III ("I will have an impact on others.")	Initiative vs. Guilt	Interpersonal conflict
IV ("It will move me to serve others.")	Identity vs. Identity Confusion Intimacy vs. Isolation Generativity vs. Stagnation	Collaboration

38

controlling another) or internal (controlling or strengthening oneself). Equally important, drawing on the work of psychoanalyst Erik Erikson, McClelland suggests each power orientation corresponds to a specific stage in individual development. Thus, how people view and take up power is linked to their past developmental accomplishments and their present challenges. Figure 3.1, adapted from McClelland, and Table 3.1 summarize the power orientations and their links to Erikson's developmental stages.

A Developmental Concept of Stages and Phases

Erikson (1963, 1968) suggests that human development involves progressing through stages defined in terms of internal and interpersonal dilemmas. The infant—and later, the child, the adolescent, and the adult—confronts others in the world and demands that their relationship satisfy certain expectations related to its biological condition and social history. Success at any developmental stage—for example, the older child's need to learn to exercise aggressive initiative without guilt—depends on continuing success at all previous stages and permits advancement to the next challenge. When someone fails a particular developmental test, he or she may remain effective at preceding tasks but have difficulty advancing. This person may have partial success at later tasks, but most of his or her effort is concentrated on the unmet challenge. For example, employees who cannot take initiative without feeling guilty not only will have difficulty presenting their position when this means challenging someone, but also will have problems working competently and securing a work identity. Instead, they will continually practice acting aggressively.

Sometimes a person who has passed a particular developmental stage may encounter a situation that presents a challenge corresponding to that stage, which cannot be readily mastered. When this happens, the individual "regresses" to concerns with the developmental dilemma of that

FIGURE 3.1. Classification of Power Orientations

Object of Power	*Source of Power*	
	Other	Self
Self (to feel stronger)		
Intention:	"It" (God, my mother, my leader, food) will strengthen me.	I will strengthen, control, direct myself.
Action:	Being near a source of strength.	Collecting, accumulating information, things.
	I	II
Other (to influence)	IV	III
Intention:	It (religion, laws, my group) will move me to serve, influence others, to do my duty.	I will have an impact (influence) on others.
Action:	Action on higher principle or purpose.	Competing with, affecting others.

Adapted from McClelland (1975), p. 14.

stage, almost as if it were being confronted for the first time. For example, a man who has normally been able to take initiative without guilt may run into a supervisor or situation that makes him feel guilty about how he works or anxious about his or others' aggression. As a result, he will have difficulty continuing to work competently. Losing self-confidence, he may become fixated on the problem of aggression and react to many situations as simply being tests of his ability to take initiative.

The following discussion describes Erikson's developmental stages and shows how they are related to the power orientations McClelland discovered.

Types of Power

Type I: Power and the Stage of Trust Versus Mistrust. The infant relating to the mother encounters the first question, in Erikson's terms, of whether it should regard the world with "basic trust" or "basic mistrust," whether it can depend on the mother to provide the fundamental support needed for living. Someone who as an adult still seeks reassurance of the world's basic trustworthiness is likely to take a Type I orientation to power ("It strengthens me"). Not only does this orientation provide security; it also represents the only orientation of which such a person is capable. It expresses a wish to feel powerful by working for someone else who is powerful and who can therefore be trusted to provide a secure world. It may characterize someone who chooses to advise an elected official or top manager and takes satisfaction in the closeness of loyal service to someone strong.

This does not mean that a staff advisor who enjoys drawing on the strength of a line executive is simply a baby. Everyone to some degree continues to seek the reassurance of a nurturing environment in later life; rather, adults differ in their need for this confirmation. People who hold the Type I power orientation may especially need or take pleasure from such reassurance. Similarly, the motives for becoming a staff advisor, for example, are infinitely more complex than those of the infant who wants just to be fed. Moreover, nothing in any unconscious connection between particular advising roles and earlier concerns about a mother's trustworthiness diminishes the validity and value of the activity. Indeed, this power orientation may especially suit someone for advising work. These observations are true for the other three power orientations as well.

Type II: Autonomy Versus Shame and Doubt. Once an infant feels it can trust the world and its agents, it encounters the second dilemma, of "autonomy versus shame and doubt." Can it act independently in the trustworthy world without seeming too small, inept, or inadequate? A child seeks to prove its independence by collecting and controlling objects that represent the substance of the world. An adult who is still worried about

40

autonomy is likely to take a Type II orientation ("I strengthen or control myself"). It expresses a wish to feel powerful by being independent of everyone else, free of contact with others and not bound by their interests or actions. It may characterize someone who is interested in data collection. By accumulating and managing information, a person may gain a sense of control over the objects the data represent.

Type III: Initiative Versus Guilt. As the young child develops a sense of autonomy, it confronts the challenge of "initiative versus guilt." Increasingly mobile, the child asserts him- or herself against others such as parents. Can he or she take initiatives against them without feeling guilty about hurting them? The child must find an answer to this question in the specific terms of the Oedipus complex: at this time, a child normally wishes to defeat the same-sex parent in a contest for the affection of the other parent. The outcome of the struggle is decisive for later assumptions the child and adult will make about the meanings and consequences of acting lovingly and aggressively. The challenge of learning guilt-free initiative is to find ways of acting aggressively without hurting those one loves.

41

The Type III power orientation ("I have an impact on others") expresses the perspective of this period. People think of becoming powerful by doing battle with others and defeating them for their possessions or positions. Adults who have not fully resolved the Oedipal dilemma may unconsciously exaggerate the danger of conflict and the likelihood of reprisal or, alternatively, the chances of success and resultant guilt. Professionally, this power orientation may characterize strategists or organizers.

Type IV: Identity and Intimacy Versus Identity Confusion and Isolation. Erikson's last four stages present challenges posed by the search for identity, intimacy, generativity, and integrity. The first two of these are especially closely tied to the Type IV power orientation. Adolescents face the challenge of consolidating a cohesive "identity against identity confusion." They decide with which ideas, people, and, crucially, occupation or career they want to identify (and be identified) for the rest of their lives. Once adults feel secure about who they are, they face the test of being able to engage in "intimacy," rather than ending up in "isolation." Individuals must face the possibilities of closeness against the risks of vulnerability, exposure, and loss. They practice loving wishes in relations with others equal to themselves. When they succeed, the most important new intimacies are sexual, but friendships and affiliations with work organizations also provide opportunities for attachment. This intimacy is the basis for realistic identification with co-workers and work organizations.

The Type IV power orientation ("It moves me to serve others") expresses a wish to feel powerful by directing others in the name of general principles or collective interests. It involves more or less intimate interaction among people who understand who they are and accept others as their partners. People attempt to resolve differences according to mutually accepted norms, rather than individual wishes. This orientation is the most complex of the four, depending on successful development through adulthood. It entails the ability to take initiative in acting competently and intimately with others who are equal. It may be expressed by managers or leaders who act on collective interests rather than personal loyalties. "Professionals" commonly couch their actions in terms of the "neutrality" of this orientation, directing other people in the name of abstract principles.

Just as the stages of identity formation are developmentally linked, so are McClelland's power orientations. *Success at any power orientation depends on mastering the preceding ones.* For example, someone frightened by a Type III power orientation cannot understand or begin to learn the Type IV orientation. Further, he may retreat to a Type II orientation, where he can be alone, dependent only on his own efforts and resources. At most, he will see power in terms of win-lose conflicts.

In addition, as the earlier discussion suggested, power orientations and stages of identity development are reciprocally related. Political success reinforces accomplishments at a corresponding developmental stage. Failure unsettles achievements at the corresponding stage, as well as subsequent stages. For example, someone who has not found ways of taking initiative without guilt will not be secure or effective in the Type III power orientation. Conversely, someone who has trouble with conflict in the Type III orientation will have difficulty moving beyond autonomy to initiative, as well as meeting later challenges.

Types of Politics

As Table 3.1 indicates, each of the different power orientations and its associated developmental stage encourage a particular type of organizational politics. The Type I orientation leads to a politics of subordinacy, in which people look for others who are strong on whom they can depend. This orientation corresponds to unconscious fantasies about a strong, caring, "politics"-free organization, and may be expressed in wishes for an integrating culture.

The Type II orientation leads to a politics of isolation, in which people try to become self-sufficient by accumulating as many resources as possible. People may express this orientation through a cynical retreat from "politics."

The Type IV orientation, which corresponds to Arendt's concept of power, can be the basis for a realistically sophisticated collaborative politics through which workers can promote interests and resolve conflicts while feeling some attachment to co-workers and the organization. If people begin with the assumption that co-workers, including managers, will continue to support one another despite conflicts over real differences, they can assert their interests vigorously but securely. They will be able to solve problems that conventional "politics" masks. Even if specific decisions do not satisfy everyone, people will be more likely to feel the procedures are legitimate.

Finally, the Type III orientation leads to conventional organizational "politics," the politics of win-lose competition for programmatic resources and career opportunities. People characterize this politics as self-interested, rather than collectively oriented. It is concerned with winning rather than collaborating. It is devious and circuitous rather than direct and straightforward. It is selfishly calculating rather than disinterestedly rational. It favors collusion over competence.

Politics and Regression   **43**

Type III politics holds out two dangers. It induces workers with more advanced development to regress in order to participate, and it entails expressions of aggression that make workers anxious and encourage them to regress to defend themselves.

The Regressive Effects of Participation in "Politics"

For those who regard their work in terms of a Type IV power orientation—who see themselves acting on general principle, serving collective interests, or mediating conflicts—Type III politics calls on them to act in ways consistent with a developmentally earlier orientation. Someone acting with a Type III orientation makes it difficult for others to maintain a Type IV orientation: there is no commitment to reasoning together and collaborating. It is tempting—and may be strategically necessary—to step down from the Type IV position.

Sometimes people with Type IV orientations engage in Type III politics while continuing to think of the possibilities for Type IV politics. They do not regress, their previous development is unaffected, and they act relatively effectively. However, "politics" may regressively affect both power orientations and identity development. A Type IV orientation depends on a secure sense of industry, a coherent personal identity, and comfort in intimacy. Because the Type III orientation corresponds to earlier efforts to free initiative from guilt and reprisal, participation in such politics unconsciously recalls childhood anxiety about aggressiveness. Sometimes people with Type IV orientations find Type III situations so difficult they lose some of their sense of competence, identity, or ability to be intimate.

These dangers to personal identity help explain why relatively few workers feel loyal to their organizations. Continuing involvement in

Type III politics makes it difficult for a worker to be close to and care for co-workers or to identify with an organization. When workers conceptualize most of their relationships in terms of calculated triumph over rivals, they have trouble thinking of co-workers as persons whose welfare they share. Superficially, people might observe they are so annoyed by "politics" that they don't feel part of the workplace. This statement describes an unconscious connection: "politics" makes intimacy difficult.

Regressive Defenses Against the Aggression of Politics

All politics are expressions of aggression, in attempting to influence, move, shape, or harm others or the self. In different ways, Freud (1962 [1930]) and Klein (1975 [1932], 1964 [1937]) argue that social life is possible only if people have opportunities to balance their aggression with expressions of love and caring. Unconsciously, being able to act lovingly toward others compensates for imagined dangers from aggressively harming others, being punished, and feeling guilty.

Type III politics is unconsciously associated with earlier Oedipal conflicts with parents, when the risks of aggression seemed greatest. Success in earlier development depended on learning to act both lovingly and aggressively toward parents and others. At work, managerial exhortations to work hard call for aggression yet fail to provide opportunities for caring for others. Conventional "politics" similarly encourages individuals to set themselves off from others and fight them for scarce rewards. As a result, even when some people benefit from strategic action, engagement in "politics" unconsciously makes many people anxious about aggression that is unbalanced by caring. When workers think in terms of individual achievement and when they concentrate on attacking co-workers, they become isolated and are unlikely to affiliate deeply with an organization.

Workers may defend themselves against the anxiety of involvement in Type III politics in several ways. For example, some continue to work and act aggressively but try to deny any harm or express any guilt from their efforts.

Others unconsciously regress to a Type II power orientation and argue cynically that "politics" is immoral and dangerous. They will work well but independently, so they don't have to deal with co-workers, owe them anything, or risk losing to them. Some rationalize their actions in terms of a pseudo–Type IV orientation. They say they are serving "economic efficiency" or "the public interest," and their positions should overrule the selfish actions of "politicians." Claiming moral superiority, they almost magically expect power without coming into contact with co-workers.

A still more regressive defense is fantasizing that the organization is an intimate place where caring pervades and aggression is unnecessary. Regression to this Type I orientation is usually less consistent with getting work done than the Type II defense because it rules out the aggression that most work requires. It depends partly on a magical belief that, if a worker holds back on acting aggressively, identifying with the organization and managers will provide the power to get work done.

These defenses retreat from realistic relationships with co-workers and an organization. By protecting workers from dangers of aggression, they require holding back from aggressive action, not simply in social relations but also in work itself. In addition, these regressions in power orientation have regressive consequences in personal development. They redirect concern to problems of aggression and initiative, autonomy, or basic trust and make it difficult for a worker to maintain a sense of competence. Crucially, workers are developmentally unable to feel secure being close to co-workers or identifying with a real organization.

Regression and Withdrawal

Conventional organizational "politics" often presents workers with a difficult choice: risk regression in order to promote their interests and get work done. Many workers fear not only another person's power to harm or hinder them, but, crucially, *they are afraid of their own regression.* They fear losing the mastery, sense of identity, and possibilities of intimacy that have come with their past development. Workers whose development is insecure find work and "politics" especially threatening and may choose the safety of withdrawal, caring less about work or the organization.

In Sum

Workers' capacity to identify with an organization depends on the fit between their personal development and the norms of organizational politics. Type III politics is appropriate for resolving conflicts among interests where resources are scarce. However, by arousing anxiety about aggression, it encourages people to exaggerate scarcities and conflicts. As a result, people apply Type III norms unthinkingly to many situations where Type IV politics might lead to more constructive solutions (see Argyris, 1982; Argyris and Schön, 1978).

Even effective participation in Type III politics is consciously and unconsciously inconsistent with identification with an organization as a whole. Moreover, when workers feel anxious about Type III and defend themselves by regression, they take power orientations that are still less likely to deal realistically with interests and conflicts. The defenses protecting workers from dangers of aggression require them to hold back on acting aggressively. In addition, such responses as subordinacy, isolation, and unthinking aggression move workers further from experiencing an organization as a place of security and development.

When an organization seems dangerous, both personal development and political sophistication are threatened. Workers retreat from realistic relationships with co-workers and the organization to power orientations that are unlikely to get work done. Moreover, they are less likely to feel competent and secure in their work. Centrally, conventional "politics" makes it constitutionally difficult for people to identify *as adults* with organizations.

Conventional Politics and the Problem of Organizational Loyalty: Prospects for Organizational Culture

46

Can managers promote organizational loyalty and identification? They cannot significantly change workers' inner lives, but they can shape the conditions to which workers respond. In particular, managers may succeed in creating an integrative organizational culture to the extent that they support the unconscious requirements for intimacy. This analysis suggests that such a program has four requirements.

First, a culture is not simply a set of rules like work procedures, nor is it merely a compendium of stories managers repeatedly tell. A culture comprises values and norms that affect people because the accompanying actions make sense and feel right. Hence efforts to "create an organizational culture" depend on changes in day-to-day activities (see, for example, Deal and Kennedy, 1982; Martin, 1982; Schwartz, 1985; and Smircich, 1983).

Second, contemporary work, much of it intellectual and interpersonal service activity, must make new sense in two ways. The traditional work language of "production" and "productivity" does not obviously fit what many people do. They "produce" insights, decisions, or personal relationships, but this is not equivalent to producing an automobile, the prototypical work image. People have difficulty measuring themselves when they spend their days attending meetings, talking on the phone, and exchanging memoranda. Managers need to reconceptualize what workers do in terms that reveal the value of their activities.

At the same time, day-to-day activities must make workers important. They need recognition for specific efforts, such as authorship of reports. They need to see consequences to their actions, by participating in and observing decisions about whether and how their efforts are used (see Yankelovich and Immerwahr, 1983). They need to be associated with things that last, whether tangible products or programs or organizations themselves (see Denhardt, 1981; Schwartz, 1987).

People should be able to produce things they regard as useful, valuable, and lasting. If workers can care for the bit of themselves they see in their products, this loving also repairs imagined damage from working hard or occasionally working against others (see Hirschhorn, 1988).

Third, working conditions and incentive systems must have the unconscious effect of allowing people to balance aggressive work with caring work. They should have the opportunity to work collaboratively and be evaluated as team members. If co-workers come to care for one another, this affection will hold them together through conflicts among them, and it will unconsciously compensate for anxiety from working aggressively. In addition, these changes require the creation of Type IV organizational politics.

Fourth, for workers to act with the maturity needed to identify with co-workers and an organization, they must participate in a politics that enables them to discover and serve collective interests. They need ways of expressing real differences and resolving conflicts that allow them to remain connected to co-workers and invested in collective work. Type IV **47** politics, like every politics, begins in formal authority relations and spreads to other relationships. If managers and supervisors discuss issues, problems, and conflicts honestly and with concern about subordinates' welfare, subordinates may learn they can express differences and pursue interests without fear of destructive conflict or anxiety. If managers who must make decisions that displease some can honestly explain their actions in terms of general principles and collective interests, both winners and losers may remain loyal to the managers and organization.

Simply, any organizational culture that realistically develops worker loyalty must be accompanied by practices and politics that enable people to work hard, together.

REFERENCES

Arendt, H. 1958. *The Human Condition.* Chicago: University of Chicago Press.

Argyris, C. 1982. *Reasoning, Learning, and Action.* San Francisco: Jossey-Bass.

Argyris, C. and D. A. Schön. 1978. *Organizational Learning.* Reading, Pa.: Addison-Wesley.

Baum, H. S. 1983. *Planners and Public Expectations.* Cambridge, Mass.: Schenkman.

———. 1986. "Politics in Planners' Practice." In B. Checkoway (ed.), *Strategic Approaches to Planning Practice.* Lexington, Mass.: Lexington Books.

———. 1987. *The Invisible Bureaucracy.* New York: Oxford University Press.

———. 1990. *Organizational Membership: Personal Development in the Workplace.* Albany: SUNY Press.

Chasseguet-Smirgel, J. 1985. *The Ego Ideal: A Psychoanalytic Essay on the Malady of the Ideal.* Translated by Paul Burrows. New York: W. W. Norton.

———. 1986. *Sexuality and Mind: The Role of the Father and the Mother in the Psyche.* New York: New York University Press.

Dahl, R. 1961. *Who Governs?* New Haven: Yale University Press.

Deal, T. E., and A. A. Kennedy. 1982. *Corporate Cultures: The Rites and Rituals of Corporate Life.* Reading, Pa.: Addison-Wesley.

Denhardt, R. B. 1981. *In the Shadow of Organization*. Lawrence: Regents Press of Kansas.

Erikson, E. H. 1963. *Childhood and Society*. 2d ed. New York: W. W. Norton.

———. 1968. *Identity: Youth and Crisis*. New York: W. W. Norton.

Fenichel, O. 1945. *The Psychoanalytic Theory of Neurosis*. New York: W. W. Norton.

Freud, S. 1930. *Civilization and Its Discontents*. Translated and edited by James Strachey. New York: W. W. Norton.

Hirschhorn, L. 1988. *The Workplace Within: Psychodynamics of Organizational Life*. Cambridge, Mass.: MIT Press.

Klein, M. 1952. "Notes on some schizoid mechanisms." in Joan Riviere (ed.), *Developments in Psycho-Analysis*. London: Hogarth.

———. 1964. "Love, Guilt and Reparation." In *Love, Hate, and Reparation*, by Melanie Klein and Joan Riviere. New York: W. W. Norton.

———. 1975. *The Psycho-Analysis of Children*. Translated by Alix Strachey, revised by Alix Strachey and H. A. Thorner. New York: Dell.

Lasswell, H. 1958. *Politics: Who Gets What, When, How*. New York: Meridian Books.

Martin, J. 1982. "Stories and Scripts in Organizational Settings." In Albert Hastorf and Alice M. Isen (eds.), *Cognitive Social Psychology*. New York: Elsevier North-Holland.

McClelland, D. C. 1975. *Power: The Inner Experience*. New York: Irvington Publishers.

Schwartz, H. S. 1985. "The Usefulness of Myth and the Myth of Usefulness: A Dilemma for the Applied Organizational Scientist." *Journal of Management*, 11, 31–42.

———. 1987. "Anti-Social Actions of Committed Organizational participants: An Existential Psychoanalytic Perspective." *Organization Studies*, 8, 327–340.

Smircich, L. 1983. "Concepts of Culture and Organizational Analysis." *Administrative Science Quarterly*, 28, 339–358.

Yankelovich, D., and J. Immerwahr. 1983. *Putting the Work Ethic to Work*. New York: Public Agenda Foundation.

CHAPTER 4

Contemporary Perspectives on Personal and Organizational Authority:

The Self in a System of Work Relationships

Laurence J. Gould

> Man must be at peace with the sources of his life. If he is ashamed of them, if he is at war with them, they will haunt him forever. They will rob him of his basis of assurance, and will leave him an interloper in the world.
>
> —Walter Lippman, 1915

Introduction

In contemporary organizations there is an increasing need for managers and executives to function in rapidly changing, more complex, and more fluid environments—both internally and externally. Mergers, acquisitions, precipitous bankruptcies, massive layoffs, shifting alliances, and turbulence in the marketplace all conspire to make the experience of organizational stability and continuity fragile. Organizations were, to be sure, never closed systems, but in more stable times with much slower rates of change, they were experienced as self-contained and self-perpetuating. By contrast, contemporary postindustrial organizations often have quite the opposite character. They are experienced as unstable, chaotic, turbulent, and often unmanageable. There are many reasons that organizational environments are changing, including the globalization of work, rapid technological advances, the increasingly diverse nature of the workforce, and last but not least, and the subject of this chapter, corresponding changes in attitudes, beliefs, and values related to the nature of authority and the dilemmas encountered in its exercise.

Taken together, these factors suggest that those responsible for managing organizations and for organizational change and development must have the requisite psychological and systems knowledge to take leadership in their roles and to function effectively under increasingly novel conditions, including the likelihood that: (1) people at every level in the organization will be encouraged to be more self-managing in their roles because they have a sense of purpose and the requisite and appropriate authority to act. Respect will be a significant aspect of all effective working relationships and a crucial incentive for the loyalty, performance, and retention of high-caliber employees; (2) organizations will become increasingly "flat" as older hierarchical forms of authority and influence give way to more collaborative influence-based models of work relatedness; (3) by the year 2000 the majority of the workforce in America will be women and members of ethnic subgroups. This will require considerably more complex and demanding capacities for relatedness, as individuals, groups, and teams are increasingly required to work across cultural, ethnic, and gender boundaries; (4) more and more managers, administrators, and executives will have a consultation orientation, and what staff there are who hold the organization's center will not second-guess operating or field units or undermine their authority—rather, their role will be to set overall goals and enable the units to carry them out. These extraordinary changes will require new and far more sophisticated skills, competencies, attitudes, and knowledge about the psychological and systemic forces that drive and shape organizations and the people in them, and considerably more sophisticated forms of relatedness as the workforce becomes increasingly heterogeneous, and markets more globalized. A major general consequence, which is the thesis of this chapter, is that an unprecedented level of self-management will be necessary as a basis for action in the absence of prescriptions, orders, commands, standardized routines, and well-defined hierarchical structures, and that a strong sense of personal authority is the crucial determinant of effective self-management.

It is perhaps difficult to comprehend fully how much managers today must exercise a level of discretionary authority almost unheard-of even a decade ago, and this trend will continue and accelerate. The point is clear—if external authority, hierarchical command structures, and agreed-upon informal conventions that have evolved over long periods of organizational and cultural time are no longer adequate to guide behavior, managers perforce will be increasingly thrown back on their own personal sense of authority as the basis for action. That is, delegations of authority will be more in the form of guidelines rather than in the form of specific orders and requirements. More and more, managers will have general goals set for them (and they, in turn, will set more general goals for their subordinates), but how such goals are accomplished will increasingly be determined "locally." The corollary point is that those whose sense of personal authority is inadequate or insufficiently developed will have, even more than before, difficulties in managing effectively, particularly as they advance to more responsible positions in the organization. It will no longer be sufficient to be simply a "good soldier" or a good team player. Effective management will require the constant taking of initiative and managing the corresponding anxieties of being accountable for the discretion one has been delegated. Given these requirements, a crucial question arises as to the sources and nature of those personal gyroscopes that guide directed and purposeful action in the absence of clear external guidelines. It is in this context that the nature of personal authority and its relationship to organizational authority becomes paramount.

51

In the following sections, I define the nature of personal authority, highlight its links to organizational authority, examine through clinical cases how personal authority shapes organizational authority—that is, behavior-in-role—and conclude with some key hypotheses about the kind of organizational culture that facilitates effectively taking up and exercising mature organizational authority.

The Nature of Personal Authority

Since the term *authority* is used so variously, it is useful to begin with the matter of definition and to distinguish between organizational and personal authority. *Organizational authority* is defined as the authority that is delegated to roles, and therefore it gives the role occupant the "right-to-work"—that is, the right-to-work within the boundaries of the role. *Personal authority* is the counterpart of organizational authority. It is a central aspect of one's enduring sense of self no matter what role one may occupy. It is, therefore, defined as the "right-to-be"—that is, the right to exist fully and to be oneself-in-the-role. Needless to say, the right-to-work and the right-to-be also entail corollary social and ethical responsibilities, obligations, duties, and ultimately accountability for one's performance and behavior.

To elaborate further, we can say that *personal authority is experienced when individuals feel entitled to express their interests and passions, when they feel that their vitality and creativity belong in the world, and when they readily accept the power and vitality of others as contributions to their own experience. They give themselves and others permission to be vital, or in a word, to be authentic-in-role.* In this context, personal authority can be thought of as existing on a continuum. At one end of this continuum are those who have a well-developed, realistic, appropriate, confident, and robust sense of personal authority. At the other end are people with serious difficulties around their sense of authority. Such difficulties can take many forms. Sometimes they are manifested and experienced as a seeming excess of personal authority—that is, a grandiose, unrealistic, unmodulated, narcissistic sense of authority, a belief that one is permitted to do and have everything. Or alternatively, we see those who seem to have a weak, anxious sense of their own authority—that is, those who believe they are permitted nothing. Whatever form these difficulties take, adults will experience them when they attempt to exercise authority in their organizational roles.

A person's internal sense of his or her authority is shaped in the crucible of family relations as parents make manifest their desires, fears, and wishes for their children. As parents legitimate or delegitimate a child's interests, curiosity, and feelings, the child feels either authorized or deauthorized to express his or her inner vitality, his or her "real self." Most children usually develop powerful feelings and fantasies of being delegated (or denied) some important authority, and these feelings may become reinforced by the parents over a long period of time. For example, a child may come to feel the responsibility for taking care of the damaged family or a particular family member at the expense of his or her own pleasure, independence, and accomplishment. Similarly, a child may come to feel that his or her role is to be the family martyr, the family savior, the family "screw-up," or the fair-haired boy or girl.

To be sure, people are not simply passive receptacles. Some are innately more resilient; others are more easily influenced. A child's sense of personal authority emerges at the intersection of parental influences and demands and the way he or she internalizes and interprets these experiences. Indeed, psychotherapists often see in their patients powerful fantasies about their own authority—what they have been or are permitted to do—that have little relation to reality. The therapist experiences these fantasies in the "transference" as patients bring all their feelings about their own authority and the therapist's presumed authority to the therapeutic relationship. Whether the patient tries to control, gratify, please, rebel against, or undermine the therapist, he or she is enacting his or her own deepest feelings about authority.

Although a person's sense of authority is shaped by early family relationships, it should be emphasized that it can and does change and develop over the course of the life cycle. New experiences with teachers, mentors, and peers can repair earlier damage to one's sense of self. Alternatively, a severe trauma later in life can lead a person with a robust sense of personal authority to feel undermined and conflicted. Survivors of catastrophic events provide an obvious example. Because they often feel profoundly guilty, they act as if they are not entitled to any pleasure, gratification, or success. They deauthorize themselves in the sense that they no longer feel entitled to enjoy or accomplish anything.

The Exercise of, and the Relationship between, Personal and Organizational Authority

A sense of one's own personal authority deeply affects how individuals take up their organizational roles and how authorized they feel to take **53** initiative and accomplish their objectives. An inhibited person who feels entitled to very little may fail to exercise the minimum amount of authority vested in his or her role. By contrast, people who are grandiose and have an inflated sense of self may exceed the maximum available authority in their roles, leading them to deny others the appropriate exercise of their authority. Moreover, as I have already suggested, increasingly, people have significant freedom to choose how they take up their roles. This means that their own personal characteristics—who they are, what they are feeling, how past and present have combined to determine their behavior—increasingly shape the resulting texture of roles in the organization.

Three Cases

Given the above, I would like to present case material illustrating in some detail how difficulties in developing an adequate sense of personal authority may originate.[1] I would then like to suggest explicitly how such difficulties are related to the ways in which one exercises one's personal authority in organizational work roles. There is one important caveat, however—namely, the reciprocal nature of personal and organizational authority. While the purpose of this chapter, and therefore the case material, is cast in the direction of how personal authority influences the exercise of organizational authority, the converse is also true. A central assumption is that although an individual's sense of self, and hence personal authority, determines to a significant extent how he or she functions in role, important aspects of behavior and experience are critically affected by the setting. What a person is capable of doing and what parts of the self achieve expression depend on conditions that inhibit or amplify particular attitudes and potentials. In an organization, these conditions are set by its structure, group and social dynamics, culture, and operating methods.[2]

The following three therapy cases—two vignettes of Diane and Robert, respectively, and a more extended case description of Matt—highlight how issues of personal authority and the ways in which people exercise authority at work are inextricably linked. Diane experienced an inflated sense of self and thus denied others their authority. Robert and Matt, by contrast, failed to take up the authority available to them to perform successfully in their roles. I will highlight the origins of these difficulties, how they affected each person's relationship to me as the therapist, and how they became manifested in the organizational context.

Diane. Diane entered psychotherapy complaining of depression, which she explicitly felt began with her father's death two years earlier. She said she couldn't understand why it was taking her so long to get over it, and if anything, she was feeling worse and worse. As a merchandising director for a large clothing manufacturer, she was extremely competent and generally appreciated but was having increasing difficulties with her boss and subordinates. She was impatient with her staff and usually dismissed their tentatively offered advice and opinions. Further, she required, and often demanded, "pride of place" with her boss to the exclusion of everybody else, including his wife.

During the course of therapy, important features of the familial and psychological roots of her behavior became clearer. The oldest of five siblings with two younger sisters behind her and then two brothers, Diane, as her "father's little wife," was to be the competent alternative to her scattered, incompetent, depressed, and disorganized mother. Further, she felt that her mother was quite resigned to this state of affairs, which left her free to manage (quite competently, in fact) the four younger children. In her father's eyes, Diane was the antithesis of her mother. She was competent to manage all the affairs of the house and was "wise beyond her years"; her father often said to her, "You are my indispensable little girl."

In her relationship with me, she recreated many aspects of her relationship with her father, making me into a longed-for substitute. She alternatively craved my admiration and attempted to take care of me. She detailed each small victory or triumph, excoriated unappreciative colleagues and friends, and with each recounting waited expectantly for my approval, agreement, and support. When it was not forthcoming, she either became furious, bitter, withdrawn, and contemptuous, accusing me of insensitivity, coldness, and incompetence, or became tearful, hurt, and whiny. She also tried to take care of me, was solicitous if I appeared tired, proffered recommendations about my ties, and begged to undertake having my office repainted and redecorated.

Her family history and the transference that developed paralleled her situation at work. Just as she had felt contempt for her siblings, whom she characterized as "my mother's kids," she believed that she was her boss's best subordinate. Just as she became daddy's little wife, she expected and covertly demanded the undivided attention of her boss and a special emotional relationship with him. While she was undoubtedly competent, these conflicts distorted her sense of personal authority. She felt entitled to too much. Consequently, she gave less and less psychological permission to her subordinates and peers and demanded more and more authority. The trauma of her father's death exacerbated these already existing difficulties and diminished further her ability to take up her authority at work in a mature way.

Put in schematic terms, we would say that initially her grandiose sense of personal authority dominated her role and "spilled over" into her boss's and subordinates' roles. She knows best; the others are fools or incompetents. Her own role in the organization does not leave any room for others to make a contribution. The more authority she took for herself, the less she gave to others. As she made progress in therapy, she was able to redefine her authority so that it was appropriately expressed within the boundary of her role, leaving room for her colleagues and subordinates to make a contribution. She was also, as she came to understand herself, better able to relinquish her need for a special relationship with her boss.

Rob. Rob entered treatment at the age of thirty-seven following a devastating performance review. In the early sessions he told me how a reorganization and a related shift in reporting relationships "pulled the carpet out from under him." His new boss wanted him to devote all his energies to work on delayed, over-budget, new products, for which he had a major R&D responsibility for several key components, or else risk being let go. As a senior engineer in R&D, Rob felt that his boss's demand was gratuitous. What else would he be doing?

As his story unfolded, it became apparent that he was, in fact, doing many other things—many, many other things, including leading a popular company country and western band, participating on three task forces, voluntarily teaching an advanced computer course, and playing "counselor" to a large number of younger colleagues. To be sure, he was quite competent in each of these roles, as well as in his primary organizational role. He was liked by his staff and colleagues, widely respected, and always available. But despite his competence, his boss was correct: he was neglecting his major responsibilities. In early sessions, he angrily complained about being "reigned in," "squelched," misunderstood, and suddenly unappreciated by his new boss, despite his obvious dedication, loyalty, and devotion to the company. He also began to become extremely anxious.

In his relationship with me, Rob began to reenact his complex relationship to his work role. He was the man who knew about everything,

55

including psychoanalysis and psychotherapy. He also tried to be helpful and enlightening, and he became concerned about other patients whose paths he crossed in my waiting room. He talked about books, movies, politics, music, mythology, and archaeology with appropriate modesty and not the slightest hint of braggadocio. He also ingenuously offered to computerize my billing system. But it was often quite difficult to get him to focus on the subject at hand—namely, himself.

In reconstructing his family history, it became apparent that he was indeed cast in the role of "needing to know it all and be it all." His parents were academic and professional bluebloods, both multitalented, who shared an attitude of patronizing, intellectual noblesse oblige. To be competent at one thing was to be, in his family, a narrow "specialist," a term uttered with unconcealed disdain. He learned early that this was the fate of his older sister, who not only flagrantly rejected these lofty parental injunctions, but had the bad grace to be a chronic problem child with episodes of destructive and self-destructive behavior and, later, a constant series of minor delinquent entanglements. So he became the offical "good boy," manifesting his goodness by becoming a caricature of the Renaissance man he felt his parents could wholeheartedly endorse. Thus he could uphold the family's good name, as he ruefully later said, "unto the next generation."

In parallel with his therapy, Rob reproduced these family dynamics in his organizational role. As his boss's impatience suggested, he was not fully committed to his work. That is, he did not commit his passion and intelligence to the task at hand of developing the new product. Instead, afraid to be what he wanted to be, he sought to satisfy everyone else by meeting them in the realm of their interests and needs. Consequently, everybody but his boss admired and appreciated him. Paradoxically, while his many-sided interests suggested that he was an expansive person, he was in fact severely inhibited. He could do only what others wanted, not what he wanted to pursue or enjoy. This behavior mirrored Rob's earlier attempts to satisfy his parents. Not entitled to pursue any single interest or to identify his own passion, he pursued many to satisfy them. Indeed, whenever he began to immerse himself in any single activity, he became anxious and quickly diluted his involvement by doing other things. However, this always left him vaguely dissatisfied, so by the time he initially saw me, well into his thirties, he had little sense of real direction or purpose, despite a rather wide range of impressive intellectual and career accomplishments.

As treatment began to have an effect, Rob was better able to focus his energies and to recognize that he had never felt free (authorized) to have a single-minded, passionate interest. With this hard-won insight, he was able to bring more of himself into his primary work role and, correspondingly, to forgo other informal roles or to invest in them more modestly.

Matt. Finally, in presenting the more extended case of Matt, I'll try to show in greater detail how a person's early history, family relationships, course of therapy, and behavior at work are all interrelated.

Matt came to treatment at the age of thirty-two shortly after getting married. At that time he was a newly minted vice-president in a large financial services company, though his boss complained that he failed to take sufficient initiative. In addition, he complained of anxiety and some marital difficulties, which he said shocked him so early in the marriage. His wife was already in psychotherapy, and her therapist had suggested he seek treatment for himself. As time passed, he increasingly framed his problem as being continually caught between the demands of his wife and his mother. His father, he said, played little role in the conflict, since he tended to be generally passive and complied with his mother's wishes. He could acknowledge some anger toward his father for this, but he also identified with his situation. When I inquired, in due course, why he felt it was so difficult to stand up to his mother or his wife, he became extremely disorganized and anxious.

Over the course of his psychotherapy, many aspects of this issue became clarified. He came to realize, for example, that his father's disinterest and his mother's intrusiveness and insensitivity felt like a cold, deadening shower on his budding interests and activities. As a result, to preserve his excitement and pleasure, he retreated more and more into a secret life that included elaborate games, hidden collections, and rich daydreams. While he could tell me about this, one obvious manifestation of his secrecy was that he almost never talked about his work or organizational role in any detail, and when he did, it was usually only in passing and in a self-deprecating way. I was able to interpret the anxiety that if he expressed his interests openly, I would, like his parents, also be a cold shower and thereby spoil his pleasure through ridicule or disinterest.

While we made considerable headway on this problem, I had the persistent feeling that something crucial was being missed. But I had no compelling evidence except a nagging feeling that "it didn't add up." I was particularly troubled by the strength of his inhibitions, since despite what seemed like considerable therapeutic work, he continued to display a high level of anxiety whenever the issue of getting into a tangle with his mother arose, and it came up more often as his wife was increasingly unwilling to submit to his mother's wishes.

During one session in which he was discussing a current conflict between his wife and mother, he said, "I really feel as if my mother is going to lose it—she gets so irrational. It scares the hell out of me, but it also makes me so angry I just don't know what to do." I also noted that he

57

became increasingly agitated as the session progressed. Shortly before it ended, I asked him, once again, as I had in some version many times previously, how he imagined his mother would respond if she didn't get her way. He gave his usual conventional response, that she would pout and make him feel guilty. In his session the next morning he reported the following dream. *I was in the downstairs hallway of the house I grew up in. My mother came down from upstairs and started to yell at me. She also might have hit me . . . I'm not sure. Then I heard a loud thumping . . . like something banging against the wall, and I became very frightened. I think I ran out of the house and tried to hide.*

He had few associations, at first, but said that the dream made him very edgy. He noted that, in fact, his mother seldom hit him, but that she did yell at him a lot. He also remembered that he would sometimes run out of the house when he was upset. In his spontaneous account of the dream, however, the oddest element, the "thumping," remained unmentioned. I pointed this out to him, and he responded by saying that it didn't make him think of anything except the phrase "banging your head against the wall." Maybe, he speculated, that showed how frustrated his mother made him feel. Suddenly, he became very quiet and finally said in a low voice, "I think it was my mother who was banging her head against the wall."

As we analyzed this dream further, we discovered that his mother had, indeed, been quite disturbed during his early years and, in fact, often became enraged and banged her head against the wall—episodes that he had entirely repressed. As he reconstructed these episodes, he gained considerable insight into his inhibitions, his need for secrecy, and his almost catastrophic anxiety at the thought of displeasing his mother by doing what he wanted to do rather than going along with her wishes. He did not feel authorized openly to pursue his interests, lest he enrage his mother or drive her crazy. Instead, he struck a compromise by asserting himself in the privacy of his fantasies and secret games, while expressing or achieving little in public except a quiet and workmanlike competence. In this way he could avoid the guilt and anxiety of hurting his mother. However, he also gained something emotionally from this arrangement. As the therapy progressed, we discovered that he took a great deal of secret pleasure in the power he had over his mother and, by implication, the privileged position he had with her vis-à-vis his father, who seemed unable to upset her, excite her, or offer her any solace. He believed that only he could make a decisive difference in his mother's emotional life—a position he relished, even though, psychologically, he paid a considerable price for maintaining it.

Not surprisingly, Matt enacted this fantasy about his power in relation to me. One day he raised, for the first time, the possibility of ending psychotherapy. He then quickly undid this by proclaiming that he still needed more time, since he had not fully resolved some important issues. A few moments later he blurted out, "I hope you're not upset that I'm thinking that the end is in sight." I responded by saying, "You make me feel as if you need to stay here to keep me happy, rather than my being here for you for as long as you think it useful." He immediately acknowledged that he was anxious that his wanting to leave would upset me and that, in fact, he had been having thoughts of ending for several months, but kept pushing them out of his mind. I then said, "If you become independent and don't need me anymore, you're afraid I won't be able to survive—just like you've always imagined your mother wouldn't be able to survive without your continued support, compliance, and availability."

Now that we are in the process of ending therapy, he wrestles with the anxiety of being independent of me and accepting that I, for my part, can flourish quite happily without him. He experiences the prospect of independence ambivalently. While he felt inhibited by his mother's fragility, he also felt powerful since he, rather than his father, could keep her emotionally stable. While his mother's constant, self-referential demands burden him, his belief that she desperately needs him is enormously gratifying. As I have interpreted this gratification, he has become mildly depressed, but he is now groping toward a more realistic but scaled-down sense of personal authority that is both less secretly grandiose and more open and available in character.

These changes, not surprisingly, have also had a considerable effect on how he takes up his organizational work role. In the beginning he invested little personal authority in his role. Instead, he kept his own thoughts, feelings, and desires hidden and simply did the bidding, or the perceived bidding, of his superiors. He followed his "marching orders." As the therapy progressed, the reasons became much clearer. He dealt with his boss in much the same way he dealt with his mother, and then with me. He was self-effacing to a fault, got excited only privately, and became very anxious whenever he started to feel as if he knew better than his boss or had an independent idea or perspective. This occurred despite the fact, as he came to understand, that his boss welcomed his input. While obvious self-promotion can certainly be a problem, Matt, by contrast, had difficulty showing himself sufficiently, that is, directly contributing and taking responsibility for his ideas and analyses. So he operated on a split level—publicly he was a good obedient boy, but all his vitality and enthusiasm were kept private and hidden. Further, in casting his boss in his mother's image, Rob completely misread his boss; and although Rob got good reviews, they were far from the enthusiastic endorsements they later became when he started to contribute more openly to the unit, as he increasingly brought to his role aspects of the self that he had previously kept private.

Creating a Culture of Mature Authority Relations

Managers and executives in contemporary organizations must exercise great initiative while delegating substantial authority to those below them. It is no longer adequate simply to give and take orders. But as people experience greater freedom in their roles, they must also confront the anxieties and conflicts that bedevil them when they exercise authority. The external world of work is shaped increasingly by people's inner feelings and interior experiences. When people cannot take up their authority freely and without undue conflict and anxiety, they fear that authentic self-expression, the full flowering of their resources and vitality, will hurt them. As the three cases presented above suggest, in the face of this prospect some people will behave in inhibited ways, while others will mask their insecurity and neediness by overreaching and demanding too much. In this sense, we can say that people are relying on what Winnicott (1959 [1965], 1960 [1965]) calls a "false self," as opposed to a "true self," to take up their roles. They will, as a result, lack flexibility and vitality, and instead they will often behave in repetitive, constricted, non-task-oriented, and frequently self-defeating ways.

Clearly, however, we cannot improve organizations by asking all of their members to engage in psychotherapy. But senior executives and managers can help to create a "culture of authorization" that supports the individual's wish to develop as a mature, self-initiating contributor. I suggest that such a culture would sustain the following norms and values at all levels in the organization.

Taking Behavioral Responsibility for Oneself. Principally, taking behavioral responsibility involves reclaiming one's projections of difficulties onto others and forgoing using others as repositories for one's own dilemmas or lack of clarity. If this is done, scapegoating and the pervasive sense of paranoia and suspiciousness that are the consequence of such projections will markedly diminish. Those with a mature sense of personal authority recognize that one always looks to one's own behavior first as a source of difficulty and that the best way to influence the behavior of others is to modify one's own behavior. This is an especially important consideration for those in positions of authority with regard to their subordinates, who, given their positions, are especially vulnerable to destructive projections and scapegoating.

Taking Emotional Responsibility for Oneself. Contemporary psychological requirements for managers include tolerance for and the capacity to contain powerful, emotional states; tolerance for complexity, uncertainty, and ambiguity; and tolerance for anxiety. A mature sense of personal authority is marked by the capacity to tolerate and contain difficult, painful, and distressing emotional states, rather than denying them or, as noted, projecting them onto others. Since anxiety, uncertainty, and complexity are steady states in contemporary organizational life, managers without a capacity to contain their own feelings, as well as the projections of others, will be impaired in their decision making. The capacity for such containment largely depends on the acceptance of these feelings in oneself, as well as the ability to recognize that the projections of others are a function of the role that one occupies (that is, one's authority) and should not be overpersonalized. Having attained this emotional perspective, managers are then in a position to use their own internal states and such projections as vital clues about the state of the work group, team, or the larger organization. Finally, a manager's ability to accept these projections, especially the negative ones of subordinates (e.g., dependency, hatred, envy), without retribution or retaliation helps to create what Winnicott terms a "holding environment"—that is, an environment that provides a sense of psychological safety within which work can productively be accomplished and people can grow and develop in their roles.

61

Taking Ethical and Moral Responsibility for Oneself. Those with a mature, robust, and well-developed sense of personal authority "metabolize" all organizational delegations of authority. That is, no delegations are uncritically accepted or taken at face value. Rather, they are internally filtered and, if necessary, modified as a basis for renegotiation with the source of the delegation. Those with a mature sense of personal authority do not simply and uncritically follow orders or abdicate responsibility for the consequences when they do so.

Fully Recognizing Interdependence. Individuals can no longer effectively guide or manage complex systems. Given contemporary levels of organizational complexity, no single manager or executive, no matter how brilliant or talented, can have a full understanding of how the organization functions or what needs to be done to make it function more effectively. At all levels, those in authority must depend on one another and on subordinates for insight, wisdom, and perspective. A corollary is that all managers, and especially senior managers, need to recognize, understand, and take some responsibility for how the whole organization functions, as well as their own functional spheres.

Conclusion

In concluding I'd like to return to the quote with which I began. The peace with the sources of one's life that Lippmann suggests, represents an ideal state. It is a state that under felicitous conditions we more fully approach as we develop through adulthood, but that we never fully attain. However, we can attain a certain sort of grace, and an increasingly more robust, adaptive, and refined sense of personal authority as development proceeds. T. H. White, author of the wonderful and charming *Once and*

Future King (1966), in an extended aside regarding the foibles and follies of youth, comments on the development of a seventh sense—"a thing called knowledge of the world, which people do not have until they are middle-aged. It is something which cannot be taught to younger people. Only in the long years which bring one to the middle of life does a sense of balance develop. And balance—the sixth sense—is a precondition of the seventh. The seventh sense—knowledge of the world—is the means by which both men and women contrive to ride the waves of a world in which there is war, adultery, compromise, fear, stultification, and hypocrisy—and this discovery is not a matter for triumph" (White, 1966, p. 24). I would add to this a parallel knowledge of the self, similarly informed by the guilt, shame, and disappointment that one has not lived up to one's ideals. Such discovery and self-knowledge is also hardly an occasion for triumph, but if it leads, as it often does, to self-acceptance, it can be the basis for new possibilities of wholeness, vitality, and an emotionally rich and unconflicted sense of personal authority. However, this is not only a lofty human ideal in the individual and personal realm, but the core of effective management and leadership, since mature authority relations will increasingly become the hallmark of enlightened and successful organizations.

62

NOTES

Acknowledgment: I would like to express my thanks to W. Gordon Lawrence (1979, and personal communication) for some of the language of these perspectives, as well as for his seminal ideas regarding the management of the self. These have influenced my thinking about the issues of personal and organizational authority in fundamental ways.

1. In presenting clinical material to illustrate dilemmas in taking up the authority of one's work roles, I do not wish to imply either that all such difficulties are "pathological" nor that psychotherapy is usually required to deal with them. Rather, clinical examples of more extreme and persistent forms of these problems simply highlight their ubiquitous nature and bring them into clearer focus. That is, no one is entirely free of distortions in authority relations. However, within a quite broad range, the majority of successful people have learned—in many different ways, from lived experience and intimate relationships to high-quality management development programs—to understand better what drives their behavior and affects their role performance. As underscored in this chapter, such self-awareness has great value that potentially can be translated into more adequate self-management.

2. The group relations training conferences pioneered by the Tavistock Institute (see, for example, Miller, 1989) are especially important in this connection. These conferences are aimed at illuminating how one's sense of authority is profoundly influenced by group and social processes and how individuals are "used" by the group to express underlying collective anxieties and concerns. In the context of this chapter, the direct implication is that one's sense of personal authority, no matter how robust, is always conditioned to some extent by the group situation.

REFERENCES

Lawrence, W. G. 1979. "A Concept for Today: The Management of Oneself in Role." In W. Gordon Lawrence (ed.), *Exploring Individual and Organizational Boundaries: A Tavistock Open Systems Approach*. Chichester: John Wiley and Sons.

Miller, E. J. 1989. *The "Leicester" Model: Experiential Study of Group and Organizational Processes*. Occasional Paper no. 10, Tavistock Institute of Human Relations.

White, T. H. 1966. *The Once and Future King*. New York: Berkeley Publishing.

Winnicott, D. W. (1959) 1965. "Classification. Is There a Psychoanalytic Contribution to Psychiatric Classification?" In *The Maturational Process and the Facilitating Environment*. London: Hogarth Press.

———. (1960) 1965. "Ego Distortion in Terms of True and False Self." In *The Maturational Process and the Facilitating Environment*. London: Hogarth Press.

63

PART II

The Case Studies

CHAPTER 5

Professionals, Authority, and Group Life:

A Case Study of a Law Firm

Larry Hirschhorn

Introduction

Group life is difficult because it poses the often insoluble conflicts and challenges of rivalry, authority, and leadership. To skirt these issues, groups live in many kinds of "halfway houses." They may, for example, accept the authority of one person who introjects all the denied aggression of the group and then rules them like a king. They may simply prefer to operate as a nominal group in which relationships are shallow and cynicism shapes day-to-day life. Or they may struggle to create the image of a "good" group, the collegial and egalitarian group that creates good feelings by suppressing key differences, denying feelings of unfairness and entitlement, and repressing aggression.

Professional organizations may face particular problems here. Trained to act as individual performers, professionals resist group life, fearing that

Reprinted from *Human Resource Management*, vol. 28, number 2 (Summer 1989), pp. 235–252. © 1989 by John Wiley & Sons, Inc. Reprinted by permission of John Wiley & Sons, Inc.

the group could limit their authority, their right to judge a situation as they see fit, and their right to use their own time according to their own preferences. Moreover, behind such anxieties lies a deeper fear that were they to judge and constrain one another through group action, their repressed rivalries would undermine their relationships. Collegiality may be used as a method for ensuring a professional truce.

This chapter examines these issues through the medium of a case study. Examining a law firm to which I consulted, I show how its collegial and egalitarian culture functioned partly as a social defense against the politics of group life—against the dynamics of authority and leadership in groups. In the first section, I describe the firm and link its defensive structure to its partners' fears of aggression. In the second, I examine a partner retreat I facilitated and show how, despite their collective defenses, the partners' regard for one another and their commitment to mutuality helped them resolve critical developmental problems. Their collegial culture was a developmental source of strength as well as a system of defense. Finally, I consider the general theme of professionals and authority and suggest that the triangular relationship between professionals' skills, their persons, and the way they perform their professional role distances them from their own feelings. I argue briefly that themes of this case are increasingly relevant to managers throughout the economy as they organize professional teams in order to pool their knowledge and increase their productivity.

The Firm

Roberts and Carey was a small but fast-growing law firm in the Midwest specializing in litigation and real estate. Established by a group of lawyers who had graduated at the top of their class from a prestigious law school, the firm had a reputation for high-quality litigation work, for the high intellectual standards of its partners, and for its capacity to attract lawyers who had clerked for Supreme Court and well-known federal judges. While earlier in its history it had experienced the expected difficulties of a start-up firm, it was now growing rapidly, adding six lawyers to a staff of eighteen just prior to my work with the firm.

The firm had developed and sustained its early egalitarian and collegial tradition. There was no executive management committee, partners did not vote their shares at partner meetings, and their conversation and discussion were suffused with a sense of camaraderie and pleasure. Indeed, my many conversations with the partners from my first encounter to the present confirmed the special character of the firm's culture. Jokes and playfulness rounded out partner meetings, and partners trusted one another while respecting their junior associates.

Though justifiably proud of their unique culture, the partners were increasingly facing problems created by their egalitarian traditions. In interviews with me, the partners emphasized the personal and historical bases for their collegiality and the structural arrangements that were sustaining that environment. In contrast to most law firms, Roberts and Carey had more partners than associates, thus avoiding some of the typical problems associated with sustaining a "two-class" system. They could maintain their egalitarian tradition by avoiding the cultural splits between the few "top dogs" and the many "bottom" ones. In addition, the most productive partners, that is, those who brought in the most clients and contracts, did not make much more money than the least productive, and the lower-paid partners did not make much more money than the higher-paid associates. These two structural features were linked. Since partners could not make money from so small a number of associates, high-performing senior partners who wanted more money could get it only at the expense of their low-performing colleagues. Since their egalitarian tradition inhibited such a redistribution from the "weak" to the "strong" (as one partner described it), the salary distribution among the partners was compressed.

When a firm partner contacted me, this arrangement was falling apart. John Carey was the most productive member of the partnership, well known throughout the city for his unique talents as a litigator. He felt increasingly unrewarded and unacknowledged for his unusual efforts and successes. Moreover, facing growing college tuition costs for his children and resentful of some of the other partners who had family money, he started asking his partners to recognize his value by giving him a significant salary increase—one that would substantially skew a relatively egalitarian distribution of income.

Not surprisingly, his request made his partners anxious. The firm was planning a retreat to review key business issues, Carey was insisting that the salary issue be addressed at the retreat, and several partners worried that, denied his request, Carey would leave the firm and perhaps destroy it. Recognizing that they faced a critical turning point in the firm's history, the partners asked me if I would help facilitate their retreat.

Groups and Authority

My interviews in preparation for the retreat highlighted the dangers that Carey's request had created. One partner noted, "Carey wants to use the retreat to discuss how to reallocate the pot. This discussion could really be divisive. Carey should be making more, but there is a potential for disaster if we wind up talking about the issue." Similarly, another noted, "We can't take dollars from those who deserve less and give to those who deserve more with the firm still surviving." Finally, a third, describing the difficulty in talking about compensation, noted, "People are honest here, but there is a certain amount of unspoken issues here. We don't evaluate each other as partners; this is a consensus-oriented group."

My interviews suggested that the issue of compensation masked a more general problem of leadership and authority in this collegial group. In assessing the future of the firm, the partners seemed unsure of its potential and development, and the stories they told of past decisions described a firm that seemed to be drifting. Though growing rapidly, they held no common understanding of how large they should become; they agonized over the prospect of moving to a new building, fearing the possible cost and disruption; they worried about losing large, well-paying clients, believing despite their track record that they would not find new and equally remunerative work; and they periodically imagined and hoped that they might merge with a larger law firm.

Indeed, I found the last hope puzzling and paradoxical. In my early interviews, each partner in succession told me with pride about the unique character of the firm, its intellectual caliber, egalitarian culture, and special reputation as the "law firm's law firm." Yet several told me the story of a recent attempt to merge with a larger law firm, which fell through after their prospective merger partner walked away from the negotiations. Upon hearing this story, I asked the partners how this was possible. How could partners so proud of their firm be willing to bargain away their uniqueness and special character? One denied that the merger would pose significant challenges to their culture and mode of operation, but two others gave me more realistic and more poignant answers. One noted that part of the reason for pursuing the merger was "a feeling that we were missing the boat—that we couldn't compete, and weren't making money." Another suggested that the partners lacked conviction in the firm's future and that in seeking a merger they were looking for "a big brother to supply us our clients and take care of our needs." Moreover, he noted, if the firm merged, it would mean that it was a noble experiment that failed—"And what was so bad about that? Nothing is permanent anyway."

Aggression

As these quotations suggest, despite their success, the partners felt unable to compete among the "big boys" in the marketplace. Instead, their feelings of being special and unique masked an underlying sense of dependency, a wish that someone could protect them and take care of them. Paradoxically, they wanted a leader, a big brother, to protect them, but as their resistance to Carey's request suggests, they seemed unable to authorize any one or any group of their members to become the leader. They seemed caught between the wish for an egalitarian culture and an all-powerful leader. How and why had they created such a bind, and why might such a dilemma lead them to throw away their future as an independent firm?

My interviews suggested that their culture and process were built upon the tacit assumption that aggression must be inhibited. They were afraid of striking out, standing apart, and making claims within both the firm and the broader marketplace. Firm partners treated the "business of business" with disdain and discomfort. Partners postponed billing clients for work completed; they were slow to collect receivables; they did not market their services, believing that quality work attracts its own business; and they frequently charged below-market rates for their services, feeling that only the "big firms can scare people by their size and fame." One senior partner, well known for his litigation work, complained that it was difficult to estimate prospectively the cost of a litigation effort and he now feared sending his client a bill for thirty thousand dollars even though that represented the full cost of his excellent work. "He will go through the roof when he sees the bill," noted the partner.

71

Similarly, partners had no organized marketing effort and felt uncomfortable "hawking" their services. One partner took pride in not using his client connections to generate further business. "We don't push for business," he noted. "I don't use the line 'you owe me one.' There was a title company that I gave 15 to 20 million dollars' worth of referral work to but I didn't ask for business. They finally gave it to me. Professionals are recognized for the quality of the work they do and this should be enough." Indeed, their dependence on litigation work enabled them to skirt their ambivalent relationship to the marketplace.

Since much of the litigation work was taken on referral from other law firms, the latter (often big firms charging high rates) rather than Roberts and Carey negotiated the rates of pay with the client. Roberts and Carey lawyers were thus price takers rather than price makers, obtaining rates by depending on the rate structure of the larger, more aggressive firms in the city. "Referral rates are like manna from heaven," noted one partner.

Projection: Inside and Out

As these examples suggest, the partners wanted to feel comfortable and protected in the marketplace. Moreover, since these feelings were based in part on their inhibited aggression, on their reluctance to demand resources and opportunities, their wish for a big brother suggests that they needed and wanted to project their inhibited aggression into a fantasized protector, thus sparing themselves the difficult dilemmas of feeling angry, tough, and mean.

Their conflicted relationship to aggression highlights the deeper and more enduring links between Carey's request for more money, their dependency culture, and their collegial relationships. Carey wanted to stand out; he wanted to be recognized and claimed what he felt was his entitlement. By placing aggression back into the group, by reclaiming it from the fantasized big brother, merger partner, and big-boy law firm, Carey's request simulated the partners' aggressive feelings toward one another. The collegial culture was thus a defense against aggression, enabling partners to contain their own rivalries while also limiting the firm's ability to shape its own future in the marketplace.

Indeed, throughout my interviews partners spoke of potential leaders in stark, aggressive terms. "We don't have business leadership," noted one, "and if we did, we might hate it." "A czar would not work; the founders are ungovernable," noted a second. "I don't want an autocracy; I left a firm like that," noted a third. "One of the things that I like about the firm is that I don't like a king because kings want tribute," noted a fourth. And finally, one partner worried that the money discussion would destroy the "veneer of civilization that prevents the strong from eating the weak." The terms "czar," "king," "autocracy," "eating," "strong and weak," and "hate" all suggest that the partners, in thinking about a firm with leaders, feared that new leaders would create a climate of uncontained aggression and destruction.

Indeed, the partners got back at such imagined bad leaders in a contained and sublimated way by establishing a management committee composed of the most junior and least respected members of the partnership. The committee managed small administrative matters, taking tentative initiatives to track payables and receivables, but operated only because other senior partners tolerated its functioning. As one partner noted, "The members of the committee are the exact opposite of what you would expect." Establishing and tolerating this committee, the partners were able to express their contempt for the leadership function without actually attacking real powerful leaders. Finally, the difference between their fantasized inside king and outside protector highlights the difficulties they had in creating a relatively whole image of leadership. The fantasized outside big brother, the large firm that gave them referral work at good rates, protected them, while the fantasized inside leader exploited them. They could not develop an image of the "good-enough leader" who protected them and made substantial demands on them at the same time. Sustaining such a split image, they reproduced their stalemate of wishing for a good leader from without while denying a place to potential leaders from within.

Dependency

The tendency to create split images of leadership inhibited the firm's ability to create and support naturally emerging leaders in the group,

72

not by aggressing against them, since in general they inhibited aggressive feelings, but paradoxically by *depending excessively on them*. During my interviews, many partners told me of an early firm founder, Henry Spielman, who was passionately identified with the firm's future. He had aggressively marketed the firm to potential clients throughout the city, but then left after going through a bruising process of asking for and obtaining more money from the other partners. The partners described the experience as a painful one, particularly since they felt they had acceded to Spielman's request, he had agreed, and then he reneged by leaving. Since then they referred to all demands for "more" as "Spielmanesque." Naturally, the memory of Spielman's leaving amplified their anxiety as they anticipated dealing with Carey's similar demand. Many believed that the firm could not survive the departure of one more partner.

I never met Spielman and could not fully understand what drove him out, but an incident involving Carey several months after the partner retreat suggested what might have happened to Carey himself. Facing rapid growth, the firm was offered a chance to occupy prime space in an old and once glorious mansion that was being renovated as an office building. The rental rate was good, but the firm faced risks in occupying an expensive building that might fail to attract new tenants and the promised upscale shops. The firm's partners converged one night to discuss the building and, as it was described to me later, all eyes focused on Carey. One senior partner turned to him and said, "John, if we take the office space and the going gets tough, will you stick with the firm or leave?" Carey (who had gotten the salary increase he had asked for) turned to him and said, "I can't make any promises," and the remaining partners responded, as one noted, "as if someone had popped the balloon." When discussing this incident with me some weeks later, Carey noted that he could not say, "Of course I will stay," because he was thinking of Spielman.

At the time I did not push Carey to explain himself further, but as I reflected on the Spielman story it seemed to me that Spielman and Carey had both experienced the burden of standing out and excelling in a dependency culture. The leader in such a setting is overburdened with the risks of leading the firm, and the firm's members passively aggress against him by simply overrelying on him. Rather than acting as collaborating followers, they become passive. While I believe Carey faced his own internal conflicts about acting leader-like, I suggest that his response that night was shaped in part by the prospective burden and anxiety he felt in leading and comforting such a lumpy group of followers. Indeed, this is one reason firm partners pursued their negotiations with their prospective merger partner despite their misgivings. As one partner put it, "If a partner really took the risk of smashing the idea of the merger, then he would be the new leader *and what if he were wrong?!*" In other words, leaders in dependency cultures face a great sense of risk and burden. Their mistakes

73

are not tolerated, and expecting miracles, their followers are quick to hate them when they fail.

Thus in constructing a shared image of leaders, the firm's partners enacted two splitting processes. They split fantasized outside leaders who were beneficent from fantasized inside leaders who were domineering czars, and they became passively dependent on actual leaders within the firm while having contempt for the impotent pseudoleaders on the actual management committee.

Drift

It is clear to me now why the firm seemed to be drifting and why its partners were ready to give the firm away to a beneficent big brother. Fearing aggression, the firm could not tolerate leadership, and unable to sustain leaders, the firm had no interpersonal system for containing the anxiety implicit in the firm's uncertain though certainly hopeful future. Since no leader was authorized to worry, everybody did, raising the overall level of anxiety in the firm as a whole. This is why the partners seemed so lacking in confidence despite their remarkable achievements, and why they were willing to sell their hopeful future down the river to a bigger law firm.

In Sum: The Firm's Defensive Structure

The firm's collegial culture functioned partly as a social defense against aggression. While developing genuinely collegial and playful relationships with one another, partners could sustain these relationships only by unduly inhibiting aggression. Fearing the consequences of rivalry and intent on suppressing differences that could provoke angry or difficult feelings, the firm sustained its collegial culture at significant cost. Developing a split image of leaders who were either beneficent big brothers or mean czars, the firm hoped to find its good leader on the outside, in the form of firms who protected it, while overburdening emerging leaders from within. This culminated in a salary system that could not acknowledge differences, in a management committee composed of the weakest partners, and in a sense of drift and uncertainty that suffused the firm's working process.

But like all defensive structures, this system provided its compensations (secondary gains) as well. Unlike other firms who dealt in the dirty world of money and business, the partners could imagine that they were special, that their "noble experiment" was unique and precious, one that stood above the fray of streetwise lawyers fighting for money. As intellectuals, they imagined they could avoid this world, and if they failed, their stance had been worth the try.

Schwartz's Model

Roberts and Carey's structure raises interesting questions about social defenses in general. In a landmark article, Schwartz (1987) constructed a psychodynamic theory of the "organizational ideal" in which organization members, unwilling to face their imperfect selves, imagine that the organization contains the secret route to their ideal selves. Projecting their hidden grandiosity onto the organization, they repress their own sense of limits and failure and come to believe that the organization and its leaders are perfect. In such a culture, members have contempt for one another, or for at least those who stand nearer the bottom of the organization, since only by rising to the top can a person prove that he or she approximates the organizational ideal. Competition between peers is then justified, since the organization's perfection can be protected only if the unworthy are eliminated or put in their place. Mutuality between peers is consequently inhibited and feelings are denied. While Schwartz does not link his theory to Bion's (1959) thinking, one might imagine that this relationship between the organization and its members creates a powerful "fight culture" as members willingly allow the perfect leaders of the omnipotent organization to harness and express all their projected aggression.

75

The law firm described here highlights a different constellation of forces. Schwartz's organization is a fight culture, in which love is inhibited and leadership idealized, while the law firm created a dependency culture in which *aggression* was inhibited and leadership *devalued*. In the former the belief in the organization's omnipotence and grandiosity is primary, while the resulting relationships between organization members are secondary. In the law firm, the contained and controlled links between the organization's members were primary, so that aggression between them needs to be contained, while the fantasy of a precious and special organization is a secondary compensation for the pervasive feelings of anxiety and drift.

This difference suggests that we might construct an organizational typology based on the difference between the inhibition of mutuality and the inhibition of aggression. The former, based on primary grandiosity, creates a fight culture, while the latter, based on the concept of a community of peers, creates a dependency culture. Table 5.1 highlights these differences.

Just as psychodynamic typologies enable us to construct developmental theories of personality, this typology suggests that the latter organization is more mature, that its members are part of what Klein and Riviere (1964) might call a "depressive-position" culture, while the members of the former are in what she might call a "paranoid-schizoid" culture. It is

TABLE 5.1. Two Models of a Professional Culture

	Inhibition of	Basic Assumption	Primary Drive	Secondary Gain
Schwartz Model	Mutuality	Fight	Grandiosity	Identification with the powerful
Alternative Model	Aggression	Dependency	Community	Preciousness

ironic, then, that the former organization might nonetheless prove to be more successful, since the latter, by avoiding aggression, relinquishes the fight culture's basic assumption to a more primitively organized setting.

Finally, this diagram highlights the poignant and important quality of the firm's struggles. The partners suffered and were threatened with demise because they sought mutuality. They had learned to love but now needed to learn how to fight those they loved without undermining the basic mutuality that lay at the foundation of their relationships. They faced a sophisticated developmental problem.

The Retreat

Mutuality as a Strength

As I noted, the firm partners first asked me to consult to them as they contemplated holding a retreat devoted to business development issues while addressing Carey's request for more money. The retreat was a success, though it suffered from the common and present dangers posed by a dependency culture's hope that a consultant can save its members. Organized into four phases, the retreat began with a discussion of a "working note" I wrote to the partners based on my interviews with them. It then moved to a review of the firm's strategic options, then to a discussion and agreement on compensation that partly met Carey's requests, and concluded with the establishment of an executive committee composed of the firm's most dominant and important partners. The retreat climate was alternately humor-filled, serious, and difficult but never rancorous or withholding. The partners' fundamental connections to one another, their affection for one another, and their commitment to mutuality helped carry them over the anxious periods of working through key differences. Their very weakness was the source of their strength. Three events highlight the strengths of their collegial culture.

Event 1: The Salary Compromise

First, they resolved the problem of compensation when several junior partners simply proposed that the salary schedule for the coming year (not yet implemented) be revised to reflect Carey's contribution, demonstrating that some partners were willing to take significantly smaller salary increases to acknowledge Carey's accomplishments. Their willingness led to a succession of "give-backs" as each partner in turn acknowledged that he or she too was willing to forgo some part of his or her projected increase in salary.

The salary conversation was initially difficult, with several founders arguing that Carey could not claim that he unilaterally brought in several key contracts. The obvious and primitive rivalries between the most senior and productive partners emerged when Brent (a senior litigator) argued, with a slip of the tongue, that there were insufficient facts to prove that Carey was the most "popular, I mean profitable, partner." In other words, the rivalries evoked the more rudimentary struggles between classmates for popularity. As the senior members argued over entitlements and credit, I remember thinking at the time that the junior partners were silent, compliantly allowing the senior partners to fight among themselves (though Carey was subdued and gentlemanly throughout), even though they gained directly from the egalitarian salary schedule. It was as if the senior members were enacting a primitive fight for dominance in front of the rest of the "herd," and the juniors, fearful of participating and silenced by the power display, could not talk.

But after a break, the tone and process changed completely. Three junior partners returned and proposed a new salary schedule. Their affect had a healing and reparative tone. Their spokesman, Paul, talking in a caring way, noted that he had been discussing this issue with his two other colleagues and now wanted to propose a way to satisfy Carey. They posted their proposed salary schedule in which they but not others would accept smaller increments to give Carey a substantially larger one, and two other senior partners additional (though less significant) increments. Carey's dominance on the new salary schedule was obvious, though he still did not have all he had asked for, while the overall schedule shifted money from the least to the most productive. Silence followed as people viewed the list. Others then joined in, proposing that they too could take smaller increments. When the flow of concessions was over, people waited for Carey to respond. He noted, first slowly, that "140K is not the number I asked for," and then added strongly, "but I would be a jerk not to accept it." In effect, the act of sacrifice first initiated by the junior partners led everybody to accept a compromise in which Carey's unique contributions to the firm could be acknowledged. The junior partners who had profited from the firm's egalitarian compensation system sacrificed money to acknowledge the difference between Carey and the other senior partners and between the more and the less productive members of the firm. In a firm uncomfortable with aggression, the senior and more productive partners could not demand their entitlements but the junior members could acknowledge their contributions.

Indeed, Paul, a leader of the junior group of partners, projected a distinctively maternal role in the firm, worrying about people's health and satisfaction and talking with pleasure about the way he took care of his wife and children. Jewish and gentle, he projected the feelings of the concerned mother when discussing firm issues. Because the firm's culture suppressed the rights of "fathers" to demand honor from their "sons," he, as a mother figure, stepped in to ask the sons to honor their father in order to safeguard the family. Reflecting the strength of the firm's culture of mutuality, the partners could draw on the maternal impulse of unilateral sacrifice, rather than on the "manly" process of struggle and compromise. By introducing the principle of sacrifice as an alternative though complementary framework for social relations, the maternal impulse revealed the unexpected strengths of the firm's culture.

Event 2: My Identifications

Second, I think the firm's commitment to mutuality enabled me to identify deeply with its dilemmas. In writing a working note to the members based on my interviews, I found myself emotionally and sometimes passionately engaged in their dilemmas, and as several of my colleagues noted, put more of myself than usual into the working note. Reaching the culmination of my proposed set of hypotheses about their situation, I wrote:

> Consider finally my fourth hypothesis:
>
> You have yet to create a partnership process that supports an authentic leadership cadre and governance system. Consequently, naturally occurring anxiety about a firm in a complex market is too widely distributed, too widely shared, and, as you react to one another's anxiety, is amplified to the point where you periodically feel adrift or panicked.

And then I went on to write:

> I am not talking here about management practices, or marketing strategies, but rather of a more developed and sophisticated institutional politics that enables you all to do quality work while authorizing a leadership cadre to take hold of the firm's developmental problems and potentials. You can buy management education, purchase market research services, and follow well-

described implementation procedures, but only through a partnership process can you create a leadership system that is consistent with your culture, helps protect it, and enables it to develop.

Forgive my cheerleading here, but I don't see why this can't be done. I don't know why, with your deep competence and shared appreciations for one another, your "noble experiment" can't mature. As partners at midlife entering the peak period of your productivity, why can't you develop a more sophisticated partner-associate boundary that rewards the former without exploiting the latter? Why can't you develop a more sophisticated firm-market boundary in which you continue to practice an intellectually based form of law while acting more planfully and strategically? Why can't you preserve your collegiality while developing a more differentiated partnership in which leadership and performance are unambivalently acknowledged?

The Baby-Boom Cohort. Rereading these words now, I see my own struggles as well as the dilemmas of Roberts and Carey. In interviewing the partners and feeling connected to their community of equals, I discovered my own struggles for adulthood, my wish to go beyond sibling rivalries and to acknowledge authority and come to terms with my own relationship to real and fantasized leaders in my world. Sensing that they were grappling with these problems in a contained way, that despite their difficulties they felt supported by their regard for one another, I could find my own voice in their words.

Identifying with them, I came to believe that I and my law-firm clients, most of them baby-boomers like myself, shared a broad and unconsciously experienced set of cultural assumptions as well as developmental problems. Growing into adulthood when institutional authority had failed, the baby-boom generation had carved out a simultaneously developmental and regressive relationship to adult authority. Believing that authority had to prove its legitimacy rather than win it from past accomplishments, the baby-boom generation brought rational scrutiny to social institutions. But in questioning authority and denying its legitimacy, the baby-boom generation also amplified the perpetual dream of Oedipus that children are their own fathers. Believing that they have willed their births, they fall prey to the narcissistic dream that they are immortal as well. This wish leads to a cul-de-sac represented by the cohorts' lack of commitment to the next generation, their disinterest in children and in their own generativity. Indeed, the firm's apparent fragility and the partners' willingness to sell it away signified their inability and unwillingness to create or generate a future world they and their followers could occupy. Looked at as a developmental problem, *they did not so much lack the aggression to compete as the aggression to generate.* In turn, their preciousness not only justified their passivity but confirmed the narcissistic overtones of their culture.

One senior partner expressed this complex relationship in a poignant way. Reflecting on the problems that compensation created, he not only noted that senior partners were unrewarded, but asked, "What kind of firm are we creating for the younger associates?" The junior members were committing their careers to a firm that might prove unviable in the long run. In other words, by denying the differences among them, the partners were not behaving responsibly to the younger generation.

Their Identifications. My identification with the partners enabled them in turn to identify with me, and with my role as their consultant. On the first night of the retreat, as the partners talked about their feelings and fears, their reactions to the working note, and their hopes for the retreat, one senior partner, Will, noted how "moved" he had felt by one section of the note. In assessing their dilemmas of growth, I had written: "This [growth] is a complicated knot of problems, but I wonder if at bottom you have overestimated the actual risks that size poses. I wonder if you don't face a problem of nerve and confidence rather than of markets and budgets."

Will noted, "There I was sitting at the hockey game reading Larry's paper, and I came across this sentence about our confidence and I thought, 'Jesus he's right, we've been together fifteen years and we still lack confidence.' I was f . . . g moved." A person is "moved" when his fragmented and incoherent feelings are brought together by a powerful stimulus so that he feels more coherent and grounded. He is "moved" to a different ground of experience by the combined force of the stimulus and his response. My prose, however, was not particularly powerful or beautiful, and my insight, though important, was clearly available to many of the partners. After all, I got my ideas from my interviews with them. I suggest that Will was "moved" in part by the emotional character of my own writing, by its evident seriousness and commitment. In seeing that I took his reality seriously, that I identified with it, he could open himself up to his own potential insights and associations. The note, in other words, functioned as the medium for an initial working alliance between Will and me. I projected my feelings and identifications into it, and he, sensing my commitment, projected his own feelings into his reading of it.

Event 3: Appropriate Dependency

Third and finally, the group's capacity for mutuality enabled the members to trust me and accept my proposed design for their retreat. As I noted, on the first evening of the retreat they reviewed their reactions to my note and their hopes for the retreat. After they had finished going around the room, it was clearly my turn to provide some framework for both reviewing their thinking and proposing some next steps. Clearly, Carey's request was uppermost in their minds and was the cause of substantial anxiety. During their review of the note and their thoughts, several had addressed Carey directly, arguing that he could not claim full credit for the contracts he was supervising. Carey said little, noting only that he disagreed but did not want to pursue the issue that evening.

I then proposed that they not immediately work on his request but instead turn to the more general business issues they faced. I believed that they needed to see the context for their current conundrums and hoped that the process of working through other issues might help them surmount the obstacles to resolving the conflict between Carey and the other partners. One partner responded skeptically and sensibly, wondering if the initial discussion would not prove too artificial in light of the "real" problem on their minds. I agreed but proposed nonetheless that they give my design a try, understanding that if it did not work they could change it at any time with my help. They agreed, not with shouts and cheers to be sure, but with enough assent to indicate that the design was "good **81** enough" and by implication that they had a "good enough" relationship to me. They were ready to trust me.

Basic Assumption Dependency

Of course, their basic assumption dependency behavior played a role here as well. Since I was their consultant, it was appropriate for them to rely on me for good advice and sound design ideas, but I suspect that their wish for saviors was partly projected into me as well. This became most clear as the retreat neared its closing. In the excitement of resolving the compensation problem and in response to the themes of my note, the group of partners decided to establish an executive committee then and there. I felt the rush of their excitement, the sense of their achievement, though the austere voice of analytic reflection whispered to me, "This may be flight." But the moment seemed like too much fun and the austere voice resembled a stingy aunt unwilling to share in life's pleasures. So I said nothing and relished in the pleasure of their apparent development. At the end I caught myself and weakly noted that perhaps there may be some felt losses that are not being faced—would those not elected to the committee feel that they lost, feel that they have been displaced? No one could imagine what I was talking about.

Some weeks after the retreat, when I contracted with the newly formed executive committee to meet with them on a monthly basis, these losses became more apparent. One member of the old and contemptuously regarded management committee was depressed, somewhat bitter, feeling that his work had not been appreciated. I felt badly, as if I had conspired to kill him psychologically and that he now had to work through his depression alone rather than with his partners at the retreat.

The Dinner Meeting

A dinner meeting of all partners and associates, led, conducted, and orchestrated by the executive committee, typified the complex character of the firm, with its intermingling of mutuality and the partners' adolescent character, their search for a concept of authority and leadership that was consistent with their valued history, and the limits of a retreat shaped by dependency as well as genuine work.

In contrast to all prior meetings it was held as a dinner meeting in the most prestigious business club in the city, amid pictures and trophies of the city's male elite, extending back to the nineteenth century. As the occasion was ostensibly held to enable associates to talk to partners, the dinner tables were arranged to create a master table with two tables as legs with people sitting on either side of the two legs. Almost no one could see everyone else's face. At or about dessert, Gary, the most WASPish of the senior partners, rose to conduct the meeting and moved through an agenda full of self-congratulations for the excellent work of the firm and its rosy future, though as always the ample supply of unexpected jokes lightened the proceedings. But I was upset. The committee, far from working to develop its authority in a manner consistent with its past, drew upon stereotypical images of male authority that, even if present and available in today's culture, nonetheless had a musty and outmoded feeling to them. "Maybe the retreat had been one big exercise in basic assumption flight," I wondered. Afterward several of the senior partners came up to me to ask me how it was. Reluctant to be a nay-sayer, I moved my hand to signal ambivalence and said no more.

I puzzled over the event and my own behavior in the week before my next scheduled meeting with the executive committee. Should I confront them, I wondered; should I write Gary a brief note telling him what I observed? I wasn't sure, and my confusion puzzled me. I was identified with them, that was clear. But despite the stuffiness of the meeting, their humor and affection was present as well, and I came to feel that the event had a peculiarly adolescent character, like boys trying on men's clothing. I realized then that one reason I didn't confront the partners at the dinner meeting was that Gary seemed to be having such a good time and who would want to pop the balloon of such a nice fellow!

At the next meeting the executive committee worked on some of its pressing business and then Gary turned to me to ask me what I was thinking, what I had observed. I saw my chance and told them what I thought of their meeting, that it was stuffy, unengaging, and probably turned off a lot of people. Most were surprised, though one partner confirmed that some of the others felt the same way. But then Gary and John Carey both asked why they had not heard more protest from others in the firm. I then told them of my own ambivalence in confronting them, ending with the sentence, "And who would want to be mean to such a nice bunch of guys as you?" They laughed, feeling, I think, that I touched a piece of truth they could acknowledge, and indeed in later conversations with other partners I found that my experience matched theirs. While other partners resented the dinner, nobody wanted to ruin Gary's and the executive committee's show; they seemed to be having too much fun.

This event typified the obstacles and challenges awaiting the firm's development. They needed to construct a sophisticated boundary between leaders and followers which authorized both while supporting the mutuality and respect that characterized their basic relationships. The dinner meeting was a parody of authority, but a playful one, so that the executive committee's missteps in the developmental dance were contained by its capacity for affection.

In sum, by holding the retreat, meeting Carey's request, and forming an executive committee, members of the firm had taken the necessary first steps toward developing a more mature partnership process. Their collegiality and dependency (both a strength and a weakness) had enabled them to restore their relationships to one another and to form a working alliance with me, though both qualities also periodically waylaid them with the attractions of fantasized images of authority that could only undermine their hopeful future.

83

Conclusion: Professionals and Authority

I have suggested that professionals resist group life, with all its opportunities and dangers, in order to skirt the issues of rivalry, authority, and mutuality in groups, and they do so by creating an ideology of collegiality. *The ideology of collegiality functions as a social defense to denude group life of its passions.* As anyone who has attended academic seminars knows, when professional academics come together in a room, collegiality is dissipated as the members attack one another's ideas and then turn on the seminar itself as a failed medium for work and discussion. They confront one another, and then, facing the despair that their jointly produced alienation creates, they retreat from one another. Trying to create a group life, they disappoint one another and so over time they avoid one another.

But why does group life bother professionals? Let me return to the theme of aggression. Professionals, particularly lawyers, learn to be aggressive through the use of a set of techniques and tools. They can use aggression in their professional work because they feel that it is objectively deployed and is independent of their actual character and feelings. Thus in their professional work they are not faced with the dilemma of integrating mutuality and aggression, the good and the bad, because these are not *their* feelings.

By contrast, general managers, with no specialist skills, face the problem of aggression more directly. To direct, lead, and support, they do not rely on techniques, but rather must draw on their own personal and emotional resources to shape their thinking and acting. Consequently, when performing their role effectively, they mature. The general manager is not afraid of the bad or the good and comes to appreciate the complex and often hopelessly contradictory character of group life. The practice strengthens his or her managerial links to other people. By contrast, the professional is successful often because he or she separates the person from the role, thereby not taking the work personally. This is why, for example, an ambivalent and passive person can function as a ferocious lawyer in the courtroom or as a razor-sharp literary critic.

Professionals' alienation from their affects are both the source of their individual strengths and the basis for their weak group life. But we may be moving beyond the era of the individual professional as the complexity of professional practice forces professionals into teams and groups. As we enter the knowledge economy, managers in many settings will need to organize such professionals as engineers, scientists, accountants, and market researchers so that "intelligence," the firm's intellectual capital, can be pooled and systematically deployed. As managers help create professional teams, they may find that they cannot rely on traditional norms of professional life to link the work of one professional to another. They and the professionals they manage will need new values, norms, and processes to create an effective and satisfying group life.

We have yet to see how a new balance will be constructed between the individual, his or her professional skills, and group life. But as professional organizations confront these issues, they are likely to face the kind of problems that Roberts and Carey have just begun to confront.

NOTE

Presented to the Second Annual Conference of the International Society for the Psychoanalytic Study of Organizations, New York City—October 24–25, 1987.

REFERENCES

Bion, W. 1959. *Experiences in Groups.* New York: Basic Books.
Klein, M., and J. Riviere. 1964. *Love, Hate, and Reparation.* New York: W. W. Norton.
Schwartz, H. 1987. "The Psychodynamics of Organizational Totalitarianism." *Journal of General Management*, 13(1), 41–54.

CHAPTER 6

How Organizational Culture
Can Affect Innovation

Steven P. Feldman

What can we learn from the study of American culture that can be most useful for stimulating innovation in large, complex organizations? To address this question, we must first broaden our understanding of "organizational culture" to include societal-level cultural forces that affect organizations. Once this is done, a whole body of knowledge from the social sciences can be used to generate insights into the role culture plays in organizational innovation.

In this chapter, organizational culture is seen as a set of meanings created within the organization but influenced by broader social and historical processes. Organizational members use these meanings—norms, roles, plans, ideals, and ideas—to make sense out of the flow of actions and events they experience. I will use this concept to investigate the influence of culture on attitudes toward and capacities for innovation in a medium-size electronics company; I will then make recommendations on how culture can be used to stimulate innovation.

Reprinted, by permission of publisher, from *Organizational Dynamics*, Summer 1988. © 1988 American Management Association, New York. All rights reserved.

The German sociologist Max Weber was one of the earliest researchers on the effects of culture on the work ethic. Weber believed that culture played a primary role in the explosion of entrepreneurial activity that created the Industrial Revolution. He wrote that this cultural development was built around the Protestant condemnation of personal pleasure and the avoidance of close personal relationships. As Weber saw it, this suppression of pleasurable activities redirected human energy into impersonal calculation and hard work. The result was a tremendous upsurge in economic activity.

By the late nineteenth century, however, much of the explicitly religious impetus for economic activity had lessened, though it had left an undeniable influence on the American psyche, encouraging economic production and the pursuit of wealth. The most successful members of this new breed—Andrew Carnegie, John D. Rockefeller, and Charles A. Pillsbury, for example—established huge concentrations of capital and labor that led to the "bureaucratization" of much of American industry. By bureaucratization I mean the development of large systems of hierarchically structured, functionally interdependent offices used to manage extensive and complex operations.

Along with the bureaucratization of industry came new developments in American business. In 1950 David Riesman published his seminal work on American culture, *The Lonely Crowd: A Study of the Changing American Character*. He stated that the motivation of the Protestant entrepreneur—which he termed "inner-directed" because it was based on the internalization of ideals—had become generally absorbed into American culture. However, he argued that the tremendous increase and concentration of population growth in the twentieth century had led to a new development in American culture: a much greater sensitivity to interpersonal relations. In bureaucratic organizations, this cultural development—which Riesman termed "other-directedness"—was reflected in the radar-like sensitivity used by career aspirants to conform to the likes and dislikes of bosses and peer groups in order to be accepted. The "organization man" had arrived.

The inner-directed entrepreneur—the individual who was motivated by internalized ideals of self-reliance, strict self-control, and a strong need for achievement—had limited effectiveness in bureaucratic organizations where teamwork was essential. But the other-directed bureaucrat, with his sensitivity to the preferences of others, was a boon to organizational cooperation.

This cultural development had mixed effects on innovation, however. Other-directedness led to a weakening of the commitment to personal achievement in the form of economic productivity, replacing it with interpersonal acceptance as an end in itself. In the large bureaucracies, acceptance meant gaining status; hence the need for achievement was still with us, but it was redefined to emphasize social rather than economic accomplishment. Other-directedness does benefit innovation, however, because it encourages compromise by focusing the worker's attention on being accepted by others. Compromise is a stimulus to innovation in bureaucratic organizations, where decision making involves multiple specialties and functions. Nevertheless, the willingness to compromise has a negative effect on innovation because it undermines passionate commitment to goals, which is essential to overcoming the difficulties inherent in the innovation process.

Since the upheavals of the 1960s and the patterns of social behavior that followed, the success of the early entrepreneurs has given birth to more than organization men. Students of American culture have noted a strong tendency toward what the sociologist Peter L. Berger has called "hyperindividualism." Hyperindividualism is concerned almost entirely with the self, its goals, and its pleasures; the multitude of self-realization and self-fulfillment movements so common in the 1970s and 1980s are part of this cultural development.

Hyperindividualism also has a mixed effect on innovation. To begin with, the concentration on one's own desires has weakened group control over individual behavior. This can be a stimulus to innovation because when individual desire is limited by little more than itself, the whole social and physical environment becomes open to change. In a culture of hyperindividualism, change and creativity are the only constants. But the focus on one's pleasure makes the hyperindividualist wary of sacrifice and long-term commitments, both of which are needed in innovative activity. In addition, focusing on one's own interests makes teamwork all but impossible.

In summary, then, idealism, conformity, and selfishness are three characteristics of American culture that influence business behavior. All three have both positive and negative effects on innovation in large, specialized organizations.

Research Orientation

In this chapter, I will present a case analysis of an entrepreneur in terms of the way in which his commitment to certain ideals helped to create his company's organizational culture and that culture's ability to support innovation. I will carry out the analysis using an interpretive concept of culture; that is, I will focus on how organizational participants used their experience—stored in such things as ideals, ideas, memories, plans, and stories—to create a situation in which certain kinds of behavior were encouraged. The advantage of this approach is that it provides a description of important, shared categories that stimulate some activities and constrain others.

The case data can certainly be interpreted in many other ways. For example, an organizational developmental consultant might rely on group process theories; a strategic management analyst might find a problem that is unclear or inappropriate goals and organizational structures; and a leadership theorist might find the problem in the entrepreneur's decision-making style. All these approaches have a contribution to make to their practitioners' purposes. But the interpretive concept of culture achieves something that these other approaches overlook: the collective predispositions organizational members create through their shared history, predispositions that influence them to understand events, react to situations, and solve problems in certain ways. This chapter will demonstrate how the organizational culture, formed from and in reaction to the deeply held ideals of the founder, influenced organizational decision making and new product development.

Case Analysis

"Smith Electronics" was started by Mr. John Smith (a pseudonym) in 1950. By 1985, when I carried out my fieldwork, the company had grown to three hundred employees with sales of thirty million dollars and three major divisions, all of which were involved in the production of electronic products. Mr. Smith, who was chairman of the board, had begun delegating control of the company to his top management team in the mid-1970s because of the growing complexity and size of company operations; before this, product innovation had been under his direct control. When he tried to decentralize, however, the cultural influences that had evolved along with the company over the previous thirty-plus years undercut the organization's ability to develop innovative suborganizations. The inability to achieve a balance between corporate control and suborganization autonomy is a central problem in the management of innovation in large, specialized organizations, and Smith Electronics was no exception.

Idealism and Leadership

The central fact that gave interpersonal relations at Smith Electronics its particular character was that from 1950 to the late 1970s, the number of employees was small enough so that all of them knew Mr. Smith personally. This personal interaction was generally positive. For his part, Smith demonstrated a dedication to his employees by providing job security, a pension plan for retirement, and recognition of their contribution to the company (in the form of such activities as "employee appreciation" days). The employees in turn felt trust and affection for, and commitment to, Mr. Smith. The employees told stories that expressed this sentiment; for example, during a financial crunch that had occurred in 1964, Smith's employees had lent him money to help him remain in control of the company.

The relationship between Smith and his employees was the focal point from which the employees' diverse cultural backgrounds and potentialities were structured into a more limited set of organizational cultural patterns. The employees carefully interpreted Smith's formal exercise of authority, his informal comments, his criticisms, and even his jokes in order to extract his preferences and assumptions. The employees perceived these as important information about what would or would not happen and what they should or should not do. Because of his effect on their work lives, Smith became the center of their work culture. In addition to his concern for his employees' well-being, however, Smith tended to dominate organizational decision making. This combination— kindness and control—led his employees to become dependent on him. As one manager stated about his own decision-making style, "I always ask myself, what would John do in this situation?"

89

Thus the cultural milieu that developed at Smith Electronics encouraged employees to be sensitive to and to follow Mr. Smith's lead. This sensitivity reflected a strong other-directed orientation; Smith, on the other hand, with his self-motivated style and commitment to the ideal of employee security, reflected an inner-directed orientation. Because of these differences in orientation, when Smith tried to set up a decentralized organization in the late 1970s by delegating responsibility for innovation to the divisions, the other-directed employees were not self-directed enough to innovate on their own. Smith's idealism had led to a positive work atmosphere, but it also had encouraged his managers to become dependent on him.

Idealism and Strategy

Smith's idealism did not end with his dedication to his employees. Two of Smith's strongest ideals, which were also explicit company goals, were his commitments to product quality and customer service. One manager who no longer worked for the company said that Smith's commitment to product quality was so strong that it seemed as if he wanted personally to sign each product as it went out the door. This idealism, however, which was undoubtedly a company strength, led to an internal focus on product engineering at the expense of an external focus on market dynamics and customer needs. Even though top management intellectually recognized this imbalance and tried, through training and the use of consultants, to correct the problem, it was never adequately resolved.

Part of the reason for the great resistance to developing a marketing orientation was the strong engineering background of the management group. This group could easily understand Smith's dedication to product quality and customer service, as it was primarily concerned with technology and technological development. There was a deeper reason, however, that had to do with what role this understanding played in organizational life. Marketing requires getting to know the customer's needs by understanding his specific situation and his specific perceptions. However, Smith's ideals of product quality and customer service were used to block the development of marketing skills because the fact that his goals were idealized made them unchallengeable in the decision-making process. Managers were faced with conflicting goals—for example, service or profits, or quality or timeliness—but because of idealized commitments to quality and service, these conflicts were prematurely resolved before marketing issues were systematically considered. Hence, by defining quality and service technologically and by idealizing them, Smith built a technological bias into the company's work culture; there was no real way that marketing perspectives could be effectively incorporated into managerial action.

The lack of a marketing focus led to a second area in which culture undermined strategy. Because Smith managers did not have an intuitive grasp of customer needs and market dynamics and lacked the inclination to achieve them, the result was a conservative, cautious, risk-avoiding decision-making style. One manager described Smith's attitude as one in which he tried to see not how much money he could make, but how much he could avoid losing. The manager called this a "defensive" management style; yet at the same time, Smith set ambitious goals for growth and profits and expected them to be achieved. A "slow growth" culture, to use the words of one long-time manager, undermined a strategic-planning system based on fast growth; hence the lack of an effective marketing capability led to frustration in implementing strategic plans and in meeting financial goals.

There was a further consequence of the tendency to idealize customer service that had important ramifications for management practice and strategy. By defining customer service in terms of technology and then idealizing it, Smith managed to idealize the company's relationship with its customers. Instead of the category of "customer" signifying the customer's situation, in the Smith culture it emphasized the user of Smith technology. There was talk of the customer's business situation and his preferences, but it was anecdotal rather than systematically analyzed for potential customer needs and relations between needs. To be sure, a few marketing managers did think in terms of customer needs, but to the extent that they did not understand the technology, they were not taken seriously and were considered marginal in the Smith culture. Like the Protestant entrepreneur of the nineteenth century whose idealized commitment to "brotherly love" enabled him to forgo warm, personal relationships, the Smith employee's idealized commitment to the technological component in "customer service" enabled him to forgo getting to know any of his customers in particular.

The impersonalization that resulted from the tendency to idealize, however, was not limited to problems with marketing. One extremely important organizational goal that had uncertain success was to improve the quality and quantity of innovations—mostly in the form of new product development. This happened because Smith's inner-directedness led him to follow his own ideals rather than anyone else's. When creative, self-confident managers came to work for Smith Electronics, they usually found the "slow growth" culture and the emphasis on "teamwork" stifling. One highly independent entrepreneur-manager, who was responsible for a significant increase in sales between 1978 and 1980, eventually became involved in a conflict with top management and left the company.

Because of Smith's anxiety about the innovative managers' self-centeredness and aggressiveness, he was unable to adapt to them, even when such an adaptation could have helped him reach his goals. His tendency to idealize (or to impersonalize) made him poorly equipped to understand their personalities, and he was unable to broaden his own personal relationships to make a more diverse group of individuals feel comfortable in the company. Smith once remarked how unacceptable a highly successful manager's aggressive behavior had been by calling him an "empire builder." The irony of this statement succinctly points out the inherent contradiction in a manager who both idealizes his own beliefs and tries to decentralize his organization: the innovative manager was being condemned for precisely the attitude that was needed to reach Smith's growth goals.

Although Smith was admired for his integrity, he was perceived as not always expressing his feelings, not always being at ease with the exercise of power, and tending to delegate emotionally difficult matters such as firings. This discomfort with the interpersonal aspects of management led him to delegate many of these problems to the president or vice-president of personnel. This led to further problems, however; for example, the vice-president of personnel, who was on the receiving end of many of the most difficult problems, developed a reputation for doing the organization's "dirty work." In other words, in certain areas Smith institutionalized an emotional buffer between himself and the rest of the organization, which led to problems of jealousy, conflict, communication, and alienation. Eventually the vice-president, who had the job of emotional buffer and who received the blame for the problems, was perceived as being ineffective and resigned. Thus Smith found that he needed strong managers, but that he was unsettled by "empire builders" and had poor results using the emotional buffer concept of management.

Smith tried to resolve this dilemma by hiring consultants or temporary entrepreneurs. He hired everyone from technologists to psychologists, labor relations experts, marketing experts, accountants, strategic planners, and general management consultants. Since his relationship with these consultants was short-term or occasional, Smith could minimize the emotional aspects of relationships that were unavoidable in daily work interactions.

However, Smith's attraction to consultants was based on something deeper than his need for talented and nonthreatening managers. The opinion of manager after manager, on both the top and middle levels of the company, seemed to concur with the words of one vice-president, who stated that Smith "tended not to believe insiders" but had an "extraordinary faith in outsiders." Thus Smith did not prefer consultants simply because he found aggressive managers intolerable; he also had a preference for outsiders in general. It was common knowledge that top management many times had, in the words of one division head, turned a "deaf ear" to employee ideas, although it was quick to act on the recommendations of consultants.

Here again the phenomenon of impersonalization was responsible. Smith had a tendency to focus on the ideal aspect of commitments rather than on the interpersonal. Unlike his relationship with his employees, which was usually personalized through daily interactions (though here too, as we saw, buffers were created), Smith could relate to the consultant not as a person but as an expert. Because the relationship was framed in this way, the tendency to idealize consultants' opinions naturally resulted. Smith did not like to focus on the personal aspect of relationships, so he tended not to develop them with particular employees, although he was kind, as we saw, to the employee group as a whole. However, because he could relate to consultants almost solely in terms of their skills, their reputations, and the reputations of their organizations (there was a preference for consultants from prestigious consulting firms and universities), Smith was much more comfortable and confident with them. For this reason, consultants largely carried out functions and tasks that traditionally belonged to top and middle management.

The cultural tendency to idealize (and thus impersonalize) therefore had a significant influence on what information was used in the strategic management process, on who participated in that process, and on who had power to affect its outcome.

Cultural Contradictions and Managerial Conflict

Not only do cultural influences affect the strategic management process; these processes also affect the culture. The way the strategic management process was carried out at Smith Electronics led to the establishment of a culture riddled with internal contradictions. Many middle-level and some top-level managers were not involved in central decision-making and planning processes; as a result, they became alienated from the goals and objectives these processes created. As was noted earlier, many ambitious, aggressive managers were not attracted to Smith Electronics, and many of the ones who did come did not stay long. Many of the managers who stayed did so because of job security, comfort, or an interest in technology, not because of ambition and enthusiasm. But Smith himself was very ambitious and set ambitious goals for the company; thus he created a cultural contradiction that encouraged conflicting goals.

93

Smith was a self-confident, strong-willed entrepreneur, but because he did not show confidence in his employees' judgments or tolerate ambitious, self-confident managers, there were general feelings of alienation and a lack of self-confidence among middle and upper management. Instead of managers developing to their full potential by being assigned tasks of increasing responsibility, managers often relied on the opinions of consultants or, in some cases, on the ability of consultants to do the manager's work. Smith needed a strong, ambitious management team to create and implement strategy, but instead he had an inhibited group of individuals who were unsure of themselves and disappointed because they were removed from the real decision-making process.

Another similar factor that was responsible for this situation was Mr. Smith's tendency to idealize his company's goals. He was primarily in business not to make money, but to build an organization that would bring him substantial recognition from society. One vice-president once bet another vice-president that if Smith was confronted with the choice between a $70 million company with $5 million in profits and a $160 million company with no profits, he would choose the latter. When Smith was asked, he did indeed choose the latter, with the rationale that he could work on profits. Despite Smith's reasoning, he chose size over profits and, more to the point, his vice-presidents often interpreted his wish for a larger company as a wish for more visibility and recognition from society. In the words of yet another vice-president, Smith wanted to be a "leading American industrialist."

Smith's tendency to idealize both consultants and the company's goals created conflicts between himself and his employees. His other-directed employees were interested in winning status by being accepted by others and by doing the "right" things; their focus was on appearance. For Smith, achievement was to be demonstrated through productivity, not through status. In a financially successful year, Smith reinvested profits back into the company, whereas many of his managers and engineers spent their bonuses on sports cars. The employees wanted to develop themselves; Smith wanted to develop the company. The employees wanted to be accepted; Smith wanted to be respected.

These cultural contradictions affected almost every aspect of the business. Smith's primary attitude toward the customer was not that he was someone to make money from, but that he was someone from whom to win recognition. The other-directed managers did not see customers as part of their peer group, and the few self-oriented and aggressive managers desired money rather than status, so both types had a more socially neutral attitude toward customers. The same conflict was behind varying motivations for product quality and customer service.

Cultural contradictions also played an important role in competition. Because of his wish for recognition, Smith's attitude toward competition was restrained, but competition in the electronics industry was very intense and at times even unethical. One time a competitor called Smith and threatened to sue him because Smith's salesmen were telling potential customers that the competitor was about to go out of business, thus discouraging the customer from buying his product because it would not be serviceable. According to my informant, who was working for another company in the electronics industry, this kind of sales tactic was not at all unusual. Smith's reaction, however, was to demand that his salesmen stop talking about competitors; further, he made his sales manager call the competitor to apologize. Regardless of the validity of Smith's reaction, his salespeople saw it as exaggerated and inappropriate.

There are, of course, always differences of opinion between managers and their employees. But in the case of Smith Electronics, these problems were never resolved and resulted in the institutionalization of cultural contradictions—all because of the leader's cultural orientation. By idealizing or impersonalizing important relationships, Smith blocked out information about personal relations. Several managers mentioned somber officer meetings, and others mentioned that Smith did not attend to political relationships. As the company grew, he did hire managers capable of constructing a sophisticated financial system, but the impersonal nature of financial information made this relatively easy for him to do.

The cultural contradictions at Smith Electronics thus led to conflicts in both company goals and managerial behavior. Smith wanted an innovative organization, but his commitment to preestablished ideals discouraged self-motivated employees and instead attracted employees who wanted either to please him or to please themselves. Innovation was not possible because individuals from the first group tended to leave the company, members of the second group concentrated on securing organizational status by winning Smith's favor, and people from the third group gave little attention to organizational goals, pursuing instead their own interests in technology. Hence there were no people left with the passion and determination to set up their own suborganization, fight off innovation-stifling organizational procedures and preferences, and concentrate on doing something new.

Managerial Implications

What can managers learn from this case analysis about using culture to stimulate innovation? We can make four points here, but we should first quickly summarize the case results. Smith's commitment to ideals clearly reflected an inner-directed cultural orientation; we saw, however, that his commitment to his own ideals made it difficult for him to share power with others. In a sense, he was a perfectionist who had to have things done his way. This trait in turn attracted employees who preferred following to leading; in some cases, these employees simply wanted to pursue their own personal interests. These two types of employees reflected on the one hand the other-directed and, on the other, the self-centered cultural orientations. The result was the organization's inability effectively to decentralize because there were too few organizationally committed, self-motivated individuals to take positions of leadership.

The first managerial implication that can be gleaned from this case history concerns the effect cultural ideals have on decision making. As we saw, the idealization of product quality led to an excessive focus on engineering at the expense of marketing. When particular goals or functions are idealized, other goals or functions tend to be devalued. This is not a statement against ideals; ideals are needed in the innovation process for clear communication, strong direction, and powerful motivation. Hence ideals must be used, but their effect must be premeasured against the strategic planning system so that they do not undermine it by emphasizing some goals at the expense of others. As we saw, when one goal is idealized at the expense of another, it becomes overemphasized, or more precisely, politicized, in the decision-making process. This retards rational decision making because it disassociates the symbolic value of a goal or function from its empirical relevance. Managers must always manage conflicting goals, and the use of ideals must always take this into consideration.

Second, the decision-making bias brought about by excessive idealization is subtle because it tends to become hidden in poor performance. At Smith Electronics, the lack of marketing skills was a constraint on sales growth, but because engineering was idealized at marketing's expense, the lack of marketing effectiveness generally went unnoticed. Engineering's prominence in the new product development process appeared natural and appropriate because its idealization seemed to validate that importance. Hence the bias from excessive idealization often goes unnoticed because it creates a "reality" that justifies the behavior it encourages. The solution to this problem is to insist on multiple viewpoints, using each to evaluate the bias in the other. If Smith managers had been able to think in terms of an idealized view of marketing and its implications for action, then the existing bias toward engineering would have been more apparent.

Third, idealization of goals or functions limits the development of interpersonal skills. As we saw, at Smith Electronics the idealization of customer service meant the "customer" was defined in terms of Smith technology rather than in terms of his own perceptions. In other words, Smith managers could forgo getting to know the customer in terms of his own work context because this context was defined by how it used Smith technology. Thus Smith managers tried to understand "customer needs" solely in terms of the needs of their current technologies, while ignoring their strategic, organizational, and personal plans and preferences. This limited Smith's ability to maintain its customer base by continually developing its own products along with its customers' developing needs.

Idealization had the same tendency to impersonalize relationships inside the organization. Smith's idealization of certain goals made it difficult for him to tolerate entrepreneurial managers who emphasized other goals. Thus, whether it defines the customer in terms of his use of technology or whether it impedes the acceptance of entrepreneurial managers, idealization has the same effect: it blocks information about the interpersonal consequences of action, especially some of the emotional effects. Before marketing could be improved and entrepreneurial managers integrated into the management system at Smith Electronics, the company would have to decentralize its idealization process; the creation of competing ideals would have to be tolerated in the different functional areas and in the middle-management ranks. Unless the chief executive officer (CEO) can be a one-man management system, innovation cannot be accomplished without both a decentralized management structure and a decentralized culture. Homogeneous cultures are antithetical to innovation because they limit the sources of creativity to top decision makers.

Fourth, because of the tendency to idealize and the resulting lack of interpersonal sensitivity toward entrepreneurs, there was a need for talented managers who did not have many interpersonal needs. At Smith Electronics, consultants met these requirements. Since consultants were not a continuous part of the daily work routine and since they were viewed as experts, they made few interpersonal demands and could be easily put into an idealized role—one in which their advice and opinions were also idealized. However, this idealization stifled the learning process and undermined the consultants' effectiveness because it encouraged the acceptance of their advice without integrating it into management's past experience. Since the consultants' advice was difficult to implement, consultants had to be continuously involved. As it stands now, this problem can be solved only if management develops an open but critical attitude; without this, the idealization process will make the consultants' advice little more than an impossible dream.

NOTE

Acknowledgment: I would like to thank Chris Argyris and John Van Maanen for their comments on earlier drafts of this essay.

SELECTED BIBLIOGRAPHY

For a more detailed discussion of the concept of culture as it applies to organizations, see my essay "Management in Context: An Essay on the Relevance of Culture to the Understanding of Organizational Change" (*Journal of Management Studies*, 23, 587–607, November 1986).

My understanding of the entrepreneurial nature of American business culture is grounded in Max Weber's work *The Protestant Ethic and the Spirit of Capitalism* (Charles Scribner and Son, 1958); see also Thomas Cochran, *Business in American Life: A History* (McGraw-Hill, 1972). My understanding of the tendency to conformity in American bureaucratic organizations is grounded in David Riesman's work *The Lonely Crowd: A Study of the Changing American Character* (Yale University Press, 1950); this is still one of the best books written on contemporary American culture. For more up-to-date studies of conformity in bureaucratic organizations, see Rosabeth Moss Kanter, *Men and Women of the Corporation* (Basic Books, 1977); Robert Jackall, "Moral Mazes: Bureaucracy and Managerial Work" (*Harvard Business Review*, 61, 118–130, September/October 1983), and Steven P. Feldman, "Culture and Conformity: An Essay on Individual Adaptation in Centralized Bureaucracy" (*Human Relations*, 38, 341–356, 1985). My understanding of self-centeredness in American culture has been developed from three main sources: Peter L. Berger, *The Capitalist Revolution* (Basic Books, 1986); Daniel Bell, *The Cultural Contradictions of Capitalism* (Basic Books, 1976); and Christopher Lasch, *The Culture of Narcissism* (Warner Books, 1979).

For the importance of the centralization-decentralization problem in regard to organizational innovation, see Robert Burgelman, "Corporate Entrepreneurship and Strategic Management: Insights from a Process Study" (*Management Science*, 29, 1349–1364, December 1983).

For the central role of leadership in the formation of culture, see Edgar Schein, *Organizational Culture and Leadership* (Jossey-Bass, 1985). And for the strong tendency of entrepreneurs to have difficult personalities, see Manfred Kets de Vries, "The Entrepreneurial Personality at the Crossroads" (*Journal of Management Studies*, 14, 1977).

97

CHAPTER 7

Group Self-Esteem and

Group Performance

Glenn Swogger, Jr.

Introduction

When managers are asked to describe the "best" work group they were ever a part of, their answers fall in three categories. They speak of the group's ability to accomplish its task. They describe its internal cohesion and high morale, and how individuals within the group were treated. And they describe their own feelings of satisfaction and fulfillment and the personal meaning that the group had for them. They find corresponding qualities in their leadership: a task orientation, combined with fairness and sensitivity to members of the group that lead them to feel bonded with their leader, admiring, and appreciative. Reflection on these sentiments, and on my consulting experience, led me to wonder how personal satisfaction and self-esteem become linked with membership in a work group and how the group's level of pride, morale, and cohesion relates to its performance.

We know that how people function in their work roles often makes a significant contribution to their self-esteem. Work roles thus assume an emotional importance that overlays their utilitarian and economic functions. Individuals who are bound together in a work group with a common task have a shared sense of their own efficacy, of common values and experiences. This shared, felt appraisal of the group may be thought of as group self-esteem and acts as a common source of emotional satisfaction or threat. The nature and dynamics of this shared sense of self-esteem may vary considerably from group to group, depending on existing psychological contracts, the position of the group in the organizational context, and its history, leadership, turnover, and current stresses and problems.

Group efforts to maintain positive self-esteem need to be understood by leaders and consultants because they may facilitate or impede work performance. This chapter attempts to develop a useful conceptual framework for understanding group self-esteem and to derive from this understanding some suggestions for consultants and leaders as to how they might help work groups to become more productive. After first defining self-esteem at the individual level, I discuss manifestations of group self-esteem and define the concept of group self-esteem in its intricate relationship with individual self-esteem. This will allow us to examine the dynamics of self-esteem in working groups and the impact of efforts to maintain self-esteem on performance. Several cases from my consulting practice highlight key issues. The chapter concludes with a discussion of the implications of group self-esteem dynamics for consultants and leaders of work groups.

Self-esteem is a feeling, an appraisal, and an attitude. It is usually ascribed to individuals: the *Oxford Universal Dictionary* defines it as a "favorable opinion or appreciation of oneself." The feeling aspect of self-esteem is elemental, hard to describe: "feeling good about myself," "I like myself," "proud," "satisfied," as contrasted with feeling "hung up" or depressed or ashamed. This global or core feeling is often tied to an appraisal: "proud of what I accomplished," "done good," "hung in there," as opposed to feeling self-critical of some thought or action, ashamed *of* something one has done or revealed. Having a high self-esteem usually goes along with self-confidence, a positive expectation about what one can do or accomplish—indeed, an expectation that one's favorable opinion of oneself will be nourished and reinforced by further contacts with people and tasks. A positive self-esteem is a self-fulfilling prophecy. Similarly, those with low opinions of themselves often lack confidence in their ability to handle new tasks or relationships, and this too has its effect.

Psychoanalysts recognized early that the superego and ego ideal function by regulating self-esteem. This insight integrates the "feeling" and "appraising" aspects of self-esteem: we *feel* guilty because we *judge* that we have done something wrong or failed to live up to an ideal. Kohut (1985, 1987) and his followers have given self-esteem a more central role in psychological maturation and functioning. They have pointed out that self-esteem develops along two lines. In part we feel good about ourselves in connection with our pride and satisfaction in vital body functions and in our abilities, which we exhibit to others for reassurance, admiration, and confirmation (the grandiose dimension of self-esteem). As adults, our work roles, talents, competencies, and achievements can serve this function. Even in people who are otherwise quite insecure, any special skill or talent serves as an anchor to self-esteem and successful adaptation.

In the second, "idealizing" dimension of self-esteem, we feel good about ourselves because we relate ourselves to people, groups, organizations, and ideals that we look up to and admire as perfect and exemplary. We identify with and become a part of that which we idealize. By doing so, and by trying to live up to and in accordance with ideal persons, groups, and creeds, we partake of some of their goodness and enhance our own self-esteem. Harry Levinson (1990) has long focused on this aspect of motivation for work roles through his use of the concept of the "ego ideal." He has emphasized the importance of assessing a person's ego ideals in deciding whether he or she is suitable to be placed in a particular role and organization. If there is a mismatch between personal values and ideals and the requirements of a particular position or the overall goals, values, and culture of an organization, then poor performance and mutual unhappiness on the part of organization and employee are likely to result. If there is a fit between person and organization, so that a reciprocal psychological contract can be established, then a strong and important element is added to work motivation and the appropriateness of the employee for the task. A mutually satisfactory and productive relationship between employee and organization is likely to result. Levinson (1976, 1984) focuses primarily on the person-organization relationship and does not concern himself so much with relationships within small working groups.

Self-Esteem and the Group

Individual self-esteem is linked to group membership because confirmation of oneself by others plays an essential role in the development and maintenance of self-esteem. (Even criticism, if honest and helpful, can confirm our self-esteem: we have been taken seriously and with an expectation that we can be better.) Many studies have emphasized the crucial role of competence and efficacy in peer relations and self-esteem. Work-related skills are a source of praise and status for individuals in the group; they mediate the achievement of group goals and values; and they form the basis for the group's collective sense of its own competency, its ability to get the job done successfully. Thus the "grandiose" sense of pride for individual ability shown to others, described by Kohut, can become linked with a shared sense of pride and optimistic expectation: "We can do it!"

It is clear that those people and groups that we become involved with and committed to, and that to some extent our self-esteem rests on, become important to us. Along with fears of rejection, being shamed, or loss of individuality that our vulnerability exposes us to, it is with and through others that we confirm ourselves, achieve our goals, and express our ideals. When groups of people work together on a common task, the group itself becomes both an instrument for achieving personal goals and an embodiment of the hopes and aspirations of individual members. The group becomes a "we" that is valued and is seen as needing and accepting individual efforts and responding to them with support and praise. The group also may be seen as the embodiment of the ideals expressed in the task of the group and as a praiseworthy and competent means of achieving that task. Thus the group becomes a carrier of the self-esteem of its members and is seen as being a "good" group, with positive qualities: "fair," "care about you," "never give up," "can always count on them." Of course, the opposite can happen, too: a group can be experienced as negative, harmful, backbiting, unfair, unreliable, and incompetent. It is this range of variation, with its many subtle twists of group culture, that we mean when we talk of group self-esteem. Just as in the case of individual self-esteem, there are elements of feeling, appraisal, and attitude. The feeling component may be expressed as team spirit, high morale, caring, acceptance and respect of each member, and cohesiveness with a wish to be or remain a part of the group. Feelings at the other end of the spectrum may involve disappointment, pessimism, low morale, apathy, a sense of isolation, withdrawal, and rejection of the group. Appraisal may take the form of "we're the greatest," "number one," feelings of specialness, satisfaction, or even complacency; or bitter self-criticism and self-depreciation, with splitting or disintegration of the group as it struggles to decide who is to blame, who represents its valid ideals, or who can lead it out of its morass. A group's attitude is measured by its sense of competence and confidence with regard to its task. Is there a sense of being able to overcome obstacles, a "can do" feeling, an eagerness to jump in and get started, nourished by past successes? Or is there a sense of hopelessness, of pessimism, of uncertainty, and perhaps even avoidance of the task or just "going through the motions"?

There is a complex and slippery relationship between individual self-esteem and group self-esteem. Conceptually, this is related to the perennial debate in psychology and sociology over whether individual traits reflect fixed differences or are products of a relationship or context. Within the psychoanalytic domain, interpersonal and object-relations approaches emphasize that enduring intrapsychic structures are products of a relationship. Guntrip (1971), who exemplifies this approach, also points out that interpersonal considerations played a significant role in Freud's thought. Object-relations theories, as well as those of Kohut (1987), postulate that key relationships, along with associated affects and feelings of positive self-esteem or worthlessness, are internalized and become an enduring part of each person. But the process does not stop there. Through attitudes, expectations, and processes of projection and identification, internalized object relationships are reenacted with individuals and groups in new relationships. Furthermore, current relationships are not merely replays of earlier experiences, but contain within them the possibility for new learning and change in personality structure. The boundary between individual and group is a shifting process of internalization and projection, learning and identification. In my opinion, the sense of self-esteem is both an individual trait and a reflection of past as well as current relationships. People vary in the degree to which they have a stable sense of self-esteem and in the situations in which they feel most secure. Some are enviably self-confident in a variety of situations and in the face of setbacks and problems; others are exquisitely vulnerable and constantly needing of affirmation. But it appears that all of us need some ongoing nourishment of our values and value.

103

The dichotomy between individual and group self-esteem is similar to that between nature and nurture or, more generally, to the question of the degree of coupling between a system and the suprasystem of which it is a part (Buckley, 1967; Swogger, 1975). How much stability and independence does a smaller unit of a larger system have, and how much is the smaller unit influenced and controlled by its relationship to the larger system? When framed in this way, "how much" implies a quantitative answer: "some of both," rather than "either/or." We are all victims of our language and of our tendencies to think digitally: it is much easier, even emotionally settling, to see things one way or another, rather than as a complex and qualified "both." The relationship between individual self-esteem and group self-esteem is a dynamic process with shifting boundaries between person, relationships, and group.

When a group of individuals jointly invest their mutual relationships with personal importance, through the processes described above, then this pattern of relatedness—the group—becomes an entity independent of each member. As such, the group is valued and evaluated as a carrier and manifestation of important personal needs. Group self-esteem reflects this appraisal. Because of its emotional importance, members of a group will make efforts to maintain their collective positive self-image. As we shall see, these efforts may have variable consequences for the group's ability to function effectively.

It should be mentioned that this dialectic between individual and group self-esteem is an important part of the process whereby a person enters a group and becomes a member of it. New members or potential members test and evaluate groups in terms of whether the values and competencies of the group will enhance, or repair, their self-esteem. Groucho Marx's famous comment that "I wouldn't want to belong to any country club that would have me" reflects a paradox of entering a group (or a relationship) for someone with low self-esteem. Conversely, groups evaluate potential members in terms of whether they have the values and competencies to enhance the positive image and feeling of the group.

Small-group and organizational researchers of the 1950s and 1960s carried out many studies of group cohesion and morale, defining these concepts in a manner very similar to what I have called group self-esteem (Katz and Kahn, 1966; Krech and Crutchfield, 1948; Seashore, 1954; Bonner, 1959). They pointed out that when working groups are cohesive and have high morale, they are more productive in terms of their own goals. They observed how the goals of the group became incorporated as part of the individual's value system and identity. They also observed that cohesive, high-performance groups choose their own goals, which are sometimes in conflict with organizational demands. They raised questions about how the needs and dynamics of working groups and teams fit into, and were influenced by, their organizational context. Later studies pointed out that employees could be motivated by appeals to their values, a finding that has had the potential for allowing both more committed and satisfying work roles, as well as manipulation and exploitation in the name of values.

104

Earlier studies tended to view morale and cohesion as static entities related to demographic variables. I would like to suggest that a psychodynamic approach to understanding the dynamics of the work group can help us to understand how fluctuations in self-esteem affect the group and to recognize the unrealistic attempts that groups sometimes make to maintain their sense of pride and competence. For group self-esteem is not simply a passive reflection of shared values and goals and the degree of competence. Because of its emotional importance, efforts are made by groups to maintain their self-esteem in the face of threats or setbacks. Individuals attempt to save face, to avoid feeling shamed or blamed. So do groups. Sometimes these efforts are self-defeating and counterproductive.

This is very clearly illustrated in the work of Zander (1977) in his book *Groups at Work*. He devotes a chapter to "group embarrassment." Here he describes his studies of what groups do when they fail. He finds that their response is split between efforts to do whatever is necessary to improve the group's effectiveness and efforts to reduce feelings of shame (i.e., to protect their collective self-esteem). The more a group has failed, the more it will focus in subsequent efforts on avoiding embarrassment rather than ensuring future success. This behavior will increase the likelihood of further failure. Strategies for avoiding embarrassment mentioned by Zander include setting impossibly high goals, depreciating the goals of the group, denial of demands made on the group, lowering the goals, denial of shame felt in response to the failure of the group, blaming others outside the group, and increased self-criticism. Thus, while a positive sense of group self-esteem may be related to an increased capacity to work effectively, attempts by groups to maintain their pride and avoid shame and guilt may have the opposite effect.

Case Illustrations

In practice, I have witnessed dramatic instances of fluctuating self-esteem and its negative effect on performance. It should be emphasized, however, that the dysfunctional aspects of group self-esteem may arise in situations of previous strong group cohesion, pride, and commitment. The four cases illustrate some processes of change in group self-esteem and the impact of these changes on the group's task performance.

Case 1: Forensic State Hospital

The Menninger Management Institute was asked to conduct continuing education workshops at a large state forensic hospital. The rushed and poorly planned request and the inaccessibility of some key members of the leadership suggested to us that what was desired was the appearance of high-quality training rather than the reality. The hospital was under heavy attack: media attention to suicides and other conditions in the hospital, litigation, critical state audits, and concerns about accreditation. Our preliminary contacts with the hospital revealed a staff under great pressure: staff shortages, a hectic and at times disorganized pace, considerable splitting between various discipline groups, paperwork that appeared to be excessive and to have defensive rather than patient care functions, impulsive decisions by the hospital leadership in response to emergencies, and a perceived gulf and lack of support between the hospital leadership and various levels of management and staff. In initial interviews and group sessions with staff, their self-image emerged in the following comments: "Caretakers of the House of the Dead," "Masochists." Staff expressed a perverse pride in handling the toughest cases. Their attitude toward the Menninger staff was expressed by one staff member as, "Let's see what mistakes you make!"—which we interpreted as a projection of their own feeling of being scrutinized for mistakes and failures.

After these initial contacts, I conducted a team-building workshop for staff members from three units. I began by sharing my impressions of the hospital, as described above. One staff member indignantly complained that I was too negative and began to describe a therapeutic community meeting on his unit that he felt was very effective. Others joined in, and the entire morning was spent discussing this program, how well it worked, how it might be applied to other units, and so on.

At lunch with several staff members, I was again treated to an unbroken litany of complaints and pessimism about the hospital and its efforts. At one point I asked about their accreditation and whether it would be renewed. One staff member said he didn't think they deserved a renewal. After lunch I asked the group how they had gotten into the issue they had discussed in the morning. After some discussion, I suggested that they vacillated between a stubborn pride, mixed with bravado, that they persevered in treating such difficult patients and fulfilled their professional responsibilities, versus a feeling of helpless, angry despair. There were further expressions of despair and disappointment in the hospital and in the workshop. I shared my awareness of their feelings and their impact on me and added that there seemed to be a wish to negate my efforts, for fear that I might make them feel even worse by telling them there was something they could do about their situation and leaving them to struggle and perhaps suffer another failure. I might also make them feel worse by acting as yet another condemning outside judge of their efforts.

Following my comments, one staff member made an eloquent statement that there was much they could be proud of in their work, which they took for granted. She recounted the assaults and attempted rapes that had occurred to people in the room, going around the room and pointing out people one by one. She said that despite the "oppression" by responsible authorities, they all hung in there and tried their best to help their patients. She pointed to improvements in patients known to herself and others, occurring over long time periods such as six months or more.

The group was very moved by this statement. After a pause, everyone clapped. After some discussion, I suggested that the group break up into the teams from each of the three units, and that each team talk about some things they were doing right and what they appreciated in one another's efforts. The teams did this and then reassembled to report on what had been discussed. A considerable list of ways in which they had worked successfully together and supported one another was generated.

In the course of presenting these items, the groups also developed an agenda of things that needed to be done (this task had not been assigned). It included items such as ways to improve communications between shifts, as well as critical but helpful feedback to one team leader.

Comment

While the therapeutic community meeting discussed in the morning session was probably a very useful part of the treatment program, the focus of the group on it at that time was defensive, a reaction to the narcissistic injury suffered by the group in response to my feedback on their hospital. As predicted by Zander, this defensive maneuver prevented group members from working more than superficially on their problems. It was only when this defensive pseudo-self-esteem was abandoned, and the reality of their situation and their feelings acknowledged (in both positive and negative aspects), that the group was able to work together productively. In this context group members were also able to be realistically critical of one another. This case also illustrates the splits and the connections between the team level of functioning and the organizational level. Staff members were able to find a positive sense of themselves only in their team and professional roles. There remained an unbridged leadership gap between this level and the larger organization. But the unit teams were not insulated from the larger organization. The lack of leadership and communication in the organization severely hampered the functioning of the unit teams.

The next case illustrates some problems experienced by a project team with very high self-esteem when it completed its task. In many organizations temporary groups are now frequently used to accomplish a variety of tasks: project teams, task forces, and so on. For such groups to be successful, they also must attract a high level of commitment and team spirit. This imposes certain responsibilities on the organizational leadership to set the context for effective functioning of the team and to deal with the aftermath of its breakup when the task is completed. The following case shows how one organization met these responsibilities and also how a temporary project team reacted to its own dissolution.

107

Case 2: ChemTech

The ChemTech plant, with five hundred employees, is a subsidiary of a large corporation. A major force in the small town where it is located, it is the flagship plant in the company for its product, and younger managers are sent to ChemTech for training. Employees are proud of the plant's safety and antipollution records, and that there have been no layoffs in three decades. Nevertheless, there is concern because of increasing competition, which has reduced profitability, and because major patents on key products are due to expire. Therefore, the previous plant manager, with support from central management, decided to initiate a process of reorganization in the plant, leading to self-directed teams, fewer levels of management, and the organization of all functions around production. A greater emphasis on training and empowerment of employees was envisioned.

Managers asked for volunteers for a fifteen-member redesign team; sixty-five people volunteered. Those selected were a broad cross-section of the entire plant; they were given a 50 percent time allocation to devote to the redesign team. The team had been in place for sixteen months when I first met its members; during this time the plant manager had moved on to another position. The redesign team had gone through a long process of development: it had floundered at the beginning, then had taken initiative and become very proud of its autonomy. The team hired consultants as needed, visited other plants, sought and obtained relevant information from management, and produced a thick and comprehensive written proposal. A pilot project in one area in the plant had begun, others were planned, and management was reviewing the team's proposal for further implementation. There were unresolved issues about compensation recommendations and some other loose ends, but basically the work of the redesign team was completed and the group was scheduled to be dissolved.

I was asked to meet with the redesign team because for the two months before my visit there had been increased conflict and polarization within the team. There was suspicion of management—would it adopt the plan? There was conflict about how detailed the guidelines for implementation were to be: some felt that instructions should be very explicit so that employees would get it right; others felt that detailed instructions for implementation were contrary to the goal of developing self-directed teams, who would of necessity have to make changes as experience in implementation was gained, as well as to adapt to changing conditions in the plant. I was requested to meet with the team all day and to attend an awards banquet. Two members of the team chose not to attend, because of their feelings about team conflicts and their concerns about management.

In the morning session, I asked team members to talk about the process they had been through and how they were feeling at that point. The following were the main themes.

Loss. "Like giving up a child—it [the proposal] is ours." Whether to let go or stay involved. "Hard to let go." "A memorable experience." For some, the experience of loss was associated with a feeling of bitterness and depreciation of the team: "Glad it's over." Some felt depressed.

Self-Criticism. "Did we take everything into account?" "Did we communicate enough with peers?" Was what they had done "real"? Was it "perfect"?

Concerns about Relationships with Peers Outside the Group. The redesign team was the target of cynicism and envy; it was dubbed "the Dream Team," and some saw it as an extension of management. Team members felt ostracized. Blue-collar members of the team felt especially uncomfortable: "Going back to a group you no longer belong to."

Suspicion. "What will be implemented?" "Want a response!" There was concern that original supporters of the team, such as the plant manager, were gone. There were feelings of being let down, betrayed, and manipulated. "I may oppose the implementation of the plan." Some blue-collar members of the team also felt that they had attended meetings more punctually than members from management and that they had more to lose: "Hourly people don't move away—they have to live with the outcome."

Burnout. "Fatigue." "Overcommitted." "Sixty-hour weeks." "Want weekends free again."

As can be seen, the overall tone of the morning session was very negative, and we discussed this at the end of the session. To begin the afternoon session, I had planned to discuss with group members their anxieties about creativity (which I hoped might be relevant to their feelings about the task they had accomplished). I asked the group members for a few examples of what they thought were creative efforts in their work as they designed the plan. To my surprise, this led to example after example, covering four flip charts. The examples given covered in part specific items in their proposal—for example, reorganization plans that cut across hourly/salary and production/maintenance distinctions. These overlapped with examples that represented valued characteristics of the team: developing leadership from within the team, taking risks, crossing boundaries, making new friendships. The very positive feelings and comments that emerged, the strong positive group self-esteem, helped me to understand the importance of the loss that group members were experiencing. We spent the rest of the afternoon discussing these losses and what could be done in response to them.

Plant management had offered to train team members as facilitators in the implementation phase of the redesign project, and several had accepted. Management was also forming a monitoring committee to oversee implementation, including redesign team members. The awards banquet, a very elegant affair, was attended by the plant manager and other senior management. The former plant manager who had initiated the project and representatives from central headquarters flew in to attend the banquet.

Comment

It is clear that strong bonds were formed between members of this very effective project group. Its end meant not only the loss of the group, but also reentry problems for its members. In this context, conflicts emerged within the team, and the group's self-esteem fluctuated wildly between angry depression, with excessive self-criticism and depreciation of their experience and their work, and pride and satisfaction in their efforts. Here, as in Case 1, only when these feelings were acknowledged and explored could the group appraise itself and its situation more realistically and begin to consider further productive contributions to the task of implementing the members' proposal.

The emotional bonds that develop in cohesive and productive groups are threatened not only when such groups are disbanded, but also by the

109

loss of key members or leaders and by the addition of new members. In my experience, such groups may manifest their need for reformation by becoming more conflictual and less effective.

In contrast to Case 1, and in a variety of practical and symbolic ways, the leadership of ChemTech showed support for the redesign team's efforts. One member's comment about opposing implementation of the plan reminds us of the fact that cohesive groups may either support or oppose company goals; but the overall tendency in this group was to respond positively to company support.

Productive work and a sense of pride depend not only on intragroup dynamics but also on organizational context. Morale and team building do not take place in a vacuum, and a high group self-esteem is not an end in itself. The leader's role in managing the boundary between work group and organization—relating the overall goals of the organization to the tasks of the group, providing resources and feedback, and accurately and fairly monitoring performance—sets the context for the group to function effectively. This both reinforces and is reinforced by positive group self-esteem. The work group's development of a sense of self-esteem based on competence depends on the group's ability to work effectively at the organizational task. At the same time, the values expressed in creating a good workplace may support the idealizing dimension of self-esteem. This means not only general supportiveness, but also that the leadership delegate sufficient authority to working groups and give them sufficient information so that they can creatively and effectively accomplish their task. We can see how the wide latitude given the redesign team at Chem-Tech was important to its development of the autonomy and initiative necessary for it creatively to accomplish its goal.

Inspirational and "excellence" approaches to increasing employee motivation and productivity are correct in recognizing the emotional well-springs of high-level performance (Peters and Waterman, 1982). In the absence of clarity and fairness in the overall relationship between employees and company, however, exhortations to "excellence" become a form of exploitation and demand for workaholism (Levering, 1988). I recently saw an illustrative instance of this in a woman who worked for a large, successful family business. The company set high standards for employees, with the expectation that management would work long hours. In return, employees would partake of the excellence of the company and be considered "family." My client, who had suffered many personal losses and had always striven to please a distant and demanding father, strove desperately to meet company standards. While she did well in her work, she was acutely aware of the sacrifices this meant for her family. When asked why she didn't limit her hours or if necessary look for a position in another company, she replied, "Because then they would say I just wasn't —— Company material." It was clear that her needs for self-esteem were

110

so linked with the company that it was very difficult for her to consider these alternatives.

Cases 1 and 2 offer contrasting examples of the relationship between work groups and organization. Staff members at Forensic State Hospital struggled to maintain their collective sense of professional self-esteem in the face of what they perceived as the lack of trust and support by their leadership, to say nothing of the fact that they were attacked and scapegoated by a whole array of interest groups outside the hospital. It is not surprising that their sense of self-esteem was brittle, defensive, and tinged with self-pity and tendencies on their part to blame and scape-goat their own leaders. In contrast, the leadership of ChemTech made consistent practical and symbolic efforts to recognize the importance and value of the redesign team's efforts. This helped mitigate the negative effects of the team's dissolution and helped individual members maintain an ongoing commitment to organizational goals.

111

When teams are created to deal with specific problems or tasks, managers wonder what they can do to accelerate the process and help teams to become more effective. Attention to issues of self-esteem is an important component of this process.

Case 3: Finanserve

In this case a manager in a large financial services company reported on teams she had put together to design user materials for computer programs. The teams were composed of individuals who had previously worked on such problems independently. Problems developed when team members criticized each others' contributions. Feelings were hurt, especially if the individuals involved considered themselves experts on the subject. The resultant "win-lose" conflicts were difficult to handle. "Secret society" subgroups formed, to protect themselves and gain advantages by not sharing information. The manager and the group developed some strategies to handle these problems:

- public recognition of group accomplishments
- public recognition of individual accomplishments
- referral of disputed issues to an impartial "miniteam" designated by the leader
- careful and thorough consideration of objections raised by team members. In one instance when a member's viewpoint was rejected he was able to accept the decision because his opinion had been heard.

Despite these efforts, the manager wondered whether the group approach was worth the effort in terms of results and whether the group had developed sufficient capacity to be self-critical.

Comment

Case 3 illustrates a problem of using teams in a corporate setting: how to get from the "I" to the "We." Many factors make this process difficult: our emphasis on individual accomplishment and careers; the "egos"— intense concerns with self-esteem needs—of those involved; and the difficulty of getting commitment to a team effort. As Peter Drucker points out, this process is easier if the organization has a practice of frequently using the team approach. However, team members are often suspicious of subordinating their interests to a group; they fear they will be exploited or their contributions will not be recognized. In addition, many are uncomfortable with conflict and feel that someone has to be a "loser" in a conflict if his or her suggestions are rejected.

112

In Case 3, this manager's strategy of making sure that team members are heard is very important in modeling a norm for the group: that each member's best efforts will be taken seriously and respected. Some individuals, whose self-esteem is very fragile, may exhibit great vulnerability in group situations. Although persons with this tendency may be quite talented and successful in the eyes of others, they may grossly overreact to minor slights and personal disappointments. They may rationalize their shame and rage by taking rigid positions "on principle." Persons with such vulnerabilities may simply not be capable of working in group settings; they may need a more rigid, distant, one-to-one management style.

Leaders have a crucial role in promoting successful group development. In addition to setting clear goals and evaluating the progress of the team, they become the emotional center and are in the best position to deal with anxieties that develop. Leaders can model behavior and through their actions communicate implicit messages that gradually are absorbed by the group as a whole. Such modeling is most successful when members feel their efforts are successful and personally rewarding.

Strategies used by those taking leadership roles in work groups can contribute to the development of group cohesion and self-esteem. They must demonstrate that they are committed to getting the job done and not play favorites among members of the group. Favoritism and alliances contribute to fears of "winning" or "losing" and make it difficult or impossible for members to identify with the team and commit to it. The leader must show a strong commitment to fairness and respect for diversity and dissent—and this is not always easy. In most situations we "hit it off" with some people more than others. Fairness does not mean pretending to like everybody or making excuses for those who do things wrong. Such behaviors usually increase anxieties about what the leader really thinks. Fairness does mean viewing each member's behavior from the perspective of what it contributes to the task, rather than what it reveals about the member's personality. Fairness also means removing a member from the team who isn't able to carry his or her load and who thus is a burden to other team members who depend on that person.

Recognition of the accomplishments of the group is another important use of the leader's emotional leverage. Many leaders, especially those who are overly critical and demanding of themselves, feel uncomfortable praising others for successfully completing a task. They tend to breathe a sigh of relief and go on to something else. Such leaders may also feel drained by their efforts and feel that praising others is an additional responsibility they do not want. However, most of us are very sensitive to whether our efforts are recognized and appreciated. It builds both self-esteem and "we-ness" to recognize and enjoy a success. It also makes it easier to tolerate discussion of setbacks and criticisms.

Paradoxically, recognition of individuals in a group also promotes a collective sense of self-esteem—if it is done fairly and consistently and not on the basis of favoritism. In terms of the group, it says, "One of the ground rules in our team is that people get recognized for what they do." Thus, realistic praise of individuals builds a group norm and offers every member an incentive to make his or her best contribution.

113

Development of a strong sense of group self-esteem based on values and idealism is a powerful motivator. The next case suggests that at times such motivation can be overdone.

Case 4: Southwest City

A just-hired city manager, and city council, sought consultation services that extended over sixteen months. The previous city manager had been requested to resign in the context of intense conflict and polarization among members of the city council. In addition to not being able to work together, council members concentrated on citizen complaints and management details. Group members felt a sense of guilt about their problems with each other and with the previous city manager; they also felt they had failed the ideals of public service that motivated their political involvement.

The new city manager was idealized as "a pro" and was himself highly motivated for personal reasons to do the very best at his new job. As a result, in a planning retreat, the group set a comprehensive and ambitious agenda (which contained many important and worthwhile goals and projects). The city manager plunged full tilt into its implementation. Perceiving much pressure from the council, the city manager and a small group of department heads drove themselves to complete projects ahead of schedule, often without adequate consultation with those involved. This led to symptoms of burnout in the leadership group and strong anxiety and opposition among departments within the city government that feared rapid change and/or loss of vested interests. Despite these problems, the city manager and council pushed ahead with a major bond issue that represented important needs of the city but that also aroused significant opposition. The defeat of this bond issue, and of several council members, eventually led to the forced resignation of the city manager.

Comment

This case illustrates "the tyranny of the ideal": a group with high ideals and integrity became so committed that it ignored realistic constraints and the time dimensions of change, and did not succeed in efforts to achieve some valued goals. Appealing to ideals is like letting the genie out of the bottle. The genie of idealism can be a powerful motivator for commitment and corrective action. But idealism can also be corrupted by guilt or by a lack of reality testing. In other settings, it can also boomerang: sometimes appeals to values and ideals are made that are hypocritical and lack serious commitment, or that have not been thought through in terms of realistic implementation. Such proclamations may be long remembered and come back to haunt the organization when contradicted by events, or they may lead to disillusionment and cynicism.

114

Conclusion

In reflecting on all four cases and on my overall experience with manifestations of group self-esteem, I am struck by the fact that recognition of the importance of group self-esteem helped me to understand some surprises: the contradiction between the low morale and difficult working conditions of the Forensic State Hospital staff, and their stubborn insistence that they were doing fine; the intense, angry self-depreciation of a cohesive and high-performance group; and the ruinous overcommitment of a very ethical and dedicated leadership in a city government. The cases of ChemTech and Southwest City also illustrate that high morale, cohesion, and investment in group self-esteem are not an unmixed blessing; careful ongoing understanding of the effects of high commitment on individuals and groups is crucial. The case of Finanserve reminds us that the development of an appropriate sense of group self-esteem and helping individuals to make an emotional investment in work groups are difficult and perennial management tasks.

The findings illustrated in these four cases have important implications for practicing managers, as well as for consultants and researchers. The most salient can be summarized as follows.

1. High positive self-esteem is both an indicator of a work group's potential for high performance and part of the emotional engine for

achieving the cooperation and commitment necessary for successful efforts.

2. For organizational leaders and consultants, an awareness of the feeling state of working groups is of critical importance in promoting optimal levels of functioning. It is worthwhile to develop the empathy necessary to pick up fluctuations in group self-esteem and to spot maladaptive defenses against failure, shame, and criticism.

3. Strategies for promoting higher group self-esteem include showing realistic respect for individual group members' efforts to maintain and enhance their self-esteem, so that this becomes a norm of the group. Methods include

(a) realistic, thoughtful, and helpful criticism, as opposed to either attacking and belittling individuals or avoiding criticism altogether;

(b) appropriate and public praise;

(c) manifesting a sense of fairness and equity toward all members of a work group;

(d) setting realistic goals, so that individuals' efforts to enhance their self-esteem do not lead to burnout, imbalance between work and family life, and a sense of exploitation by the organization; and

(e) recognizing the importance of major changes in the group when membership turnover and/or task completion occurs.

4. A second major strategy involves enlisting commitment to meaningful tasks and promoting the group's sense of pride in its accomplishments. Methods include

(a) setting clear goals and tasks and obtaining the resources for their accomplishment;

(b) praise for achievement of group goals, including recognizing and rewarding individual contributions to group efforts;

(c) conveying a sense that individuals are measured by their contribution to the task and not by extraneous characteristics; and

(d) developing norms of using conflict and criticism within the group that maximize the value of individual diversity and talent within the group and are not unduly hurtful of individual self-esteem. Conflicts should produce contributors, not winners and losers.

5. No work group, from the executive committee to the shop floor, works in isolation from the rest of the organization. It is essential to be aware of values, norms, and psychological contracts within the larger organization that either promote and reward productivity and confirm group and individual self-esteem, or do the opposite. In some instances managers may be able to clarify policies and mandates, or initiate rewards and recognition, or gain acceptance of the group's

115

efforts in the larger organization. In other instances, managers and consultants may have a responsibility to make the organizational leadership aware of the negative consequences to group self-esteem and productivity of organizational policies, structures, and communication gaps between different levels of the organization. Efforts to promote group self-esteem and productivity, when these are undermined by larger organizational trends, are likely to be ineffective or manipulative. Since group self-esteem is partly tied to values and ideals, ethical questions and questions of the larger purpose and goals of the organization cannot be excluded.

REFERENCES

Bonner, Hubert. 1959. *Group Dynamics—Principles and Applications.* Chap. 3, "Cohesive and Disruptive Forces in Group Behavior." New York: Roland Press.

Buckley, Walter. 1967. *Sociology and Modern Systems Theory.* Englewood Cliffs, N.J.: Prentice-Hall. [See especially pp. 42–45.]

Drucker, Peter. 1974. *Management—Tasks, Responsibilities, Practices.* New York: Harper and Row. [See especially pp. 564–571.]

Fenichel, Otto. 1945. *The Psychoanalytic Theory of Neurosis.* New York: W. W. Norton.

Freud, Sigmund. 1955. *Group Psychology and the Analysis of the Ego.* Edited by James Strachey. The Standard Edition of the Complete Psychological Works of Sigmund Freud, volume 18. London: Hogarth Press.

Grunebaum, Henry, and Leonard Solomon. 1987. "Peer Relationships, Self-Esteem, and the Self." *International Journal of Group Psychotherapy*, 37, 475–513.

Guntrip, Harry. 1971. *Psychoanalytic Theory, Therapy, and the Self.* New York: Basic Books.

Hirschhorn, Larry. 1988. *The Workplace Within: Psychodynamics of Organizational Life.* Cambridge, Mass.: MIT Press.

———. 1991. *Managing in the New Team Environment: Skills, Tools, Methods.* New York: Addison-Wesley.

Katz, Daniel, and Robert L. Kahn. 1966. *The Social Psychology of Organizations.* Chap. 12, "The Psychological Basis of Organizational Effectiveness," pp. 336–389. New York: John Wiley and Sons. [See especially pp. 340–346 and 362–368 on the self-concept.]

Kohut, Heinz. 1985. *Self-Psychology and the Humanities: Reflections on a New Psychoanalytic Approach.* Edited by Charles B. Strozier. New York: W. W. Norton.

———. 1987. *The Kohut Seminars on Self-Psychology and Psychotherapy with Adolescents and Young Adults.* Edited by Miriam Elson. New York: W. W. Norton.

Krech, David, and Richard Crutchfield. 1948. *Theory and Problems of Social Psychology.* Chap. 11, "Group Morale and Leadership." New York: McGraw-Hill.

Levering, Robert. 1988. *A Great Place to Work: What Makes Some Employers So Good (And Most So Bad).* New York: Random House.

Levinson, Harry. 1976. *Psychological Man.* Cambridge, Mass.: Levinson Institute.

———. 1984. "Reciprocation: The Relationship Between Man and Organization." In Manfred F. R. Kets de Vries (ed.), *The Irrational Executive: Psychoanalytic Studies in Management.* New York: International Universities Press.

———. 1990. "Ego Ideal and Commitment to the Organization." Levinson Letter, March 15, Cambridge, Mass.

Mack, John E. 1983. "Self-Esteem and Its Development: An Overview." In J. E. Mack and

S. L. Ablon (eds.), *The Development and Sustaining of Self-Esteem in Childhood*. New York: International Universities Press.

Peters, Thomas J., and Robert H. Waterman, Jr. 1982. *In Search of Excellence: Lessons from America's Best-Run Companies*. New York: Harper and Row.

Seashore, Stanley. 1954. *Group Cohesiveness in the Industrial Work Group*. Ann Arbor, Mich.: Survey Research Center, Institute for Social Research, University of Michigan.

Swogger, Glenn, Jr. 1975. "Systems Theory and Small Groups." In *Interdisciplinary Aspects of General Systems Theory: Proceedings of the Third Annual Meeting of the Middle Atlantic Division*, pp. 74–81. Washington, D.C.: Society for General Systems Research.

Zander, Alvin. 1977. *Groups at Work*. Chap. 5, "Group Embarrassment," pp. 63–74. San Francisco: Jossey-Bass.

CHAPTER 8

The Psychodynamics of a
Cultural Change:
Learnings from a Factory

Larry Hirschhorn and Thomas N. Gilmore

Companies and their operating units increasingly face rapidly changing markets and technologies that pressure them to "change their culture." Nowhere are these changes more dramatic than in industries that have also faced deregulation. The leaders of such organizations feel pushed to empower the line workers, to demand more creativity and problem solving, to seek more collaboration and participation across the historically powerful divisions and functions, and to reduce organizational layers (Schein, 1985; Block, 1987). In sum, they are recontracting with employees for a different relationship than has historically prevailed. Rather than relying on workers who are obedient to their superiors and to the established rules and procedures, the company needs workers to exercise

Reprinted from *Human Resource Management* (Summer 1989), vol. 28, number 2, pp. 211–233. © 1989 by John Wiley & Sons, Inc. Reprinted by permission of John Wiley & Sons, Inc.

personal authority in identifying and resolving technical and interpersonal problems.

This transformation of the psychological contract and the culture is not easily accomplished. At the individual level, the changes in relationships of leaders and followers uncover deep issues of individuals' psychodynamic relationships to authority, their comfort with aggression, and their responses to dramatic increases in uncertainty. At the organizational level, the switch to a fast-changing competitive environment from the protected status of being regulated raises many similar issues for the company as a whole as it recontracts its relationships with suppliers and customers. The enterprise must channel the aggression necessary to compete and begin holding people internally accountable in ways that reflect the deregulated company's new situation of being evaluated by its markets.

120

Progress under these circumstances proceeds via a complex interaction between regressive and progressive forces. Often, specific actions that are taken to bring about the desired entrepreneurial, participative culture contain their own undoings. What Eric Trist has termed the "internal saboteur" often unconsciously undermines what is attempted at the conscious level.

The following case study explores the psychodynamics of a cultural change and seeks to deepen an understanding of the transformation process in companies and industries experiencing deregulation. We see how the changes in the dependency relationships on the boundary (from regulators to customers) ricochet within the organization, altering the dependency dynamics among levels of the hierarchy. We describe how aggression, which is functional when directed at the work and at competitors, can lead to scapegoating, mutual recrimination, and guilt when it is channeled into blame as the organization goes through the inevitable difficulties of transformation. We then examine the relationship between parallel structures (training events, ad hoc groups, diagonal slices, off-site retreats) and the chain of command in bringing about changes. Finally, we discuss the struggles over evolving new models of leadership, in which different levels and roles can be magically looked to for salvation but inevitably end up failing to meet expectations.

Knowledge of this case comes from our work with first-line supervisors at Electrosystem, a large electronic factory. Asked by upper management and the training department to develop a supervisory training program, we conducted four seminars with a total of eighty supervisors. Eschewing the traditional approach to supervisory training[1]—that is, teaching interpersonal skills—we conducted each session instead as a learning seminar in which we worked with the supervisors and upper managers to understand the supervisory role, its changing nature, and its links to other roles in the plant.

Organizational History

Electrosystem produced a wide range of circuits for the switching network of a formerly regulated national utility, using state-of-the-art clean-room and assembly equipment and manufacturing to specifications and standards set by a large engineering group.

At the corporate level, the organization had historically exchanged the privileges of being a regulated monopoly for giving the society a valued, universal service. This dependence on the external boundary was mirrored inside; workers depended on upper management, which was viewed as being in control and, in fantasy, as being omniscient and powerful. Prices were set by state commissions, and capital costs could be built into the rate bases for determining tariffs and thus revenues. The core task was to win rate cases. Now under deregulation, the company and its factories faced a more disciplining, competitive environment. Because the company no longer functioned in a cost-plus system in which inventory, capital, and building could be part of the rate base for determining prices, inventories had to be more strictly controlled and production better matched to some estimate of customer demand.

The factory's situation regarding new product development had changed dramatically as well. The company no longer had the luxury of developing high-quality products and fully testing them in a pilot fashion prior to handing the fully specified production model to the manufacturing side of the house. Instead, slack had to be drastically cut out of the new product development cycle, and often production had to begin before bugs were completely worked out.

These shifts predictably led the company's plant leadership to undertake a number of initiatives aimed at responding to these new conditions.

1. They created a participative forum, called the shop council, that would bring different functions and levels together to resolve various problems. Under the umbrella of a plantwide council, different ad hoc teams were charged with studying and recommending responses to identified problems.

2. They contracted with Edward Deming's training company to put every shop floor worker through a quality control program. Deming, a well-known quality control expert with enormous influence in Japan, has played a significant role in helping senior factory managers understand the links between quality production and organization processes. The sessions introduced methods of quality control and productivity gains that emerge from a climate of problem solving. Deming's trainers and materials argued that a modern factory culture should drive out fear and create a team system. Sessions were structured so that teams of operators, after being exposed to the Deming

concepts, were given the opportunity to "vent" their complaints and frustrations, listing problems and ideas on flip charts that senior managers reviewed at the end of each training cycle.

Indeed, as a result of their learnings from the Deming system, Electrosystem factory managers made important changes to the factory's sociotechnical system. They eliminated the punch clock for operators with good attendance and dismantled the entire industrial methods divisions through which factory jobs had been rated and people received production bonuses. People could come and go and were trusted to do a fair day's work without the pull of incentive pay. The level of direct supervision and policing declined. In other areas, such as appraisal, Deming's ideas were not adopted.

3. The factory leadership began introducing a "Just-In-Time" production system in response to this new environment. With J-I-T, upstream activities must shut down if for some reason downstream activities have been stopped. Hence, an error or problem in one part of the factory shuts down the entire factory. Since the other parts of the factory can no longer keep busy by producing to inventory, the entire factory is under pressure to solve the particular problem that has halted production. J-I-T thus becomes a method for more quickly exposing flaws in the production stream and correcting them. It is a more efficient system and can potentially create knowledge, learning, and increased interdependence.

Not surprisingly, the role of the first-line factory supervisor began to change. As a result of interventions such as those mentioned, the supervisors had shifted their time from directly supervising shop floor operators to functioning more as boundary managers or spanners who integrated the upstream and downstream sections of the production process.

In the past, the operators had interacted almost exclusively with the supervisor in relating to the rest of the plant. "We never looked behind their authority; they were God," commented one, adding that, at that time, you had no idea who your department chief was, meeting him only on an anniversary date talk. Moreover, others noted, supervisors had to wear white shirts and discipline was strict. Acting on behalf of a distant and all-powerful authority, the supervisor simply told operators what to do. Now maintenance, engineers, and customer representatives had much more visibility and influence with a section.

Yet predictably, these substantial shifts—to a less policing culture, to a more cost-sensitive production system, and to a supervisory process that emphasized the supervisor's work as a boundary manager rather than boss—had problematic psychological and cultural effects. The Deming seminars, for example, while ostensibly empowering workers to discuss the factory's work and culture, also resulted in a great deal of "dumping" on the supervisors themselves, who consequently felt blamed for the factory's dysfunctions and squeezed between their upper managers and the operators they supervised. In a group discussion assessing the Deming seminars, supervisors noted that "first-line supervisors lost respect" when upper management took all the operators' complaints "at face value" and let management be "blamed for all the problems in the plant."

In the shop council, supervisors felt they were not free to talk openly, that the council's work itself lacked direction, and that they were constantly being judged by their own bosses. Some supervisors developed a persecutory fantasy that the senior managers who attended knew each supervisor's rating and listened only to the highly rated ones. They progressively abandoned the council.

Thus, the very mechanisms designed to empower the operators on the one side and provide for open deliberations on shop issues on the other had caused the supervisors to feel blamed and scapegoated. Indeed, as we soon discovered, one reason the company sought out our supervisory training program was to repair the damage that these other efforts had themselves created.

123

What was going on here? The experiences and stresses on first-line supervisors frequently highlight wider issues of authority and organization in the company as a whole. The supervisor is the link between the administrative and production systems, between people with careers and people who just have jobs, and between union and nonunion employees. Organizational changes, when meaningful, transform these relationships—for example, by more tightly linking administration and production or creating careers for shop personnel.

The Organizational Ideal and the Judging Culture

Schwartz's Theory

Why did the factory's culture discourage people from acknowledging feelings of dependency, learning, and failure? What are the roots of such a culture?

Schwartz's theory of the organization ideal (1987) is an important place to begin to answer these questions. Schwartz argues that an image of a company and its senior managers as "perfect" or "wonderful" plays a fundamental role in shaping psychological life in many hierarchies. Confronting the demands of their own superegos for perfect performance, adults frequently project their private images of the ego ideal onto the company; they identify their image of the "perfect" with the company's history, its officers and achievements. Then, just as they are likely to feel judged by their own insufficiency when compared to their ego ideal, so they are likely to feel judged and watched by the company's officers and superiors far more than the actual appraisal process warrants. People are afraid to make mistakes and are therefore unable to learn because they fear being punished by the projected image of their ideal, now represented by the company itself.

The Organizational Ideal and Structural Conditions

We suggest that Schwartz's theory of the ego ideal, while compelling, may be too one-sided, focusing too much on intrapsychic roots of experience and not enough on structural conditions that stimulate new fantasies and thoughts as well as archaic and infantile ones. Although many adults suffer from feelings of worthlessness, the conditions and experiences of adult life can also stimulate feelings of competence and value. For example, consistent evidence shows that people who own their business, however small and vulnerable, are more satisfied with their work than those who are employed by others; this suggests that when people can control their work and understand the links between their efforts and outcomes, they feel more effective and valuable despite the greater risks and uncertainties they face.

Schwartz's theories of the organizational ideal, we believe, most closely describe reality under specific structural conditions. Feelings of being judged are linked to the psychodynamics of companies with strong monopoly positions facing little market discipline that can therefore waste resources and underemploy people. The culture of judgment based on the image of the corporation and its senior managers as perfect, while rooted partly in archaic fantasies as Schwartz suggests, is also a psychological defense against the reality of a company's dependency on political relationships to its environment and on the latent superfluity of positions and levels in the company itself. *The manifest image of perfection plays counterpoint to the reality of waste.* The image of the perfect company and its great leaders compensates people not only for their inner feelings of worthlessness but for the structural basis of their feelings of superfluity and consequent vulnerability.

Superfluity

Electrosystem highlights some of the links between images of perfection, a culture of judgment, and superfluity. Its former monopoly position had distorted the economics of its practice. Looked at strategically, its primary task was to win rate cases so that its revenues would match expenses. Not facing the discipline that the marketplace imposes on resource use, it could, like many monopolies, support bureaucracies that wasted resources.

Consequently, many of its control systems had the double character of posing as systems of tight bureaucratic control while also being wasteful and irrational. For example, when we first arrived, the plant was still operating under its inherited standard cost system that reflected costs allocated by headquarters and internal transfer prices that one division of the company charged another. Plant managers could not make sense of their actual achievements, their productivity, and their profitability. The pricing structure, far from reflecting market prices and discipline, was tied up in company politics of resource allocation. Moreover, the company had created an elaborate measuring system that assessed many features of the production systems and could presumably judge all aspects of plant and section performance. Yet its factories frequently amassed such large stocks of inventories (a reflection most likely of independent and uncoordinated action taken by different sections in a plant pursuing its own goals) that senior managers had to lay off people just to squeeze out the excess stock. The elaborated and apparently rational system of measurement was matched by key disjunctions between production and sales. Indeed, the enormous difficulty that the company has encountered since deregulation in competing successfully within the information marketplace is a sign of the limits of its prior culture and practice.

125

Throughout our work with the factory we had a sense of how much the shadow of superfluity and of excessive people, machines, and materials affected cultural and psychological life. Three examples are suggestive.

1. Meetings without Purpose. Supervisors frequently complained that they were pulled into an excessive number of meetings called simply to put their own bosses in the know, so that the latter could in turn answer questions from their senior managers. It was as if the bosses, lacking real tasks, or a sufficient number of them, had to dip down into the hierarchy and "steal" work and information to look productive. As one supervisor noted, "Our bosses justify taking our authority by saying that we can be with our people more, yet they call us into meetings because they don't know the shop . . . we could spend all day in meetings."

Indeed, one of the authors (Hirschhorn) attended two such meetings and was struck by their seemingly ritualized character and purpose. One maintenance supervisor argued that the meetings he attended rarely contained surprises and that they were talking about issues that most had discussed on the shop floor. In other words, the meeting simply duplicated informal work processes. A similar meeting between the shop and engineering also appeared quite ritualized. Indeed, the manager running the meeting sat to the side of the table, leaning back against a window as if he had no relationship to the group.

The entire process of information flow seemed burdened by the number of levels in the organization. The plant manager described how, in responding to the demands of an irate but important customer, he would set off a chain reaction of managers seeking out information about delays until, reaching the bottom, the shop floor supervisor or engineer could report on the exact status of a shipment. Facing the prospect and anxiety of not knowing something when the boss wanted information, managers in the middle naturally called meetings frequently so they could be informed. But the resulting use of managerial time cloaked the fact that the organization might be better off if there were fewer organizational levels and information moved more quickly up and down the chain of command. The meeting system could disguise management redundancy, while management redundancy could paradoxically justify the meeting system.

2. Redundancy and Special Needs. In the course of our work with the supervisors we learned that the plant tolerated a culture of exceptions based on individual needs in which, despite the pressure on resources, operators could substantially influence their work assignments. For example, operators, reluctant to work in clean rooms because of dress code requirements, could arrange to get medical notes excusing them from the presumably more stressful work. This "deal-making" and the consequent waste of resources was a legacy of the factory's membership in a broader corporate system that tolerated waste and excessive costs.

There is, of course, nothing inherently wrong with a culture that permits such "deal-making" at the margins of the workplace; it may humanize the setting, though it always threatens to corrupt social relationships within it. In the more "rational" workplace such deals become part of policy, and the resulting costs to the company are known and public. But we felt that supervisors and managers were particularly ashamed of this facet of factory life, suggesting that the use of resources to meet individual needs triggered underlying feelings about management's authority, effectiveness, and its own superfluity.

One example was quite striking here. We asked the labor relations department to give us a case it had worked on that would typify some of the problems supervisors of the factory floor faced in working with difficult or recalcitrant operators. Henry, a supervisor in the labor relations department, sent us a dramatic one. The file described a woman who was frequently absent and had succeeded in completely involving several supervisors in her life. They tracked her down in hospitals, at the homes of male companions; they lurked in factory alleys to catch her coming in late. One supervisor, frustrated by his inability to discipline, noted in her case file how he had blurted out, "You don't pay attention to what's said, and you make a fool out of me."

We wondered how the factory culture created such a climate of dependency and caretaking in which supervisors fell into the role of scolding parents, berating operators whom they viewed as "bad children" not fully responsible for their own behavior. In assuming this role, the supervisors helped perpetuate a system of making exceptions, of committing factory resources to people with special needs, just as one would do for children or invalids. In so doing, they threatened to corrupt role relationships in the factory itself. After preparing extensive documentation on this case for the next seminar, we thanked Henry for it. He then informed us that the woman was a prostitute!

Of course, we spent an enormous amount of time worrying how we could use the example (we eventually did) and then realized that we had been inducted into the culture of the factory in the process. Just as numerous supervisors had spent hours worrying about this operator and then hating her for it, so had we!

But why the induction? What was being communicated to us? We suggest that the example, like a dream or symptom, disguised a shameful reality that managers could acknowledge and distort only by presenting it in its most extreme form. Exceptions were common, operators made deals, the factory climate was one that supported chronic levels of waste and superfluity. But to hide this reality, it was projected onto the bizarre situation of the prostitute as if to signify that only prostitutes waste resources! Moreover, by inducting us into their reality, making us angry at the operator, and forcing us to deal with the problem of secrets ("Should we tell the supervisors that the woman was a prostitute?"), supervisors could also corrupt our ability to understand their lives. Indeed, in the seminar we interpreted this to the supervisors, saying that the case of the prostitute, while extreme, also represented a slice of their deal-making life. Many agreed.

3. *Lionizing the Line.* The image of superfluous management was matched by a peculiar "lionization of the line," motivated, it seemed, by the feeling that the only "real" work going on was at the line of production itself. The Deming materials promoted some of these feelings, since in highlighting the role that the operators could play in production, it quite explicitly "bashed" management for its failure to enlist operators on the one side or simply get out of the way on the other.

But we suspect that this lionization was built into the culture of the plant itself. Several supervisors expressed their frustration upon realizing that upper managers valued thoughts and complaints from the line workers more than similar thoughts from the supervisors themselves. One supervisor noted wryly that if he wanted to get an idea to his boss, he would be sure to tell it to an operator in his section who would relay it upward in a council meeting or when the boss was "managing by walking around." This overvaluation of the line was shaped by both a rational and an irrational process. On the one side, it reflected the only partly acknowledged reality that there was much management redundancy and that, particularly in a period of competition, actions on the line itself would increasingly shape the future of the company.

But on the irrational side, lionizing the line reflected a process of management abdication, a sense that since management was partly redundant and the utility was not successfully competing, management was in some ways failing the plant and the company. Therefore, the thinking went, only the line could save the company. We had two notable experiences of this implicit theory.

First, the plant manager, appearing before a supervisors' group at one of the seminars, commented that while he first thought of his role as "coach" to the plant, he now realized that he was its cheerleader. In other words, he was simply on the sidelines! In the second, talking about the importance of J-I-T, he noted that he would not be requiring progress reports on people's success in applying J-I-T because, were he to do so, it might appear as just another fad. J-I-T was too important, he noted, to meet such a fate. In other words, the formal authority system was so corrupt and lacking in legitimacy that, if it sanctioned a process, it would defeat it. Management was not only superfluous; it was truly destructive.

Clearly, of course, management was key. Operators, many of whom were women who had to manage domestic lives of their own and were members of a union with very little tradition or interest in the themes of self-management or quality of work life, were not going to take over the running of the plant. Plant management was enacting a fantasy. We suspect that part of the fantasy was simply a reaction to their sense of crisis; they might indeed fail, and it would be better not to be alone in either reshaping the plant system or watching it sink.

The Persecuting Organization

The complexity of the organization as an ego ideal is revealed by its changed meaning as a result of deregulation. There is little doubt that in the old days, as the older supervisors told us, the plant and the company was a "good object." The strict authority system was matched by a sense that one was protected for life, that if you kept your nose clean you could rise far, and that one was a member, as one supervisor noted, of a "large and happy family." The broader environment of stability and coherence created a climate of protection and certainty despite the underlying signs of irrationality.

We found that in the current climate, supervisors were not discounting the senior managers or writing them off for their own apparent failures. Instead, the supervisors had developed a more persecutory image of those managers; the "powers" that once protected them while judging them now simply persecuted them. Just as the ego ideal is in fact a mixture of the punishing superego and a loving mother, the organizational ideal is balanced between the image of the organization as good and beautiful or bad and persecuting. When the balance works, the persecutory component becomes the stimulus for effort and self-criticisms in the interests of self-improvement and advancement, so that the individual can join the "good" senior executives. But when the two components of the ideal are out of balance, the persecutory leads to feelings of despair, anger, and counterdependent rebellion. The culture of judgment, no longer softened by the protection it affords, is now seen as strictly oppressive. People consequently feel even weaker and more isolated. We had three striking examples.

1. Not Seeing Senior Management's Anxiety. By considering upper managers as persecutors, supervisors could not in fact conceive of them as people who also had to manage their own dependencies on their bosses, and who therefore faced constraints and anxieties just as supervisors did. For example, at the first seminar, Fred, the training director who first hired us, left the seminar at the end of the first day to do other work. Anticipating the moment in which the upper managers were to join the group, he said to the supervisors, "When they come, don't just ding on them; talk about training."

129

Fred left and the supervisors were furious. Like all upper managers, they felt, he was telling them what to do. "This is typical," noted one supervisor. "He is telling us what to say and how to get it right. This is not participative management."

Yet our experience of Fred's behavior was quite different. He was visibly anxious. His bosses, senior management of the plant, were to join the pilot seminar, and he was sensibly worried that they would not like it. We interpreted this to the group, but they were unconvinced. It seemed to us that the supervisors could not acknowledge the anxiety of a boss. Instead, fixed on seeing them as persecutors, they could not experience them as people who worried, made mistakes, or suffered.

2. Wanting an Enemy. We experienced the supervisors' "fantastical" images of their superiors when in each seminar we designed an intergroup encounter between the two levels; these began the second evening of the seminar and extended through the third day. In the first seminar, the supervisors were anxious about the meeting of the two groups, predicting that they would all clam up once their upper managers arrived. We helped them determine the parts of their work they wanted to share with their bosses and designed a series of mixed small groups for the first half of the last day to facilitate both groups' entry into the "intergroup." While shaped by a somewhat anxious and manic climate, the work of the two groups was nonetheless solid and, to the surprise of many of the supervisors themselves, was conducted in an atmosphere of openness and relative freedom.

As we approached a similar point in the second seminar, we could sense how different the encounter would be. The upper managers were already practiced in the intergroup encounter, and the first group of supervisors had clearly communicated to others back at the plant that conversation with their uppers was possible and even potentially gratifying.

As we approached the intergroup, there was visibly less tension, but also less excitement. Feeling this ourselves, we noted, "You can't step in the same river twice." The encounter would be less magical, less a meeting with the "high and the mighty." Instead, it would be one in which the supervisors would simply face other people who happen to have more authority. The supervisors would experience the encounter as sober but correspondingly down to earth and more genuinely personal.

130

Clearly, some of the supervisors were upset and disappointed. They had looked forward to the drama of the intergroup. But the culture of the seminar had surpassed their fantasy. "So that's it, so it's nothing," noted one supervisor, suggesting strikingly that because she was unable to deploy her fantasy of the upper managers as the high and mighty, her encounter with them could have no meaning. The supervisors needed to dehumanize their upper managers in order to construct a persecutory image of them.

3. Confusing Compliance with Collaboration. In all four seminars we asked supervisors and upper managers to write brief "critical incidents" that pinpointed some of the difficulties they faced in taking their roles. In working with a mixed group of upper managers and supervisors on the following incident, written by an upper manager, we once again experienced the persecutory image that supervisors created and sustained of their bosses.

> *Background:* Due to a sequence of events over a several-month period of time, a circuit run was back-scheduled and on the critical circuit report. The supervisor and I were working on a plan to get the circuit off the critical list.
>
> *Encounter:* During the course of our discussion, I was arguing for accepting more program during the next few weeks. The supervisor did not believe we could accept any more than what was already promised. It appeared that there was sufficient capacity. The number of people appeared to be adequate although somewhat tight. I therefore asked the supervisor for specifics of where he thought the problem might be. He could give me no specific answer. I concluded that we could accept more program. He agreed, but I felt that he didn't really believe it could be done.
>
> *Frustration:* I found this experience to be frustrating because I felt there was something the supervisor wasn't telling me. He definitely didn't appear to

believe we could make the program. He was only agreeing because I was "browbeating" him into doing so.

This incident highlights a complex set of relationships between the two levels. The upper feels that the supervisor will not authentically collaborate with him and is simply compliant. The supervisor, undoubtedly feeling judged for the backlog, does not know how to discover if the upper manager really wants his opinion or is simply browbeating him.

Most interesting, however, was that in discussing and role playing this incident, several supervisors insisted that the upper manager who had written it (and remained anonymous) was setting up the supervisor and wanted only to hear that the line could produce more. When it was pointed out to the supervisors that the upper manager was frustrated by the outcome, the supervisors could not hear it. They reiterated that the upper manager had set up the supervisor. Again, the supervisors could not see their bosses as struggling with their own feelings of failure and incompetence. Such an image of their bosses would interfere with the persecutory image they had constructed.

131

The persecutory dynamics that interfered with collaboration were not only described in the incidents but became reenacted in the seminars in the intergroup discussions. Small mixed groups (supervisors and uppers) had discussed the following incident, also submitted by an upper manager.

A forecast of the number of employees with decreasing workload was decided on for the upcoming year. This decision was made jointly by all departments and supervisors with input from all.

Some months after the surplus (i.e., layoff), unforeseen by everyone, the business picture (as usual after a surplus) turned around. The workload increased. The statement made by the supervisor was one of "I told them not to surplus anyone." This is where frustration set in.

Being the supervisor, he had a say in the overall and final decisions. I felt he did not want to be looked upon as part of a team who made the decision. When I had a meeting with the supervisor (privately) I mentioned the statement. The answer was, "Well, I get frustrated that we surplussed the people and now the workload is increasing and I felt as though my employees thought that we don't know what we are doing."

My answer was you were part of the team. If you didn't feel comfortable with the decision, you should voice your opinion and state the reasons. Also, explain to your employees how and why the decision was made, and if need be, I'll sit with them and explain it to them.

I also mentioned that this is part of being a manager and that you try to make the best decision at the time, based on the information at hand and your knowledge of the nature of your business.

The conclusion was that the supervisor admitted it was the wrong statement and he had not used good judgment. The incident and discussion helped the individual to become a better supervisor and accept his responsibility as part of the management team.

This is a rich incident. It highlights how the upper managers can feel frustrated by their inability to enroll the supervisors; it shows the link between upper management failure (e.g., they laid off too many people) and the breakdown in the relationship between upper managers and supervisors; it underscores the supervisor's fear of complaints from operators and fear of pressure from bosses. It also suggests that upper managers, engaged in wishful thinking, may see resolution and continued support for their authority where both are lacking.

We circulated among the small groups during their discussions and were pleased by the freedom with which the supervisors were speaking. In particular, many supervisors pointed out that they doubted the supervisor in the incident had indeed accepted "his responsibility as part of the management team" and may have simply been agreeing with the upper manager to avoid further conflicts.

One of us (Hirschhorn), who was leading this session, then convened the whole group in plenary and asked them to review the themes of their own small group discussions. The supervisors found it easy to characterize some of the feelings that the upper manager felt: "he felt betrayed, disappointed, frustrated." But when the mixed group of supervisors and upper managers was asked to characterize the feelings of the supervisor in the incident, the supervisors themselves took up the cudgel of judgment, arguing that the supervisor was disloyal and not a team player. The insight discussed in the small groups, that the supervisor felt browbeaten and was simply complying, was not mentioned in plenary.

This is, of course, one measure of the plant's evaluative culture and the supervisors' consequent fear of speaking up in public. But Hirschhorn's own feelings at that moment give some insight into the dynamics of the links between upper management and the supervisors. Just as the upper manager in the incident felt betrayed, *Hirschhorn also felt betrayed by the supervisors who at that moment were not supporting him in exploring the critical incident.* The feeling was profound and shocking, and Hirschhorn, talking very much out of his own unconscious voice, found himself emphatically saying, "The voice of the supervisor cannot be heard in this room." Complete silence followed.

This event and Hirschhorn's personal experience suggest that supervisors and upper managers faced deep difficulty in collaborating with one another, that the image of the persecutory upper manager split the two apart, leading the supervisor to clam up and the upper managers to feel betrayed and weakened.

The Regressive Culture

The emergence of this persecutory image of upper management helps clarify how people shape an image of the organizational ideal under different structural conditions. When Electrosystem was a monopoly, people had developed a judging culture based on their tendency to idealize powerful senior managers, while also responding to their own inner sense of wastefulness and superfluity. Superfluity amplified people's inner tendencies to feel inadequate. Yet as long as the company succeeded, the beneficent image of the company limited the burden of being judged, since judgments were in the service of being a member of the family linked to a powerful top management. Being judged is a price worth paying.

By contrast, when the company fails, the feeling of being judged does not pass. Paradoxically, people do not simply dismiss their bosses and call them illegitimate. Rather, losing the image of the beneficent company, people now feel persecuted rather than simply judged.

133

Why should this be? We suggest that this response to leadership failure continues to preserve people's underlying fantasy that their leaders are really in charge but are simply behaving more badly—with greater evil intent. Believing this, they can then sustain the hope that their leaders can in fact protect them *if only they wanted to.*

Under these conditions they believe that the offer of participation is less than genuine. One supervisor said, "Participation means: 'Guess what is on my mind.'" Similarly, as another noted, participation reminds him of the movie *Godfather II*, "[where] management makes you feel like you have a say."

While the lower level continued to see the upper as all-powerful, the uppers felt trapped by their failures and deserving of punishment from the lowers.

This dynamic was enacted in one role play in the second seminar, enacted by two supervisors. A supervisor apologizes to an operator for disciplining him in front of other operators. In the first role play, the supervisor apologizes but then justifies the content of his criticism so that the operator feels defensive and neither can reflect on how each felt when the operator was first disciplined. The pair then replayed the incident to explore what would happen if the supervisor simply apologized and waited for the operator to respond. The supervisor opened the encounter by saying, "I realized that I might have embarrassed you the other day. It was not my intention to embarrass you." A long pause ensued, in part because the new strategy initially had the operator speechless. However, as the silence grew longer, the supervisor became uncomfortable and broke the tension by jokingly saying, "Hit me."

We worked with the participants to see underlying patterns in this brief encounter: paradoxically, just as uppers could oppress lowers, lowers could oppress uppers. In many of the participative forums we suggested, such as the Deming seminars and the supervisory seminars, the uppers temporarily took one-down positions and expected to be "hit" by the lowers just as the supervisor wished to be hit by the operator in the role play. The challenges and transformation the plant was facing brought past feelings of superfluity to the surface, evoking guilt for management's waste of resources in the past and present difficulties in guiding the transformation. By being "hit," upper management would feel better for its sins. Far from creating a new space in which an adult-to-adult conversation about shared difficulties could take place, these forums sustained parent-child relationships, with occasional reversals of who was on top.

Thus a vicious circle is established: the uppers offer participation, and the lowers, feeling persecuted, withdraw. This proves to the uppers that they deserve to be punished. Uppers offer participation again, but lacking courage to break the vicious circle, they come close to abdicating, arguing that they are cheerleaders. This increases the lowers' sense of vulnerability, and as a defensive reaction, they only strengthen their view of the uppers as persecutory controllers hiding behind the facade of participation.

The Problem of Learning: The Seminar Experiences

To break out of this vicious circle, people in the plant need to be able to learn from each other and from their mistakes. But anxiety, fear, intolerance for uncertainty and error all increase the difficulty of learning.

In working with the supervisors in the four seminars, we frequently found that they imagined us to be in a judging role and had a hard time joining us as colearners trying to understand their experience. For example, in the first seminar we passed out a brief working note that outlined our conception of the changing texture of the supervisor's role and asked the supervisors in small groups to evaluate if we had understood accurately the shifts in role and performance. To our surprise, some groups of supervisors returned to the plenary after reviewing the note (which they had received before the seminar as well) asking whether they as supervisors were "off." They could not judge our theory but rather judged how fast they were making the theoretical shifts. Hearing the terms "evaluation" and "critique," they turned the work of evaluating on themselves.

Similarly, we found, particularly in the first seminar, that the supervisors had a difficult time understanding what it was like to learn along with us. For example, feeling confused on the first day of the first seminar, they asked several times, "Why are we here?" and refused to accept our answer that the purposes of the seminar were quite broad and that we could discover them together.

As our relationships to the supervisors became more articulated, however, the first seminar's work became smoother and more relaxed, and the problem of its purpose became less pressing. The supervisors were working with us. Yet strikingly, toward the end of the second day, as we began to review the work we had accomplished with them and prepare for the entry of the upper managers, one supervisor remarked, "If all of this had been clarified yesterday, we would have saved a lot of time." In other words, he could not understand that to develop working relationships and so produce clarity of vision, people needed to stumble around for a while. The muddling-through created anxiety, suggesting that mistakes were not permitted.

Indeed, this dynamic provided us with an important moment of interpretive work. In response to their complaining on the first day of the first seminar that they lived in a culture where you couldn't make mistakes, we noted that they bore some responsibility for this situation, since in demonstrating a lack of patience with the seminar itself they were not letting us make mistakes.

135

Asking for Help

When organizations and individuals enter the "permanent white-water" (Vaill, 1989) of these major transformations, they need to be able to acknowledge confusion and to ask for help. Yet we found in our work with people in the factory that it was dangerous for people to appear vulnerable and needy.

Two vignettes are illuminating. On the second evening of the first seminar, we met alone with the upper managers to review with them the supervisors' work of the first two days. A group of upper managers reviewed the set of "critical incidents" the supervisors had written, which highlighted moments of frustration supervisors faced in trying to exercise the authority of their roles. As the upper managers worked through the set of eighteen incidents, they would periodically point out one as being a particular "cry for help."

We were puzzled at the time by this phrase but realized later that by linking the term "cry" to the term "help," they were both pathologizing and infantilizing help-seeking behavior, since typically it is the alcoholic or suicidal person who in becoming drunk or attempting suicide is "crying for help." In other words, only very helpless or out-of-control people actually ask for help.

We came across this peculiar cultural mapping of help-seeking behavior toward the end of our engagement as well. We were talking with the senior plant management, outlining some possible next steps we could take in our work with the plant. The conversation deepened quickly, touching on the fundamental organization design and strategic options it faced in the immediate future. The turn of the conversation was truly surprising but in retrospect reflected our good working alliance with the plant manager and his staff. As we left the meeting, Fred, the training director who had attended the meeting, expressed great surprise at the depth of discussion and exclaimed several times, "Boy, were they helpless," suggesting that in order to reveal one's deeper concerns and vulnerabilities to someone you trust, one has to feel absolutely helpless. Again, this reveals the dynamics of a judging culture. Since it is dangerous to appear weak or vulnerable, one should ask for help only when hitting rock bottom.

Judgments Versus Experiments

During periods of considerable change, people need to be able to experiment in order to learn more effective responses. Yet at Electrosystem, the judging dynamic interfered. The following incident, written about a supervisor's encounter with an engineer, indicates the limits of learning and collaboration in the culture.

> The testing area I supervised was running flat-out seven days a week. Since testing was a bottleneck, we were keeping the test sets manned every hour, resulting in a lot of overtime for the operators. But operators in the wafer fab section, which I also supervised, were working normal hours. To give them overtime opportunities while spelling some of the testing operators, I gave the latter time off and backfilled the testing area with wafer fab people on the weekends. I trained the wafer fab people to operate the test sets.
>
> One of the codes [circuits] in the testing area began to experience yield problems. An engineer, believing that my system for allocating people had caused the yield problem (although he had no data to prove this), demanded that only testing people work in the area on the weekends. I argued but, lacking data, I had to back down, resulting in strained relationships between the engineering supervisor and the operators.
>
> This encounter highlighted several issues. Who calls the shots in the shop? Why was the engineer taking such a shotgun approach? Why didn't the engineer certify the wafer fab people? And why did I have to bow to political pressure and operate in a less efficient manner?

It is, of course, not surprising that shop and engineering have conflicts and that the latter, feeling in charge of the technical design work and responsible for a particular circuit, would try to "call the shots" in the shop. But what is most interesting is the inability of the two to address the issue experimentally, to collect data that the supervisor notes were lacking. For example, as the supervisor says, only one of the codes was in trouble, suggesting that the problem may be linked to that circuit rather than to a particular operator or group of operators. The situation, however, far from stimulating problem-solving behavior, triggered feelings of blame and defense, which led the supervisor to retreat into feelings of helplessness and the engineer to bullying. Strikingly, though the factory was presumably embedded in a scientific culture, experiments to discover the cause of problems seemed implausible.

Developmental Rhythms

The plant clearly faced significant obstacles to its development. Rooted in a culture that enforced judgment rather than collaboration, and trapped in a meaning system that gave rise to images of a persecuting authority, the plant community naturally had a difficult time transforming its systems, its management practices, and the texture of its interpersonal relationships. But our experience over the course of the four seminars also uncovered the plant's developmental strengths. Two features of our experience are important. The supervisors accelerated their learning during the four seminars, and because of their support, we became increasingly sophisticated in our own design work.

137

The Acceleration of Learning

In each succeeding seminar the work of the supervisors accelerated. They formed a working alliance with us more quickly, they came to terms more rapidly with their own fantasies about the seminar and upper management, and they established a tone of sober and realistic work more readily. Clearly, the plant culture was "taking us in," and as each cohort returned to the plant, it communicated to each succeeding cohort an increasingly more realistic and more work-oriented conception of the seminar itself.

For example, in the first seminar, we spent the entire first day building a working alliance, dealing with the aims of the seminar, the plant's history, and the differences between this seminar and the Deming seminars. On the morning of the second day, the supervisors, reflecting on the seminar thus far, dumped on themselves for being so critical of their setting and their bosses. "They gave the operators a forum and they dumped. They gave us a forum and we dumped. This is another bitch session. I am tired of complaining." We felt they were denigrating some good thinking and work, labeling it all as bitching, while also not tolerating their own struggle and necessary stumbling. We noted that they had a right to be confused and to learn as the seminar unfolded. This session marked a turning point, helping us cement our working alliance with them.

By contrast, at the second seminar, this process of reflecting on the

aims of the seminar and confronting their own anxieties and disappointment was completed by lunch of the first day. By the fourth seminar we
were able to work with the supervisors in a deeply reflective mode from
the outset, distributing notes of all the prior seminars to them and asking
them to review them and assess their meaning. At the end of the first
morning session of this last seminar, we felt that the group was in touch
with all the significant issues of the earlier sessions.

Finally, as we became calmer, we focused less on the microtactics of
design (Should we break them up now? Should we have a report out?)
and found that we could simply sustain longer conversations with them as
they sat around the hotel table. The work of thinking could increasingly
be contained simply by the protocols of conversation rather than by the
boundaries established by elaborate designs.

In short, as we learned to offer them a role as learners rather than as
trainees, we accelerated their capacity to work and reflect. But, of course,
the supervisors, the upper managers, and the training director accepted
this learner role as well. This was a sign of their developmental strengths.

138

Our Design Work

One measure of our growing sophistication and theirs was our increasingly shared capacity to acknowledge differences among them and between them. Functioning more as a huddle group in the first seminar, and
focused on how other role holders such as upper managers or operators
got in their way, the supervisors could not discuss differences in task,
shift, and grade among themselves, nor did we think of developing designs that underscored these differences. All their aggression and sense
of persecution was projected outward and upward.

At the second seminar, by contrast, we divided the group into shop
and support supervisors and had each group separately examine issues of
responsibility and authority they faced in doing their work. Finally, in the
last session we asked a group of supervisors who interacted together across
the chain of production to explore their task relationships, emphasizing,
for example, the links between production, inspection, and customer service. They did so in a sober and calm manner despite the fact that the
upper managers were about to join the seminar. It revealed to us how the
focus on the work itself and its challenges reduces the anxiety people feel
as they work across levels of authority.

Similarly, just as we and they could acknowledge and work with real
differences as the seminar itself progressed, we were increasingly able to
focus on real, plant-specific issues by bringing together roles. In the first
seminar, we worked only with the supervisors and their direct bosses. In
the second and third, we worked with labor relations personnel, engineering managers, and engineers. And in the fourth, we convened "chains of

command" that were represented in the room, asking, for example, all people who reported to the manager in charge of product line X to work together on a particular set of issues.

Training as a Transitional Space

Paradoxically, just as we were able to deepen the work of the seminar, acknowledge differences, and work on plant-specific issues, we more clearly understood the limits of the training space. At the first session, we asked the supervisors to make lists of "next steps" to be accomplished when they returned to work, as if these lists represented the "real" payoff of the training session. But in the second session, acknowledging the fantasies that such lists sustain—for example, that seminar members can make changes unilaterally and that they will continue to be a group when they return to work—we turned to the seminar members and advised them not to make such lists. While this frustrated some ("Why are we here and what can we do?" one noted), we and they were then able to design some work they could do together based on a much more realistic picture of their authority.

Ultimately, as we became more linked to the supervisors and more sophisticated in our thinking, we realized that the training encounter is a transitional space, one that lies between learning and action and provides the "appreciative" insights and "here and now" experiences that can help people redesign their work world upon their return. Like transitional objects, the training space lies between the reality of the work world and the enacted reality of the training encounter itself, in which commingled thoughts and feelings can emerge safely in a setting where the stakes, though limited, are palpable. In the transitional space, core issues often can powerfully surface, revealing the substantial challenges that this factory faced in changing its inherited culture. One difficult and poignant experience was telling here.

At the end of the third seminar neither the plant manager nor his deputy was present. Previously, the two had closed out the seminar with some final comments and reflections. How could we end it today? Hirschhorn seemed particularly anxious about the problem and, after thinking it through, proposed that we end it with a call for reflections from the plenary. Vinnie Carroll, the project director, agreed. Five minutes before the scheduled time for ending the seminar, one supervisor called out, "Let's really thank the Wharton team," and everyone clapped. Carroll then called up Gilmore and Hirschhorn, who sat down next to him. Following the plan, Carroll then asked if anyone wanted to say something to "close out or complete some unfinished work."

Silence followed, and anxiety visibly grew. No one felt authorized to speak, and we sat in silence facing the supervisors' group. After a minute or two, one supervisor broke the silence by turning to Carroll and asking him, as if he were on a television talk show, what he thought about the state of the American economy. Carroll answered briefly; again silence followed. Hirschhorn then noted that he simply wanted to make contact with the group and say goodbye. One supervisor jumped up, said "Goodbye," and sat down. More silence followed. Carroll then closed the meeting, and the supervisors fled the room.

What happened here? Anxious to find a structure for closing out the seminar and feeling perhaps let down by the absence of the two chief executives, we had created the core properties of an authority boundary. By going to the front of the room and facing the group, we created a palpable but invisible line between us and them; thus acting as the boundary keepers for the entire event, we assumed the authority role typically taken by the top managers of the plant. We thereby evoked the plant's primary struggle. Could members of the plant community work across the authority boundary without bringing their fantasies of authority to the boundary? Our experience suggests that they could not, at least not yet. The imaginary line became a projective screen for these fantasies; consequently, the supervisors were silenced, afraid, and could relate to us only as "national experts on T.V." Our experience in other settings is that as long as one person takes the authority to speak in public, then others follow. But no one among the group of thirty-five spoke, and their flight from the room was a sign of how toxic we had become at that moment.

The experience points up the underlying cultural struggles the plant community experienced. When faced with leaders who have failed you (they don't show up) and who then ask for help (for communication), can followers respond and create a new adult encounter with authority, free from images of persecution and idealization? Can leaders and followers, the two together, authentically collaborate in this situation?

Conclusion

Much of the writing about making changes in a company culture fails to deal with the culture's deeper aspects, of which members are not aware. Many of an organization's historical patterns are established both to deal with the work and to defend the organization against anxiety (Hirschhorn, 1987; Gilmore and Krantz, 1986; Miller, 1986). When these patterns begin to change, considerable anxiety is unleashed, some relating to the uncertainties about the new patterns, some linked to surfacing issues that were kept out of awareness by the psychological contracts people had with one another and with the organization.

In the Electrosystem case, we have seen how the culture in a regulated monopoly was centrally shaped by an exchange in which followers projected perfection onto their leaders and onto the company as a defense against the reality of political dependence and the waste that being a monopoly allowed. Internal systems measured level of activity, not results that were assessed by a competitive market. As these arrangements on the boundary were changed by deregulation, they in turn unsettled internal relationships, especially along the vertical spine.

Just when the leadership of such enterprises most feels the need for more reality-oriented collaboration across functions and levels, the anxieties stimulated by the changes can induce increased stereotyping. Leaders oscillate between seeing followers as compliant, lacking initiative, and lionizing their ability to save the company. Followers see their leaders as knowing but not telling, asking but not listening. Together they struggle to create a space for working on their issues, only to find that they are unable to enact the new behavior in mutually satisfying ways. Leaders either overcontrol or "get out of the way" rather than discovering **141** a collaborative middle ground.

In these settings, the participants must invent transitional spaces that protect them from the operative norms of the ongoing business. They can then begin to make more visible the deeper struggles lying beneath the slogans about becoming more competitive. The grandness of changing culture must be better coupled to the small but important behaviors that can begin a learning process—first discovering some of the dilemmas and then collaborating authentically in their resolution.

NOTE

1. Each session consisted of two days with the supervisors and a final day that the senior management attended in order to work intergroup and interlevel issues. Each session built on the previous ones rather than on repeating modules.

REFERENCES

Block, P. 1987. *The Empowered Manager: Positive Political Skills at Work*. San Francisco: Jossey-Bass.

Hirschhorn, L. 1988. *The Workplace Within: Psychodynamics of Organizational Life*. Cambridge, Mass.: MIT Press.

Gilmore, T. N., and J. Krantz. 1986. "The Splitting of Leadership and Management as a Societal Defense." Presented at the International Society for the Psychoanalytic Study of Organizations, New York.

Miller, E. J. 1986. "Making Room for Individual Autonomy." In Suresh Srivastva and associates (eds.), *Executive Power*. San Francisco: Jossey-Bass.

Schein, E. H. 1985. *Organizational Culture and Leadership*. San Francisco: Jossey-Bass.

Schwartz, H. 1987. "The Psychodynamics of Organizational Totalitarianism." *Journal of General Management*, 13(1), 41–54.

Vaill, P. 1989. *Managing as a Performing Art*. San Francisco: Jossey-Bass.

CHAPTER 9

The Psychodynamics of Safety:
A Case Study of an Oil Refinery

Larry Hirschhorn and Donald R. Young

Computers and automation create increasingly integrated production systems that, while efficient and flexible, can fail "catastrophically" (Hirschhorn, 1984; Perrow, 1972). For example, downtime in an automated assembly factory can cost hundreds of thousands of dollars. More serious examples: The failure of controls in a nuclear reactor can cause a meltdown, and the rapid flow of gases and fluids in a chemical factory creates an everpresent danger of fires and explosions. How do people manage the anxiety of working in groups in a dangerous setting? How do they work productively yet carefully? How do they remain vigilant without becoming excessively preoccupied by the dangers they face? In other words, how do they cope? While cognitive psychologists focus on how individuals deploy their attention, this chapter suggests that powerful psychosocial dynamics shape people's capacity to work safely in groups.

Reprinted by permission of Jossey-Bass Inc., Publishers, from *Organizations on the Couch: Clinical Perspectives on Organizational Behavior and Change*, ed. Manfred F. R. Kets de Vries and Associates (San Francisco: Jossey-Bass, 1991), pp. 215–240, and originally entitled, "Dealing with the Anxiety of Working: Social Defenses as Coping Strategy."

Based on a case study of a consultation to an oil refinery, this chapter illustrates how groups in organizations may develop particular "social defenses" (Hirschhorn, 1988) that help people contain the anxiety of working while actually reducing their ability to work safely. Social defenses, expressed in relationships, procedures, and organizational rituals, help people cope with the anxiety they feel while working at difficult or risky tasks. Thus, for example, hospital procedures that depersonalize a nurse's relationship with very sick patients, or rituals of decision making that diffuse responsibility, help people limit the anxiety they experience. Working in dangerous industrial settings, people in groups may also develop procedures, relationships, and rituals to help them feel safe. Paradoxically, these may create new dangers as well.

144

This chapter, divided into four sections, unpacks the structure and dynamics of a social defense system in an oil refinery. Describing two fires that prompted the refinery manager to seek consulting help, the first section of the chapter examines a core social system "split" between two production units in the refinery. The second section links this split as a social defense to the psychodynamics of safety, to the dilemmas of acting vigilantly but not fearfully in dangerous settings. The third shows how this social split supported a culture of the "good" invulnerable hero who acts alone, while stereotyping "bad" heroes whose isolation reaffirms the plant's goodness. Summarizing the argument of the chapter, the fourth and last section suggests that we need a new way to investigate accidents, based on community self-study, if we are to transcend such social defense systems.

The Presenting Situation

The Smalltown oil refinery, employing about two hundred people and producing fifty thousand barrels of gasoline a day, was the main employer in a western city in the United States. Situated on a plain with lakes in the background, the refinery dominated part of the cityscape. The city's culture was modern frontier. Blue-collar workers came from families long native to the area, while the financial and commercial managerial elites often came from elsewhere, the product of corporate transfers.

The refinery appeared orderly, with the large tanks and pipes laid out over acres of land. Two control-room structures, each a cross between an office building and a shack, stood at different parts of the refinery. "Indoor" workers sat in these buildings monitoring the flow and refining of oil into gasoline, while "outdoor" workers toured the wide expanse of the yard, checking meters and valves while looking for danger signs such as leaks and pockets of gas. Standing at one end of the refinery, the main office building was unpretentious, its corridors narrow and paneled;

senior managers' offices were sensibly carpeted and furnished. The refinery manager's office held a recently installed computer console, which gave him up-to-the-minute information on refinery operations in all the significant parts of the yard. The refinery manager was beginning to wonder what role his midlevel managers would have now that he could get information about refinery operations without going through them.

Two Fires

The previous year, the refinery had had two severe fires, one in the summer and the other in the fall. No one had been killed, but in the second several workers narrowly escaped severe injury. After the second fire, the refinery manager contacted Donald Young, the company psychologist at the corporate office, to assess how stress might be affecting safety. Young then contacted Larry Hirschhorn to help him.

145

Studies of both fires carried out by a company audit team showed that each fire had several causes. Indeed, accident audits typically highlight the system of relationships that both sustain production and lead to production failures. Like slips of the tongue, the accident provides a window into the system's dynamics. For example, before the first fire, operators shutting down the refinery were unaware of piping changes that led distillate to be pushed through an open valve and into the yard. As a result, the area around the pipe smelled gassy. Some operators noticed the distillate leaking around a pump but did not connect it to any evident safety problem. Others assumed the gassy smell was normal for a shutdown. As distillate accumulated on the ground, a flame from a nearby furnace ignited the liquid, creating a fire. Hence, the stress of a shutdown, a valve left open, operator ignorance of changes to the piping, and inattention to danger signs all conspired to create the fire.

Similarly, in the second fire, one operator tried to control seepage of oil and water through a leaky gasket. He linked the valve to an open bleeder and cleared away asphalt that was blocking the flow of liquid. Later, when other operators prepared to start up the refinery, they failed to isolate the valve from the bleeder, so that propane gas flowed through the bleeder and a plug. The gas, pushing the plug outward, rushed out into the air and created a dangerous propane fire. Later investigation showed that an improperly sized gasket had been installed in the valve. Thus, a combination of circumstances—an ill-fitting gasket, a plugged line, a start-up, and an operator's failure to isolate a valve from a bleeder—all contributed to the fire. In integrated production systems like refineries, chemical plants, and power stations, accidents highlight the systemic nature of the production system itself. Everyone and no one is to blame.

The Consultation Process

After talking with the refinery manager, George, we agreed to visit the refinery for two days to help workers and managers assess some of the issues that affected safety and organizational functioning. After conducting interviews with individual managers and workers, we met with three groups. The first group, the refinery's health and safety committee, was composed of two managers and five union members. The second group, composed of different categories of workers, was brought together during the consultation to discuss the relationships between operators and their assistants, called *controlmen*. The third group, of workers and supervisors from the "back end" and "front end" of the refinery, was assembled to focus on the development and staffing of the soon-to-be-completed centralized control room.

146
At each meeting we and George sat around a conference table and talked with between six and eight other people. We presented some general propositions about safety to the first group, stimulating it to examine when and why refinery workers behaved in an unsafe manner. The second group examined the refinery's chain of command, assessing whether its many levels made it difficult for people to feel accountable. The third group talked about the design of the centralized control room, focusing on the links between control-room and yard workers and between the back end and front end of the refinery. These conversations led to no immediate decisions. Instead, they were intended to help raise awareness about safety and bring people from different units and levels together.

A Social Split

Our interviews prior to these meetings helped us understand more about the history and structure of the refinery. It was a profitable forty-year-old refinery going through a slow process of modernization and development. Responding to a company-sponsored early retirement program three years prior to our visit, 25 percent of the workforce had left the refinery. Consequently, the refinery hired skilled operators from other company refineries as well as well-educated young people from the Smalltown region to fill these jobs, so that the overall educational level of the workforce rose. In addition, at the time of our visit, management was building a centralized control room using up-to-date computer graphics and electronic control systems to improve workers' ability to monitor and control plant conditions. Finally, George, who came to the plant in 1985, was working to improve a once-contentious labor-management relationship. The previous refinery manager, who once noted proudly that "boss" spells "double-S.O.B. backward," had little interest in working with the union to improve safety and working conditions. By contrast, George actively consulted the union president and instituted a labor-management safety committee.

But despite these important changes, the refinery was still bedeviled by tensions and accidents. Most striking was the history of a key split within the social system of the refinery itself. The refinery was divided into two units, the cracking unit or frontend unit, and the refining or back-end unit. The first unit took up the crude and divided it into fractions of different weights, while the second refined the resulting fractions. All those interviewed described the second unit, which we will call unit two, as fractious, divided, conflict-ridden, the "black-sheep group," while the first unit, or unit one, was described as peaceable, a real team, and fun to work in.

Thus, for example, people noted that the members of unit two had to deal with a difficult operator, Gerry, who constantly got into fights with her workmates, while the first unit had a nurturing woman, called "Princess," who held weekend barbecues at her house for her team. Similarly, several people, highlighting the fractious character of unit two, told us how, just before we came to the refinery, two members of that unit got into a fistfight on second shift—further evidence of the tensions besetting the group. By contrast, when management reprimanded one member of unit one for his role in the second accident, the unit's members wrote a letter of support and protest to management.

147

Why was unit two so fractious and divided? Its work, several people told us, was no more difficult, dangerous, or dirty than unit one's. One technician suggested that unit one simply received more attention and resources: "They were the first to get computers in their control room, and there may be a feeling that the refining unit [unit two] just gets less attention." Indeed, when touring the two units, we were struck by the difference in the quality of their monitoring equipment. Unit one had numerous computer terminals arrayed along a tabletop, each capable of displaying, in the brightest colors, the status of temperatures, pressures, flow rates, and composition of the different fractions of oil. In comparison, unit two's control room looked like a boiler room. A large control panel dominated the cramped space, with its meters, resembling the instrumentation in the engine room of a locomotive, seeming to fill it to confusion.

Other people, however, suggested that unit two's dilemmas were linked to its history. Unit two was not weak because it had been neglected, but neglected because it was weak. Several people thought the unit functioned poorly because it had suffered the leadership of an unsupportive and heavy-handed general foreman. John, who had led the unit for ten years from the mid-seventies, had controlled all the details of the work and would not let unit members think for themselves. When he retired, the unit just seemed to fall apart. As one person noted, "The group, at that time, looked up to John very strongly. More or less they wouldn't make a move unless he said so. I used to fill in for him, and the men would question me to make sure that John would want to do this or that. . . . He had a real upper hand on his people." His successor, Frank, lacked John's strength and experience. Instead, as several people noted, he was a likable engineer, who, since he had not come up through the ranks, was too eager to please. But he could not command respect. As one manager noted, "Frank had a lot of experience to go through and his people did not have a lot of confidence in him. They called him the 'short little boss that didn't know much.' "

At first we were convinced by the explanation. The data we gathered from our interviews suggested the following story. Unit two had grown far too dependent on John, and consequently its members could not function effectively after his departure. John had monopolized authority and therefore undermined his operators' self-esteem, but they could still function effectively by identifying with him. They were powerful because he was. After his departure, however, their own self-contempt could not be contained and so they began to hate each other. In other words, their self-contempt was projected into the unit. This interpretation suggests, moreover, that the operators had contempt for Frank's likability, not because he was simply weak or inadequate, but because they could respect only brute power. Indeed, their reference to Frank's size (he was their "*short* little boss") points to the depth of their contempt and the irrationality of their response. By hating another person's physical appearance, people turn him into a cripple, a freak, and can then use the person as a projective screen for their own feelings of self-hate or disregard. Frank, we thought, had been a victim of the group's dynamics as well as his own limitations.

This explanation satisfied us initially, but other facts continued to tug at our sleeves. Most important, the theme of splitting and division characterized many of the ways in which the refinery presented itself as a whole during the consultation. The split between the two units, while fundamental to the operations of the refinery, was one instance of the tendency of refinery members to create and sustain splits across many levels and divisions. Thus, people discussed the tensions and divisions between operators and their subordinates (the *controlmen* mentioned earlier), between union and management, and between refinery workers and the engineering staff. They also talked about the split between the bad woman Gerry and the good woman Princess and the split between Gerry and the rest of unit two's members. Beginning with the key split between the two units, it appeared as if the refinery's social system was built on its social divisions—*it was its divisions*—so that people experienced the whole system as the endless interplay between "good" and "bad."

Indeed, when touring the still-unfinished centralized control room,

148

we found that the split between the two refining units had been reproduced in the control room's design. The control room was arranged so that chairs, fixed to the ground, were placed alongside a long and narrow tabletop, much like the long countertop of a 1950s-style cafeteria. Each chair was placed up against a terminal sitting on the table. Because the new control room would convey information to the operators from all parts of the refinery, and since each terminal could display data from any part of the refinery, refinery managers and the control-room designers had many choices in designing the room's configuration. Most important, there was no longer any compelling rationale to separate the two units. Indeed, using centralized control technology, managers and operators would be able to monitor some of the important flows and changes in the oil as it went between the two ends of the refinery. Yet the tabletop was semicircular in shape, so that unit one operators, sitting on the left of the semicircle, *would have their backs to unit two operators sitting on the right-hand side.* The design assured that members of the two units would not work face to face.

149

Finally, and most strikingly, we learned during the course of our interviews that over a decade before the two fires, the social relationships between the two units had been reversed! Unit two had been the peaceable and functioning unit, and unit one, fractious and unmanageable. As one person noted, "We saw many of the same things that we see now in the refining unit [unit two] in the cracking unit [unit one]. It was a hotbed of troublemakers then, but many left to get into the mechanical maintenance group."

These observations—the existence of splits at many levels of the refinery, the reproduction of the split between the two refining units in the new control room's physical design, and the reversal in the position of the two units ten years before the fires—led us to the following hypothesis: The split between the two units was built into the fabric of the refinery's sociotechnical system. It was part and parcel of its psychosocial arrangement. At any particular moment in its history one or another unit, level, or person might be bad, or weak, or the source of conflict, but there always had to be such "bad" or problematic units.

The Psychodynamics of Safety

Splitting as a Social Defense

Psychodynamic theory provides a rationale for this process in organizations as well as among individuals (Hirschhorn, 1988). It suggests that a work group will divide internally in response to difficult or risky conditions and tasks. This division then becomes a *social defense*, a system of relationships that helps people control and contain feelings of anxiety when facing their difficult work.

Thus, for example, in many companies people describe the controller's office as "rigid," "cold," and "nit-picking," even though the controller's formal role is to account meticulously for how the company's money is spent. Uncomfortable with mobilizing the discipline and aggression they need to control their own spending, people outside the controller's office project these feelings and their associated images onto the controller's office. "We are easy, we make exceptions," so the stereotyping goes, "while *they*, the controller's office, are rigid and unforgiving." People's internalized image of the controller, shaped partly in response to their own anxieties about money and spending, thus creates a split in the social system itself. The controller's office becomes "bad" and "rigid" because everyone else wants to be good and easy.

150

Looked at psychodynamically, such splitting is closely linked to the processes of projection and scapegoating. When people feel vulnerable, inadequate, guilty, or inferior, they project these feelings onto some outsider, who is then experienced in just these ways. For example, men unwilling to acknowledge their sense of vulnerability may imagine that women are the vulnerable ones; poor whites unable to acknowledge their feelings of inferiority may decide that blacks are truly inferior; and, as we have suggested, unit two members had only contempt for Frank, "the short little boss," as a defense against their own self-contempt. Splitting is therefore a defensive operation that helps members of one group control their experience by stereotyping or scapegoating another group.

We experienced this defensive character of splitting throughout the consultation. Two examples from the meetings we conducted during the consultation are telling. When meeting with the refinery manager and a cross-section of refinery personnel to discuss some of the problems and conflicts facing operators and controlmen, Princess, the "good" woman in the "good" unit, expressed surprise and puzzlement at unit two's problems, for after all, her unit "had no such problems." In response to her expressions of surprise, we stated that it was important to acknowledge that people in the two units did experience their work very differently.

Later, reflecting on this encounter, we were puzzled by Princess's comment. Surely she was not really surprised that the second unit was divided, that people were unhappy in it, and that Gerry, the "bad" woman and an operator, symbolized the problems people were having with the operator role. Everybody talked about these issues. Rather, we suggest she was puzzled by the implicit acknowledgment that people in the second unit were really suffering, were truly in pain. It was not that the two units differed, but that these differences were important. That is why we responded intuitively, insisting that she acknowledge the other group's experience.

Projection and scapegoating culminate in just such a denial. The scapegoat becomes the repository of feelings that cause pain, and then others deny that these feelings are indeed painful.

Similarly, we experienced the defensive character of such splitting when discussing how the new centralized control room might bring the two units together. As we noted, at the time of our visit, each unit controlled its portion of the refining process from its own control room or shack. To modernize the refinery, management was building a new centralized control room with up-to-date computer console equipment. Why, we asked, should there be a distinction between the units any longer? They would, after all, share the same physical space, and the "outside" workers who repaired or adjusted equipment in the yard could then be shared by both groups.

People at first said nothing and seemed tense and anxious. The refinery manager, speaking slowly, noted that they had to proceed very cautiously, **151** and he was not prepared to consider this issue now. We did not push the point. However, as we reflected on this encounter later, it seemed to us that we had attacked the refinery's defensive system. While, as we have seen, the new technology made the division between the two units increasingly unnecessary, the unconscious system of defense required it.

Safety and Splitting

But what were people defending themselves against? If people were using the bad unit as a repository for unwanted feelings, what feelings were they projecting into it? Let us return to the challenges of running a refinery. In the aftermath of two dangerous fires we were asked to help refinery workers and managers develop a safer refinery. If the refinery presented itself to us in a manner and through a process linked to the stated purposes of our visit, then its splits were linked directly to the problem of safety.

Consider the psychodynamics of managing and contributing to a safe industrial setting. If you are to act safely and prevent accidents, you must be vigilant. This means that you must imagine that you are vulnerable to being hurt. By previewing the possible consequences of a dangerous situation in your mind, you then take appropriate preventive action. *You prevent accidents by imagining that you have already had them.* Indeed, people working in industrial settings are hurt most frequently because they ignore the ways in which seemingly minor hazards are nonetheless dangerous. Experienced operators working near welding operations stop wearing goggles and then suffer eye burns due to flashing, when they fail to turn their heads in time. A worker on a scaffold successfully avoids a weak plank but then falls through it when, under the pressure of a schedule, he steps on it rather than around it. A worker uses a ladder without rubber stops on its legs and then falls when the ladder slips along a grease spot on the floor.

Clearly, vigilance is a complex activity, because if you become excessively preoccupied with potential accidents, you will be unable to work. Moreover, your excessive anxiety is likely to infect others, disabling them as well. For example, workers who put up skyscrapers and walk the steel girders hundreds of feet above the ground shun novices who cannot keep their worries to themselves. Thus, in acting safely, workers in a dangerous setting must be vigilant without disabling their ability to focus on their work.

The refinery manager thought his workers found it hard to strike this balance. He believed that workers failed to notice dangers when they made their rounds because they "got into ruts." Similarly, he noted that when production pressure was low, backbiting and fighting among workers increased, leading to carelessness and more danger. Just as people get jumpy on weekends when they should be relaxing, feelings of danger become more prominent and disabling when people cannot contain their anxiety by working at their accustomed pace.

We suggest that the social splits at the refinery helped people manage the anxiety of working in a dangerous setting. The bad unit, we suggest, represented all that was bad and dangerous in the refinery. Projecting their feelings of being vulnerable, weak, and potentially helpless into the bad unit, people in unit one could feel safe and good. But since, to feel safe, they were acting irrationally, this splitting also prevented them from acting safely. Thus, the second fire, the more serious of the two, *happened in unit one's part of the yard.*

The Problem with Procedures

The safety director at the plant acknowledged that he felt ineffective both in enforcing safety procedures and in educating people to behave safely. Yet procedures play a critical role in helping people strike the balance between work and worry. They reduce the burdens of vigilance by helping people act safely without thinking excessively about the potential dangers that shape these procedures. Enacting the procedures without a great deal of conscious thought, people protect themselves without obsessively previewing the accidents that may hurt them. Free of excessive worry, they can focus on their work.

Reflecting on his ineffectiveness, the safety director highlighted two seemingly contradictory processes. On the one side, he noted, men often play the "hero" role by taking shortcuts, refusing, for example, to wear safety belts when working over a pit. But on the other hand, he noted, men would often employ some laborious and apparently useless procedure, arguing that "it's written that you have to do it this way." Examining old records, the safety director would find no evidence for such a procedure. Thus, the procedural system was itself split between dangerous shortcuts and senseless protocols. By using shortcuts, workers could pretend that they were invulnerable. By following senseless protocols unconnected to actual dangers, workers did not have to preview potential accidents. In each case they denied the dangerous world confronting them. The workers could not apply procedures *intelligently* and with just enough conscious thinking to assess why they were acting in a particular way. As the safety director noted, "Procedures are like a checklist, but you can't execute them if you have no understanding of them." Similarly, the refinery manager noted that "people feel snowed under by the rules, and I am not sure they can see the forest for the trees." Tied up and defended by a more irrational system of social splits, the workers could not apply procedures rationally.

153

To summarize, the social system of the refinery was defined by its psychosocial divisions. Units one and two were split between good and bad, and procedural behavior was cut off from thinking and planning. These splits, we suggest, were part and parcel of the refinery's social defense system, helping workers to contain the anxiety of working in a dangerous setting. But because these defenses blocked rational behavior, they also increased the chances of accidents.

Social Defenses and the Hero System

The safety director's allusion to the term *hero* provides more insight into the plant's social defense system.

The Hero as the Ego Ideal

Heroes are invulnerable and independent, and they do not need other people. Indeed, the refinery was located in a part of the country where heroes as loners were celebrated in local lore, and frontier practices, such as owning a gun and valuing physical prowess, shaped men's conversation and behavior. Facing a complex technology that poses dangers to life and limb, people who imagine themselves to be heroes contain their anxiety in two ways. They believe that they are invulnerable, and as "loners" they need not feel dependent on others. But by denying their dependence, they also deny the dangerous features of the technology itself. In a refinery people depend deeply on each other because each person monitors and controls an operation that affects all other operations. This is the hallmark of any continuous-process production system. Thus just as the split between the good and bad units helped people *project* their anxiety onto the bad unit, the culture and image of the lone hero helped them *deny* their anxiety.

Our experience in the consultation suggested that the plant's social defense system—the split between good and bad—was reinforced by the culture of the hero. There were two particularly revealing examples.

The Pair as Hero

Meeting to discuss safety, the refinery manager (George), the members of the health and safety committee, and a few other high-level supervisors examined obstacles to improving safety at the refinery. Describing the process of bringing suggestions from workers to management, Mike, a union representative on the committee, noted that he took workers' ideas to managers without involving or informing the foremen. Hirschhorn suggested that this could really backfire because foremen might feel that health and safety programs were designed to undermine their authority, and they might not cooperate. This statement seemed to create discomfort. People were silent, and then George noted, "Well, I don't know if people agree with that." Feeling the anxiety, Hirschhorn said, "People are not saying all that they are thinking." Then Jim, the assistant manager, got up and with an audible "Whew" said, "I guess it's time to take a break." Later, Jim noted that this had been his most important learning of the day.

Thinking back, we suggest that the dynamics of the health and safety committee itself had helped create a fantasy that George, with a few cooperative union people like Mike, could circumvent the institutional matrix of the refinery—the historically complex union-management relationship and the refinery's complex chain of command—and create a safe, happy, and productive place to work. Indeed, throughout the morning we were struck by the way Mike, a young and intense man and the most active union member on the committee, seemed eager to defend the plant and speak well of it, even though he was a union man. He sat directly opposite George, and as the morning discussion progressed, it appeared that this pair, George and Mike, represented what Bion (1959) calls the *pairing fantasy*, the wish that two special people together can help a group overcome obstacles without involving everyone in the difficult work of development. Like heroes, the pair saves the group.

Seen in this context, Hirschhorn's statement threatened to undermine this fantasy. By pointing them back to the messy world of disgruntled foremen, he suggested that this committee, despite the fantasy it enacted and contained, could not magically and heroically transform the refinery. Other people could undermine it.

Manager as Hero

Our relationship with the refinery manager, George, also highlighted this culture of the hero. While he sponsored the consultation and worked with us over the course of the two days, incidentally making himself vulnerable to us, he would at times communicate that he did not really need us, that he could go it alone. For example, sitting at the conference table, arms folded, with the three different groups, he did not lift his pencil to take notes or jot things down, as if to communicate that he either knew everything or could remember it anyway. Similarly, after the first day of work, reflecting on its value, he said to one of us, "It's useful to have the other people here learn about these issues," as if to suggest that he had personally learned nothing new. Hirschhorn replied by reminding him that he too had been surprised by the discussion of the foreman's role in ensuring safety, and he agreed. In other words, he did learn something, but like a hero, he was reluctant to acknowledge that he could profit from being with or working with others.

155

Yet while projecting invulnerability—his ability to avoid being influenced by us—he periodically expressed enormous frustration. He could not imagine how, despite any insights he might obtain during the meetings, he could actually improve safety. In a moment of frustration he said, "I guess all I can do is go out there and really start to walk around, take people on tours with me, show them what is dangerous, why this ladder can't be left in the middle of the yard when it snows." In other words, he could not imagine working *through* his organization, of leveraging his efforts through others. Instead he would be the hero, sweeping workers into his yard tours and showing them, by example, what it meant to be safe.

This idea per se was not wrong, but spoken in frustration it reflected George's sense of isolation and his compensatory fantasy that he could act heroically. As the hero, he had nothing to learn, but as a loner, as someone who could not collaborate, he could not act effectively.

The Negative Side of Heroism

The hero is a complex mythical figure, and we develop a many-leveled response to him. Most obviously, we appreciate the hero because he saves us. More subtly, we admire the hero for his courage; more primitively, we envy the hero for his independence; and most unconsciously, we hate the hero because we cannot control him. Because he does not need us, he may hurt us as well as help us. Acting out of this cultural and mythical ambivalence, assassins, while crazy in their own right, kill presidents and movie stars. Others, less disturbed but prone to worship heroes nonetheless, use the cult of a particular hero to gain access to them, and in their fantasy lives get their power and control their behavior.

While the refinery promoted a culture of heroism, it also created two scapegoats who represented the *negative* side of heroism. These scapegoats were punished because they were too independent. Just as the refinery's social defense system split the two units, it split the image of the hero in half. Some people could enact the hero role, because others represented the dangers that heroes pose.

The "Bad" Woman as Scapegoat

Consider the case of the "bad" woman, Gerry, in unit two. Everyone described her as obstinate, difficult to work with, and "someone who always thinks she's right." Indeed, toward the end of our consultation one member of unit two asked to see Don Young privately to discuss the trouble he and others were having with Gerry. People were wary of her and seemed to resent the ways in which she was different. She lived alone, could fix cars, knew the martial arts, and was separated from a man who had abused her.

Half expecting to meet an ogre, we experienced her quite differently. She had a boyish and tough look, but in an interview with Hirschhorn she appeared lively, feisty, demanding, committed to productive work, and unhappy with the laziness and inattention she observed around her. Describing the first fire in unit two, which occurred on her shift, she felt that the workers and managers knew they were using "dirty charge" but decided to forget about it and "pretend that they didn't have a problem." At the second of the three group discussions, she took the role of the fighter, to be sure, arguing that the controlmen had to be more accountable for their work. But her affect was vital, and we felt strongly that she wanted to connect to us, to the group, and to contribute to the discussion.

We suggest that people were scapegoating Gerry. An obvious reason is that—unlike Princess—she engaged in behavior that violated the gender norms that prevailed in their male-dominated work environment. But we could look at it somewhat differently. On the one hand, by noting that she lived independently and was a master of the martial arts, her co-workers were in effect describing the characteristics of a hero. On the other hand, by describing her as aggressive and obstinate, they reframed her heroic characteristics as signs of excessive willfulness and an inability to get along and cooperate with people. We suggest that people were using Gerry as a symbolic repository for the negative images of the hero. If the image of the hero evokes both positive and negative feelings, then refinery members could retain the positives for themselves—they could take heroic shortcuts—while projecting the negative traits of heroes—their uncontrollability and independence—onto Gerry.

Gerry's role as the negative hero may have contributed to the accident in unit two. On the night of the fire a controlman who officially worked under Gerry's direction openly defied an instruction she gave him. The audit did not identify this fight as the cause of the accident. But our hypothesis points to a plausible indirect connection between the two. By defying Gerry in public, the controlman created a "psychodrama," or group ritual, in which the group, satisfied that they had "destroyed" the bad and unreliable person Gerry, was now safe. Consequently, they became less vigilant and created the conditions for a fire.

Finally, Gerry suffered significantly because she was isolated and distrusted. Reflecting on the social process of the refinery, she noted, "Paybacks are a bitch here and they last forever. A person can make life absolutely hell out here. If you ever let any one see that anything bothered you they would pick at that." In short, to be safe, not from the technology but from attacks by other people, you had to appear invulnerable. Thus Gerry was saying that the negative parts of the hero role had been thrust on her. She could not risk showing her vulnerability, since people, discovering her weak points, would attack her.

157

The Would-Be Hero as Scapegoat

Bill, a controlman's helper who had recently joined the refinery as a member of the "good" unit, was also the victim of this hero system. When the propane gas blew up in the second fire, Bill, risking his life, rushed toward the blaze to shut off a valve.

But his experience as hero was to be short-lived. The day before the fire, Bill was walking by two operators who were working to start up the refinery and volunteered to climb up a steel structure to open a valve. However, he and they failed to close a bleeder that had to be lined up with the valve. While officially being supervised by the operator standing below, Bill had the responsibility to look down the line to check if the bleeder and the valve were lined up. This open bleeder was the proximate cause of the fire, and after a careful investigation, management sent Bill a letter of reprimand. A hero one day, he became a villain the next.

Toward the end of the second day of our consultation, Bill's supervisor, Tom, approached Don Young and asked if Don, as company psychologist, would see Bill. Tom noted that after receiving the letter, Bill "was really hurting." His teammates on the unit wrote a counterletter to management asking that the letter of reprimand be withdrawn. Management did not back down, but as Tom reflected, the letter of support from the unit did little to lift Bill's spirits. We decided to interview Bill together.

Several hours later Tom brought Bill to an office in the main suite. We were struck then by the image of Bill's helplessness as Tom, escorting Bill, gently pushed him by his elbow into the office, suggesting that this man had to be guided like a child or invalid. Bill sat down and began recounting the accident and its aftermath.

After describing the accident in some detail, he noted how hard it was to be a hero one day and a villain the next. He said how bad he felt the next day when people, unaware of his role in the accident, congratulated him for his courageous behavior. He mentioned how horrible he felt when passing a particular teammate in the yard who had almost been killed in the fire. He then said that he had held a job as a pipe fitter in another factory, and there, "when you screwed up, they beat you up and sent you down the road."

At first glance this creates the impression of a depressed and guilty man who has been punished by his superiors and is punishing himself. But four other parts of the conversation point to a more complex picture. First, in recounting the fire and accident itself, his face and voice were animated, as if he were describing an exciting sports event or movie. As he highlighted the initiative he took to open the valve the day before and then described his courageous behavior during the accident, it appeared as if he were telling us "you had to be there."

Second, he spoke contemptuously of his teammates' letter of support. He termed it "that little letter," saying that he did not care about it, and he criticized the first draft for being insufficiently diplomatic.

Third, testing for depression, we asked if he was having trouble sleeping or was waking up early, and he said no. "How about eating?" we inquired. "I have to lose some weight," he suggested.

Fourth, try as we might, we were unable to say anything helpful to him. "Would it help talking to the man you almost killed?" we asked. "No," he answered. Perhaps he did not like all the care he was getting and would rather be beaten up, as he was when employed as a pipe fitter, we suggested. No, he didn't think that was it. "Why did he think he was solely responsible?" we asked. "Well, I opened the valve," he replied. Unable to say anything useful to him, we began to feel increasingly helpless. Indeed, as the conversation wound down, Bill said somewhat sardonically, "Well, you guys are giving me all these theoretical ideas. I thought you were going to help me."

What was going on here? We suggest that far from being depressed and guilty, Bill was both ashamed and enraged: ashamed for his failure and enraged at his subsequent humiliation. To get back at the plant community, which was sophisticated enough to try to help him after it had punished him, he refused to be helped. In this way his own feelings of helplessness, of impotence, were transferred back onto the plant community and of course onto us. In other words, he did not want us to help him; he wanted us to feel helpless.

The Dance of Projection

We suggest that Bill and the plant were engaged in a complex dance of projection. The plant community, anxious to control its own sense of vulnerability, of helplessness, after the accident, scapegoated Bill by reprimanding him. To be sure, he was partly responsible and had been careless. But one operator, after all, was supervising him, and the other was participating in the work. More important, management was pushing the workers to work quickly so that the refinery could be started up without delay. Indeed, Bill's supervisor, Tom, who brought him to his appointment with us, told us that he worried that he had pushed the men too hard prior to the accident.

But because Bill was easily humiliated—a reflection of the omnipotence that led him to act heroically, if sometimes carelessly—he refused to be scapegoated. Instead, by refusing to be helped, he put his own sense of helplessness *back into the system*. Anxious to protect itself from feeling vulnerable, the plant community now felt helpless to help Bill. Just as social splits distributed feelings of helplessness between the good and bad unit, Bill had turned feelings of helplessness into a "hot potato," as these feelings passed from him to the refinery and back.

Clients often transfer feelings stimulated by a work system onto consultants. This is the analogue of the transference in psychotherapy. We suggest this happened to us as we worked with Bill. In making us helpless, Bill brought us to the edge of such feelings as despair, anger, and contempt. We disliked him for having made us helpless and disliked ourselves for failing. We suggest that these feelings shaped the unconscious experiences of refinery members. Feeling vulnerable in a dangerous situation and unable or unwilling to trust the "heroes" around them, people developed feelings of contempt and anger for social scapegoats such as Gerry, unit two, or the troublemakers that once populated unit one, to control their own feelings of vulnerability.

Finally, we suggest that Bill was singled out in part because of his capacity to act heroically. He was a young controlman's helper who had acted eagerly in opening the valve and had acted truly heroically during the accident. Looked at rationally, he needed both discipline and to be disciplined. But looked at irrationally, as a newcomer he was an easy projective target for people's ambivalent feelings about heroes, for their anxiety that heroes were uncontrollable, too independent, and therefore dangerous. The hero in him had to be tamed so that it could be manifested in subtler ways, in ways acceptable to the plant's culture—like violating a procedure or keeping to himself. Thus, we suggest that he was reprimanded not because he had caused an accident—indeed, much evidence suggests that he was not solely to blame—*but because he was a hero*. This

159

explains why, despite the evidence that the fire was linked to the pace of work during the start-up, Bill was singled out.

Summary

The problems just discussed point up the inadequacies of traditional methods of auditing accidents. This final section touches on the kind of broader developmental response that is needed if society is going to create safer work environments.

The Problem of Vigilance

160

People working in dangerous settings need to be vigilant without being fearful. This requires sophistication. They need to follow procedures but to do so with intelligence. They need to focus on their work but also to see the pattern of relationships, the links between pipes, valves, pumps, and controls that create unexpected pathways for the evolution of accidents.

Looked at psychodynamically, people behave safely when they care about a setting, and in integrated production environments they must care about the whole setting. This means that they must project feelings of their own self-worth onto the workplace, so that just as they care for themselves they protect their environment. But if the experienced dangers are too great, or the organizational climate promotes feelings of inadequacy, or finally, management does not develop procedures and techniques for working safely, people will split up their internalized image of the workplace—they will project their sense of danger onto one part and their feelings of safety and security onto another. This is the genesis of dangerous social splits. Thus at the Smalltown refinery, its members had developed a complex social defense in which one unit was bad and the other good; a bad, obstinate woman was compared to a nurturing princess; procedures were split off from thinking; and bad heroes who created accidents allowed good heroes to take shortcuts.

As workers project their feelings of vulnerability onto scapegoats, they feel safe without paying sufficient attention to signs of danger. More important, they do not simply become less vigilant. Rather, *they turn their vigilance inward*, away from the technology and the artifacts of production and toward the social system itself. People pay undue attention to the defensive relationships they have constructed with one another, ensuring, for example, that the bad unit would not contaminate the good unit in a centralized control room, ignoring the bad unit's dilemmas and pain, isolating negative heroes such as Gerry, and constraining their own expression of vulnerability for fear of "paybacks." The social defense system itself becomes the focus of attention. As people pay too much attention to their relationships and too little attention to the technology, the sociotechnical system is split apart.

Auditing Accidents

How can managers and operators working in dangerous settings help shape and develop a climate in which scapegoating and splitting are minimized and people at all levels can rely on each other? Accident audits provide an occasion for change and development. Typically, as was the case at the Smalltown refinery, the auditors try to pinpoint the accident's proximate causes and the people who were responsible. The audit is conducted as if it were a legal inquiry, interviews are conducted in confidence, evidence is assembled, and a report is issued that purports to be the truth.

But such a tradition denies the multicausal and sociotechnical nature of most accidents. Most serious studies of accidents show how inadequate maintenance, pressures of production, a failed control system, as well as an operator's error all combine to create the accident. Indeed, in any complicated industrial system—such as a chemical plant, nuclear reactor, or oil refinery—accidents are "always about to happen," but operator vigilance combined with good safety, effective maintenance practices, and control systems prevent them. An accident "breaks through" this system of defense when a series of failures converge at a particular moment to upset the system. There is always a proximate cause for the accident—the broken valve, the leaky pipe, the failed sensor—but invariably accident audits show that these proximate causes create accidents because other defenses, such as a maintenance protocol or a sensor, had already failed or been violated. By highlighting proximate causes and then pinpointing blame, accident audits become ritualized expressions of the same social defense system that helps create the accident in the first place.

161

New Approaches to Investigating Accidents

To break through this defense system, to create a new and less distorting social system, we need to change this tradition of accident investigation. Two recent examples of responses to accidents in the U.S. Navy are suggestive here.

In April 1989, forty-seven seamen died aboard the USS *Iowa* when a gun exploded during an exercise. The Navy's auditors blamed a single seaman, Clayton Hartwig, suggesting that he was a homosexual distraught over a failed love affair and committed suicide by blowing himself and the other seamen up. Arguing that they recovered traces of a detonator that Hartwig had presumably built, they nevertheless could never duplicate it and acknowledged that Hartwig could not have had time to build it—he did not know he would be the gun captain until the day before the exercise. While blaming Hartwig, the Navy also acknowledged that it had uncovered—but discounted—such factors as serious safety problems in a turret, poor supervision of seamen, and poorly trained gunmen. It appears as if the Navy, eager to put the accident behind itself and exonerate its systems, chose to scapegoat Hartwig by painting him as a deviant seaman. Ironically, there was no firm evidence that he was in fact a homosexual.

Consider by contrast the Navy's response to a series of accidents and fires aboard naval ships in November 1989, about six months after the explosion of the USS *Iowa*. Arguing that no single thread "tied the accidents together" (indeed, the USS *Iowa*'s explosion may have been just the beginning of this series of accidents), that there was no single cause, the chief of naval operations ordered a forty-eight-hour "safety standdown" in which seamen were to stop all normal operations and instead review all safety procedures. In other words, recognizing that there was no single cause or reason for the series of accidents, the admiral suggested that the *system* for ensuring safety was weakening. Thus he wanted people to stop acting and by reviewing safety procedures raise their awareness.

The admiral's order highlights four features of a developmental response to accidents. First, no single person or system is blamed. Second, unlike the case of the USS *Iowa*, people cannot use the audit and its findings simply to put the accident behind them. Third, safety is more readily assured when everyone takes responsibility by reviewing his or her own personal experience and responsibility for behaving safely. Fourth, people can undertake such a review if, as a *community*, they suspend action and focus their attention on the system and its safeguards.

Indeed, there is a hidden psychodynamic logic to these principles. As psychoanalysis suggests, we can start to overcome our defenses when we stop acting and start thinking, when instead of working to sustain normality we let go to extend and deepen our awareness. Similarly, instead of using the accident audit as an excuse to continue normal operations, instead of using normal operations as defense against awareness, a work community must create a place, a time, where normal operations are suspended and community members, aware of how they must depend on each other to operate safely, can deepen their understanding of their interdependence.

This suggests that the plant community, rather than simply relying on independent auditors, should study the accident; while looking for causes, such a self-study report should eschew blame. Indeed, at the time of our visit the Smalltown refinery stood uneasily between these two approaches. Conducting a traditional audit, members identified proximate causes and disciplined one worker. Yet concerned that wider cultural and social forces could shape the refinery's capacity to produce oil without incurring accidents, they invited us to help them assess how as a community they could work more safely.

To develop safe work practices in our increasingly automated plants, managers and workers need to rely increasingly on community self-study to complement the findings of a technical audit. As our consultation suggests, the struggles a community would face in managing the anxieties and conflicts associated with such a self-study would then provide it with the very experiences it needs to prevent future accidents.

REFERENCES

Bion, W. R. 1959. *Experiences in Groups, and Other Papers.* London: Tavistock.

Hirschhorn, L. 1984. *Beyond Mechanization.* Cambridge, Mass.: MIT Press.

———. 1988. *The Workplace Within: Psychodynamics of Organizational Life.* Cambridge, Mass.: MIT Press.

Perrow, C. 1972. *Complex Organizations: A Critical Essay.* New York: Scott, Foresman.

163

CHAPTER 10

The Assumptions of Ordinariness

as a Denial Mechanism:

Innovation and Conflict in a Coal Mine

Eric L. Trist

The sociotechnical approach has now made some headway in all West-ern industrialized countries, but against enormous resistance. This is not surprising, as it runs counter to long-held beliefs about how work should be organized (Trist et al., 1963). It also disturbs the socially structured psychological defenses (Jaques, 1953) that managers and workers alike have built up to adapt to conventional organizational forms. These con-stitute key elements in their identity (Holland, 1985).

This chapter outlines and analyzes an episode in an action research project undertaken by the Tavistock Institute of Human Relations in the British coal-mining industry that continued, with interruptions, for eight years during the 1950s. It shows how what Bion (1961) called the "hatred

Reprinted from *Human Resource Management*, vol. 28, number 2 (Summer 1989), pp. 253–264. © 1989 by John Wiley & Sons, Inc. Reprinted by permission of John Wiley & Sons, Inc.

of learning through experience" all but defeated an innovative collaborative endeavor by occasioning conflicts in which management and labor regressed to traditional adversarial positions.

The innovation in question introduced a new form of work organization, known as "composite working."[1] This occurred spontaneously in three different coalfields and heralded what Emery (1978) has called a "new paradigm of work." It offers an alternative to technocratic bureaucracy in which self-regulating, multiskilled work groups become building blocks for a more democratic and efficient organizational form. In so doing, it rejects the technological imperative and seeks to find the best match between, or, in systems language, the joint optimization of, the social and technical system. It has therefore become known as the "sociotechnical" approach. Under suitable conditions it leads to higher productivity and higher job satisfaction than conventional work systems.

166

The story that follows shows how psychosocial processes undermined the diffusion of this new way of working from one individual to another. It demonstrates how managers and workers used the psychological defense of denial to avoid facing the work they needed to accomplish in adapting to this innovation. Assuming that the innovation was simply a piece of "ordinary life" rather than an extraordinary one, they were quickly mired in a series of conundrums and responded to them in a psychologically regressive way.

Background

The Character of the Drift

The colliery was a village pit on which the community was totally dependent. The National Coal Board had already threatened to close it, but closure had been averted by a major organizational innovation in one of the seams—the Manley—which for the first time introduced composite working into semimechanized longwalls, then the prevailing form of mining.[2]

The success of the Manley innovation was phenomenal—in productivity, quality of output, and operating costs. It was no less so as regards earnings and work satisfaction, in relations among teams, and between labor and management. Virtually no voluntary absenteeism or accidents occurred, and sickness was halved. A major factor in this success was that component groups, which were self-selected, had previously worked together on "short walls"—a pre-longwall technology in which composite working was traditional.

The episode now to be described reports the course of events in the opening up of a new production unit in a colliery. In its early life the geological conditions were difficult in the extreme, and in the team, which was a new group put together for extraneous reasons, the majority had no previous experience of the technology or the method of working. Geological and sociopsychological circumstances aggravated each other.

The drift was separate from the other workings of the colliery, and the double unit was a new enterprise expected to produce coal equal to 25 percent of the previous output of the whole mine, whose life it would considerably extend. The venture was based on the very imperfect understandings of the Manley innovation, a main cause of the nearly complete failure that occurred.

A complement of fifty-one faceworkers was planned, with six "spare" men to provide substitutes in case of absences. The *hewing* task, carried out over one or two shifts, embraces breaking coal from the face with pneumatic picks, filling it on to the face conveyor, and setting roof supports as the face is cleared. The *hewers* are followed on the next shift by the *pullers*, who advance the face conveyors and the steel chocks. At the same time, the *stonemen* enlarge and advance the three roadways (tunnels) between and at the end of the faces on the panel.

Both management and men expected "teething troubles," but it was hoped that the advantages of composite working would begin to be realized within a few weeks. No one expected the teething troubles to last seven months or that eleven months would elapse before the planned level of output was regularly maintained.

One of the conditions of the composite agreement was that the men should make themselves up into sets of the required number. In the present case this condition was waived by both management and *lodge* (trade union local branch). The colliery was in the process of reorganization, and a number of underground workers were becoming redundant. Management and lodge agreed to draft these men into the new team, together with those who had been engaged in the development of the drift.

A meeting of the team was held by the lodge a few days before the start to acquaint the men with the agreement, to allocate them provisionally to tasks and shifts, and to appoint team captains for different task groups. Eight men volunteered for pulling, and ten for stonework, the remaining thirty-three being allocated to hewing. Three team captains were elected. Several men expressed anxiety lest they were condemning themselves to permanent nightshift and received assurance that after a week or two it would be possible to start rotating shifts.

Representatives of the lodge, together with the three team captains, then met with management to agree on final details. Although there had been a vague expectation that three shifts would be worked, it was decided to have only two, concentrating coal-getting on the dayshift (9 A.M.– 4:30 P.M.) and doing pulling and stonework on the nightshift (4:30 P.M.– midnight). The thirty-three men on the hewing shift were to be deployed

167

sixteen to each face, with one man in the main roadway, while on the nightshift there were to be four pullers to each face, six stonemen in the main roadway, and two in each of the face-end roadways. There were three deputies (supervisors), all of whom came from machine-cut rather than hewing faces. In charge was an undermanager recently appointed to the pit.

The First Week: Initial Failure

Before going in on the first morning, the thirty-three men on the hewing shift allocated themselves to places by *caviling*. Caviling is a time-honored practice for the allocation of men and groups to workplaces within a seam on a chance basis—one was more likely to receive justice at the hands of chance than of management. More than two-thirds of these men had little or no recent experience, either of longwall working or the use of pneumatic picks. The lack of hewing experience soon began to show, and it became obvious that the target advance of 4 feet 6 inches was not going to be achieved.

The manager visited the face and outlined the immediate requirements for stabilizing the situation. From this point on he retained direct control and ordered the concentration of effort on one face per shift. But managerial attention was no substitute for experience in a team confronted by bad conditions. In the early morning of Saturday, 20 yards closed completely, and it was decided to abandon both faces and win them out afresh. This took a fortnight.

Table 10.1 provides a chronology of events that transpired from week 1 through week 73 of the project.

Analysis

The Assumption of Ordinariness

This account has been a chronicle of how things went wrong. *Management, lodge, and members of the team all assumed that the drift would be an ordinary unit*, to be run in the ordinary way, and unlikely to experience more than ordinary difficulties. The untenability of this assumption yet the persistence of behavior based on it suggest that those concerned were using the idea of ordinariness as a means of psychological defense against situational elements they were unwilling and unable to recognize and confront. The principal effect was that the panel was treated throughout as a production unit under difficulties, rather than perceived for what it was—a training and development project working under the stress of a demand for full production. Though the need for support was conceded,

168

TABLE 10.1. Chronology of Events (73 Weeks)

Week No.	Events
1–2	Early morning (Saturday), 20 yards closed completely; difficulties overwhelm unorganized and inexperienced team; face closes.
2–3	Manager meets 12 of team; reinforcements arranged; production target reduced; day-wage established.
4	Saturday morning, manager meets team captains to disband existing teams and reform them; no decision made. Monday lodge meeting, overfull agenda prevents decision. Wednesday meeting of manager and team captains results in no agreement though manager wants team dissolved and new team picked, eliminating poorest workers.
5	Meeting between manager and two representatives of lodge committee and team captains; decision on dropping poorer workers deferred; manager offers further reinforcements.
6	Situation reviewed in lodge meeting where chairman supports manager, holds men back on premature demands for shift changes, and warns against hasty judgment over dropping men. Five volunteers come off (older men).
7	Three younger men leave; six spare men make up the team and are not themselves replaced. Though volunteers are called for, none come forward.
8–9	Manager enforces agreement after losing patience with poor production and inability of men to sort themselves out. Withdraws extra labor and two more leave.
10	Persistent bad conditions result in manager shortening west face by half. Forty-two men now required. Manager asks for new team, dropping nine poorest. Delegation of men wants cavils, refusing to make such judgments. Pay under strict agreement drops by 30 shillings per week. Manager refuses to pay outside the agreement.
11	Lodge insists on cavils over the nine surplus men. Previous support of manager replaced by opposition. Proposal to seek meeting with higher management. Lodge would declare dispute if refused by manager; such a meeting then automatic. Lodge committee meets with manager but no agreement. Area Labor Relations Officer visits pit.
12	Meeting of manager/lodge committee: manager agrees to visit day and night shift with representatives of lodge but refuses to take any action on pay. Subsequent lodge meeting sees committee announcing intention of withdrawing labor from the drift in the event manager won't come to terms.
13	Area Relations Officer helps management and lodge reach a new agreement. Wages improved, target reduced from 4'6" to 4'0", redundant men caviled off (only four left out of nine). Until difficulties overcome, special men to remain in key roles on each shift. Two men granted as reinforcements.
14–17	Face management steps in and creates rotation system. Within three weeks of the settlement, planned production reached, proportional to shortened face.

(continued)

TABLE 10.1. (continued)

Week No.	Events
18–21	Consolidation of team.
22–33	West face opened out. 1,000 tons per week (planned target) reached for first time in week 33.
34–43	Fluctuation about planned target.
44–72	Steady state 1,000 tons per week.
73	Better prices for single units had been obtained elsewhere in the pit, resulting in the two faces going on separate notes.

170

the time allowed (eight weeks) was no more than a token period and the underlying assumption manifested itself in a number of ways, especially in the emphasis on coal production as the primary task. Though, in words, the need for training and acquiring experience was acknowledged, preoccupation with output carried the real message of action.

The degree of unreality in assuming ordinariness may be measured by the fact that an inexperienced management and an inexperienced work team were brought together in a novel task under conditions likely to be difficult—especially in the beginning. All this was known by management and lodge when they entered negotiations. It was known also by the men. Yet it was all disregarded. The pit was under severe pressure to become economic—as soon as possible—and there was a great deal of anxiety about this; hence the preoccupation with production.

The Manley composite panels had been successful—beyond expectation and without trouble. On the Manley panels, the composite workers were multiskilled, exchanged shifts, practiced task continuity (deploying themselves as necessary to carry on succeeding tasks), and shared equally in a common pay note. Teams were self-regulating and practiced what we called "responsible autonomy" (Trist and Bamforth, 1951). The real effort, however, in the Manley negotiations had been on the terms of the agreement. Problems of work organization had been left to take care of themselves. This they had done, in a very remarkable way, but no analysis had been made of the reasons. It was simply taken for granted that such problems would take care of themselves again.

Meanwhile, reorganization elsewhere in the colliery had made redundant a considerable number of faceworkers. The lodge sought conditions for their redeployment without the relegation of any from facework status. Moreover, the one piece of "hard news" that had circulated about the Manley was that earnings were high—higher than earnings had ever been in the pit. It was an attractive prospect, therefore, to workers finishing odd jobs in older workings, and wondering what might happen to them, to join a new drift and get in on the advantages of the new type of agreement.

This led to a feature that was *not ordinary* about the drift: *the team was drafted, not self-selected,* with the result that there was no commitment to accepting the differences in skill and experience that were later discovered. Even the safeguard inherent in the traditional procedure for forming teams was dispensed with. One may infer that the pretense that special measures were unnecessary and that unusual risks were justified covered a pervasive fear that the drift would not succeed, with the serious repercussions this would have for the future of the colliery—its death. This is the underlying anxiety, intense in the change situation, which brought about the collusive denial of reality that in turn led to the initial assumption of ordinariness.

The Reactions to Failure

The reactions for what transpired after work began may best be followed from Table 10.1. It also reflects the amount of activity induced in wider managerial and negotiating systems and the levels of reinforcement, leaving, and productivity that characterized different phases in the sociotechnical history of the drift.

One might have supposed that the closure of the face at the end of the first week would have given a big enough shock to cause a radical reappraisal of the whole undertaking. Confrontation of what had happened, however, at a higher level of reality would have meant giving up the assumption of ordinariness. Instead, during weeks 4, 5, and 6 its role as the "chosen" defense was bolstered up by a series of measures that attempted to make it work in defiance of the facts. This is the latent meaning of the generous reinforcements offered by the manager (equal to one-fifth of the team's strength) and of the extent of his support by the lodge.

Nevertheless, a split in attitudes and relations was already detectable. At the same time as giving reinforcement, the manager asked the team to reorganize itself in a way that brought it into direct collision with the revered caviling rules that regulated the relations between management and workers. The men, perceiving this as an attack, started to go into opposition. This is the negative side of the collusive process, just as much lacking in task orientation as the positive side. It led into a type of impasse, familiar in industrial relations, in which *no learning takes place from what is being experienced.*

As the illusion wore thin and the impasse became more apparent, the men began to despair (by week 9 a quarter of the team had left), while the manager, desperate over costs and production and interpreting the men's lack of response as an act of hostility, enforced the agreement as regards both pay and manpower. This sudden regression to coercive control— punishment-centered bureaucracy, in Gouldner's terms (1954, p. 207)— produced the corresponding stereotype of militancy in the men's reaction, and manager and lodge found themselves in head-on conflict, with a threat of a dispute.

In the terms introduced by Bion (1961) for the description of unconscious group processes, the group enacted a fight/flight dynamic. Management and workers fought each other in common flight from the problems that had to be solved in the real task situation. In week 12 the mood on both sides changed after the visit of the Area Labor Relations Officer. In Bion's terms, basic assumption fight/flight had now been replaced in the emotional life of the group by a posture of dependency; and in this modality a settlement was reached with the help of a "wise and benevolent" figure representing the higher authority of the Area General Manager—an extremely "good object" to everyone in the pit. Within three weeks there was a dramatic improvement in productive performance, with the target reached in proportion to the shortened face.

172

The new agreement recognized more of the realities of the situation than had the original and represents a partial undoing of the assumption of ordinariness, some learning through experience having taken place. On the other hand, the working group continued in a management-dependent phase for several months, with the deputies stepping in and making all arrangements for face deployment and task-shift rotation. This had a reality component in that new skills and relationships could not be consolidated until the face was opened out again and the team built up to full strength. Some outside help on matters of organization was beneficial while task learning proceeded and new members were being absorbed. Nevertheless, it was eleven months before the production target was regularly reached. Even after eighteen months, when the panel split into two teams on separate pay notes, there was still doubt in the mind of the manager (and the observations of the research team confirmed this) as to whether the drift teams had attained the cohesive independence of the Manley panels. The original collusive denial of reality and the subsequent pattern of interactions between management, lodge, and the working group had impaired, at least for a time, the capacity to develop responsible autonomy.

Corrective Measures

With the situation structured as it was and the process started on the path taken, the subsequent course of events was to a large extent already determined. The available resources were used, the actors in all roles behaving very much according to expectation. As soon as the working group and immediate face management showed themselves unable to contain the situation, representatives of the next largest system (the colliery) stepped in, with the manager taking direct control and the lodge becoming officially involved. When the situation still remained out of hand, the even larger area system became implicated. Though a settlement was now reached, matters were put right only in the thirteenth week, after much expenditure of emotion and time, serious losses in production, and the incurrence of substantial additional costs in rewinning faces, making up wages, and remunerating reinforcements. The working group was inhibited from developing responsible autonomy, and the whole episode may serve as an illustration that *no amount of management from the outside— whether supportive or coercive—can replace effective self-regulation by the primary group.*

One may ask what measures not immediately available in the surrounding work culture—since those available were used—might have prevented the situation from developing in such a troublesome manner. To answer this question, one must ask how an assumption of ordinariness might have been prevented in the first place, which is equivalent to asking what might have permitted the negotiating group to provide leadership **173** in the reality rather than the illusory dimension (cf. Lewin, 1935).

The view is put forward that members of the negotiating group would have been able to master more of their own anxieties, which represented those of the colliery at large, and so been able to work out a more realistic scheme if they had had a fuller understanding of the reasons for the success of the Manley panels. They would then have known something of the conditions required for effective teamwork in composite longwall working and would have recognized the serious implications of their absence in the drift. At the same time, such a fuller understanding would have demonstrated that it was not impossible to make a plan that would have brought the required conditions into existence. An effective plan, however, would have entailed complete abandonment of the assumption of ordinariness—with its implications that full production was realizable after a brief period of settling in. The drift could then have been set up as a special training and development unit, with the prior task of becoming a balanced and cohesive workforce as a condition for attempting target production.

Such a step, however, would not have been easy within the norms of the prevailing work culture. These permitted the crisis to be resolved without a dispute and, in the end, a level of production to be reached better than that likely to have been achieved under conventional arrangements. *What the prevailing norms did not provide was any precedent, or "tool kit," for analyzing factors in the sociopsychological system in a way that would have broken down the assumption of ordinariness in the starting situation and avoided the consequent tensions and loss of production.*

The negotiations that led to the wages and manning agreement that had been so successful in launching the Manley panels had taken a year to complete, during which the many difficulties encountered had been successfully worked through. Matters of work organization, however, had scarcely been discussed. They were left "in the hands of the tradition," which was trusted to take care of them; that is, it was supposed that organizational matters would remain on familiar ground. In the Manley undertaking they did, as the men in various subgroups had previously worked together, often on composite short walls, and were in any case self-selected sets. None of this was the case in the drift. New ground, unfamiliar to all, had to be broken.

With the results of both the Manley and the drift to hand, the next job of the research team was to make an explicit formulation of the psychological and sociological aspects of composite longwall working. These yielded a new set of principles that could be used for converting other panels from conventional to composite longwall working.

The Institute had begun its studies of group dynamics in industrial settings by feeding in appropriately timed interventions as the work proceeded. This followed the psychoanalytic tradition and had been successful in projects such as the Glacier Project (Jaques, 1951). This, however, had not been concerned with an order of change that constituted a *paradigm shift*, as did the change from conventional to composite working in longwall coal-mining.

In such cases the research team has not only to develop an explicit model of the emergent system but to offer it to those concerned, who have a cognitive as well as an emotional problem in making the shift. For there is a discontinuity, and to encounter the novel casts doubt on familiar maps as well as on deeply held beliefs. The double difficulty that ensues creates confusion, which clears up when they can clearly envisage the alternative as an articulated systemic whole and find that it is suitable for them. In the meanwhile, they tend to be trapped in their hatred of learning through experience and usually need intellectual as well as emotional assistance in order to get out of the trap. Otherwise they remain in the grip of such primitive defenses as denial.

Comments

In his book *Experiences in Groups* (1961), Bion distinguishes between two levels of group activity: that of the "sophisticated" or "work" group (W), which involves learning and development and is concerned with specific tasks that must be met and undertaken in social reality; and that of what he calls "basic assumptions," which are unconscious. These are "dependence" (baD), "fight/flight" (baF), and "pairing" (baP). These are unlearned, primitive emotional response systems existing as internally patterned schemata that alternate with each other. Those that are not being activated belong to what he calls the "proto-mental level." Basic group organization may be in harmony or, more often, in conflict with the sophisticated or *W* organization. It is usually unrecognized by members of the group, whose level of performance may be severely impaired in consequence. The function of a consultant is to help the group become aware of its *ba* activity, so releasing the learning process. Bion later suggested that the *ba*'s were themselves defenses against anxieties described by Melanie Klein (1959) as arising in the first year of life and continuing to some extent in adulthood. Not all those who have found the idea of the *ba*'s to be useful take this further step.

Experiences in Groups has become the most influential and controversial book in group dynamics. Recent critiques of Bion's work may be found in *Bion and Group Psychotherapy*, edited by Malcolm Pines (1985). Attention is particularly drawn to J. D. Sutherland's chapter, "Bion Revisited."

175

NOTES

Acknowledgment: The original version of this chapter appeared in *Organizational Choice* (London: Tavistock, 1963), by E. L. Trist, G. W. Higgin, H. Murray, and A. B. Pollock. A new version appeared in Volume II of *The Social Engagement of Social Science: A Tavistock Anthology* (University of Pennsylvania Press, 1990).

1. In composite working all team members are multiskilled; they can thus exchange shifts and practice task continuity (deploying themselves as necessary to carry on with succeeding tasks); they share equally in a common pay note. Teams are self-regulating and practice what we called "responsible autonomy" (Trist and Bamforth, 1951).

2. A *drift* is a horizontal passageway driven from the surface into or along the path of a vein or rock layer. A *colliery* consists of the coal mine and its buildings. A *seam* is a thin layer or stratum of coal, ore, etc.

REFERENCES

Bion, W. R. 1961. *Experiences in Groups*. London: Tavistock.

Emery, F. 1978. *The Emergence of a New Paradigm of Work*. Canberra: Centre for Continuing Education, Australian National University.

Gouldner, A. W. 1954. *Patterns of Industrial Bureaucracy*. Glencoe, N.Y.: Free Press.

Holland, N. 1985. *The "I"*. New Haven and London: Yale University Press.

Jaques, E. 1951. *The Changing Culture of a Factory*. London: Tavistock.

———. 1953. "On the Dynamics of Social Structure." *Human Relations*, 6, 3–24.

Klein, M. 1959. "Our Adult World and Its Roots in Infancy." *Human Relations*, 12, 291–303.

Lewin, K. 1935. *A Dynamic Theory of Personality*. New York: McGraw-Hill.

Pines, M. (ed.) 1985. *Bion and Group Psychotherapy*. London and Boston: Routledge and Kegan Paul.

Sutherland, J. D. 1985. "Bion Revisited." In M. Pines (ed.), *Bion and Group Psychotherapy*. London and Boston: Routledge and Kegan Paul.

Trist, E. L., and K. Bamforth. 1951. "Some Social and Psychological Consequences of the Longwall Method of Coal-Getting." *Human Relations*, 4, 3–38.

Trist, E. L., G. W. Higgin, H. Murray, and A. B. Pollock. 1963. *Organizational Choice: Capabilities of Groups at the Coal Face Under Changing Technologies*. London: Tavistock.

PART III

Culture, Politics, and Race:

Organizational Psychodynamics

in Context

CHAPTER 11

The Mythological Structure of
Organizations and Its Impact

Abraham Zaleznik

Introduction

Anthropology, among its lessons, has taught us that myths are used to confront a problem and provide one or more solutions that allay anxiety, put fears and uncertainty to rest, and above all, link the individual to society. Whereas science offers rational explanations, it also tends to bypass the causes of anxiety—our primordial fears of being separate, detached, and lonely. These fears persist until some commonly held beliefs, expressed in myths, renew our sense of belonging and of the community of life. In other words, the common solution myths offer is to trust one's own family, clan, or society; to follow its norms; and to maintain the solidarity of the group. One's ultimate protection from anxiety is to belong to a strong, cohesive group.

Modern corporations, not surprisingly, have developed mythologies as

Reprinted from *Human Resource Management*, vol. 28, number 2 (Summer 1989), pp. 267–277. © 1989 by John Wiley & Sons, Inc. Reprinted by permission of John Wiley & Sons, Inc.

well, two aspects of which are explored in this chapter. First, modern corporate mythology fosters a false sense of security while dulling the capacity to understand changes in the competitive marketplace and the strategic problems within the organization. People who become CEOs of corporations dominated by a mythological structure, assuming they themselves are free from its grip, recognize that they must destroy the mythology in order to shape effective strategy and provide an environment in which "real work" can be accomplished. That is, energy must be directed toward products, markets, and customers, and be buttressed by technology, know-how, and common sense. Indeed, an advantage of the modern corporate raider is precisely that freedom of thinking, that detachment from the target's mythology. It is far more difficult for those on the inside to break the commitments implicit in belonging to an organization and believing in its prevailing mythology.

180   Another aspect of modern corporate mythology examined in this chapter is that it is not all-inclusive. Those who are included and those who are excluded are affected differently when the corporate mythology is challenged or disturbed.

Leaders and Mythology

Corporate Mythology and Teamwork

In the American corporate culture, mythology elaborates the theme of teamwork: While Americans admire the hero, the individual who has the "right stuff," they worry about his recklessness, his willingness to take risks that endanger others. Frequently the "hero" is suppressed in favor of the team player who values the performance of the group over individual recognition.

This social development was the basis for William Whyte's argument that corporate life in the 1950s had created the "organization man," the conformist who suppressed his individuality to support a corporate team. The rise of this phenomenon can be seen in the development of the U.S. automotive industry (particularly in the rise of General Motors), where paranoia and chaos reigned following World War I.

William Durant put General Motors together by acquiring numerous businesses, thereby building a mammoth corporation whose survival was not at all assured. He then hired Alfred Sloan, who, in bringing order out of the existing chaos, equated success with managerial teamwork within the top corporate group. By the 1950s, members of this group had developed a close and all-encompassing social network. They lived in the same Detroit suburbs, joined the same clubs, and attended the same parties, galas, and celebrations. The company created a way of life.

Sloan has justifiably been credited with consolidating the modern concept of management during his tenure as head of GM. Sloan's management system included decentralized operations with centralized financial controls, market segmentation between and within operating divisions, and committees to coordinate activities (e.g., purchasing, R&D) that divisions held in common. In place of the mercurial and entrepreneurial Durant, he created a system through which organization and teamwork displaced charismatic leadership.

His legacy, however, was not solely the design of a rational body of thought on how to organize and manage a large corporation. Because the social system he created was a closed one, providing its members with a secure life plan, his ideals also became a mythology—a structure of beliefs that established, in the eyes of its own corporate elite, the image of GM's invincibility. Implicit in this system was the belief that by adhering to Sloan's principles, GM could withstand competition and thus remain invincible in the corporate world.

181

But this mythology applied only to those in the corporate elite, the team members, who rose in the hierarchy and were extraordinarily well compensated through the liberal bonus program established as part of the system. First-line supervisors (who seldom expected to rise within the hierarchy) and blue-collar workers were excluded from the managerial/mythological structure. Indeed, Sloan's major management system failure was its inability to overcome hostile relations with its unionized workforce.

The public became aware of GM's mythology when, during the Eisenhower administration, Charles Wilson, the head of the company, was being confirmed as secretary of defense. At his congressional hearing, he uttered the famous words, "What is good for General Motors is good for America." Possibly, he meant that since the business of America is business, the policies that benefit corporations benefit society as a whole. But what the press and the public heard was something different: the belief in GM's (and America's) invincibility. Whether or not it was his intention, Wilson found words to express the dominant mythology of his corporation.

The existence of this mythology helps explain why GM and other domestic automobile producers, each with its own mythology, failed to meet Japanese competition in the 1970s. Focused on the inner life of the corporation, the automobile companies lost touch with the changing marketplace. The success of the Volkswagen in the 1960s was an early sign that Detroit's overemphasis on styling changes rather than function might not match new consumer preferences for efficiency and reliability. Detroit's continued emphasis on styling well into the seventies testifies to the belief in its own invincibility and its contempt for the consumer. Just as the corporate myth excluded workers and supervisors, so did it preclude real consideration of consumer preferences and needs. This story is well chronicled in David Halberstam's *The Reckoning* (1986), which attests to the collective dysfunctions that occur when managers cling to their corporate mythologies. Too often managers appear impervious to the fact that the competitive marketplace evaluates the corporation and its products from a different frame of reference than that experienced from within.

The Leader's Myth and the Myth's Persistence

Why do mythological structures persist, especially since no corporation or society is invincible and no products rationally deserve loyalty or attachment in an impersonal marketplace? This question requires two answers. The first considers the part leaders play in the rise of a mythological structure, and the second examines how the structure persists beyond the lifetime of the power figures who personify the mythology.

In the minds of their constituents, business leaders are larger-than-life figures. As charismatic creators of new products, builders of businesses, and accumulators of massive wealth, fantasies of omnipotence are projected onto them. Henry Ford, Sr., is a good example. With the development of the Model T, he personified a vision of America that went beyond Horatio Alger. A tinkerer off the farm, Ford changed the pattern of living and working in this country by producing a popularly priced car every farmer and worker could eventually own. By introducing a $5-a-day wage, he dramatized the benefits of mass production and became a national hero. There was talk of his becoming president.

The mythological structure of the Ford Motor Company centered on Henry Ford's belief in the perfection and permanence of the Model T (which competitors eventually destroyed). His vision and conviction, in turn, were products of his own attachment to his parents and his attempts to rewrite his personal history.

Facing trouble as his commitment to the Model T sustained an increasingly antiquated organization and product line, Ford refused to listen to his educated and sensitive son Edsel, who had sensible ideas for modernizing the company. Upon the senior Ford's return from a vacation, Edsel and a group of engineers brought him into a room to see a mockup of a new car that could replace the Model T. Ford walked around, inspecting it, and then tore it apart with his own hands. Attached to the Model T as a symbol of his own perfection, Ford distanced himself from Edsel and instead drew close to Henry Bennet, the head of his "goon squad." Bennet's shady background and access to gangsters and thugs only reinforced Ford's paranoia and rigidity.

Ford's life history suggests that his obstinate commitment to the Model T was rooted partly in a private psychodrama, which he projected onto his role as leader and entrepreneur. Idealizing his mother and hating his father, Ford used an overvalued Bennet as the symbolic repository of his ability to take "revenge" while his son Edsel became the symbol of the boy "in need" whose hurt could be denied by being devalued. Ford's private struggles to overcome his unresolved attachment to his parents by creating the perfect car and by proving his independence also nearly cost Ford his business. The public myth of the Model T was undermined by its private and psychodynamic foundation.

The interplay of public drama and private struggle can have a strong impact on subordinates. The power-holder's compulsion to act these conflicts out draws other executives into a corporate psychodrama, which reveals the underlying mythology. The following vignette takes us through the dynamics of such a psychodrama.

The chairman and CEO of a privately held corporation, a man in his early thirties, decided to fire his newly appointed president. The chairman had assumed his CEO position following the death of his father in an automobile accident. He gained control of the business when he induced his brother to sell him his inherited shares. With the support of his mother, the new CEO controlled in excess of 50 percent of the outstanding stock. The business appeared to be successful under his leadership, surpassing in size and scope his father's achievements.

The CEO described his problems with the president (who was also COO) as follows. The president, who was some twenty-five years older than the CEO, had been with the firm for years as the successful head of marketing and sales. He became president when the CEO decided to withdraw from day-to-day operations and instead concentrate on long-range planning and potential acquisitions. Moving into a separate suite of offices in a splendid building, the CEO left his newly designated president to handle affairs at the old offices and plants.

Almost immediately, however, the CEO felt uncomfortable with the change. He began to seek information from subordinates about the new president on various company matters. While the new president was on vacation in Europe, the CEO moved back into the old offices and began making radical changes in personnel and product lines. He even reversed course on a previously agreed-upon plant expansion. He drafted a long letter to the president and sent it to his home to await his return from vacation. In the letter, he detailed the alleged inadequacies he had found in the operations since the change and all but suggested that the president was a failure and should resign. He based these charges on information he had gained in conversations with younger executives who reported to the president. In making the inquiries, the CEO had revealed his discontent with the president to these younger executives. Clearly, he had established a climate in which he was urging people to give him ammunition against their immediate superior. These subordinates, who were closer to the CEO in age, eagerly engaged in such reporting and presented him with situations and alleged facts of which he himself had no prior knowledge.

The CEO was enacting a psychological drama and creating a mythological one. The psychological drama was based on the CEO's continuing and unconscious rivalry with his father. Not satisfied with the evident

183

proof that he could surpass his now-dead father, he used the considerably older president and COO as a target for his wish to demote the father. The mythological structure, which successfully swept in the CEO's subordinates, was based on the universal drama of the young displacing the old.

Needless to say, the mythology existed in the individual's fantasy world, and while enacted as a power struggle within the organization, it deflected attention from the changing competitive situation. Preoccupied with this internal struggle and its accompanying mythology, the CEO created instability and uncertainty, reversing, for example, expansion plans that were sensible in light of market trends. This company ultimately failed because competitors up-ended it in product design and consumer appeal.

184

Incorporating the Leader's Ideals

Corporate myths can persist after the corporate founders leave the scene. This process can set the stage for long-term decline. When power-holders in a business incorporate in their psyches the mythology of a *once* successful leader and attempt to displace rational observation and analysis with a persisting mythological structure, the corporation becomes akin to a "totemistic community." Its cohesion depends upon the continuing worship of the representations of past leadership as these become concertized, first, in the corporate mythology and, second, in business policies and decisions. The demise of the Curtis Publishing Company and its flagship publication, *The Saturday Evening Post*, illustrates this process well.

Successive management, along with the Curtis board of directors, rigidly adhered to the format, content, and image of *The Post*, which had been established by the company's founder, Cyrus Curtis, and longstanding editor, George Horace Lorimer. For these two men, their product represented America as it was at the turn of the century. Essentially rural, ethnocentric, and conservative in economic and political outlook, *The Post*, with its famous Norman Rockwell covers, became swamped by the changes occurring in the United States between the two world wars. Waves of immigration brought hundreds of thousands of eastern and southern Europeans to America. The Great Depression drove thousands from the farm to the city. The advent of the Second World War altered the isolationist outlook heralded in the magazine's pages.

Reflecting the deep-seated belief in the mythology handed down by Curtis and Lorimer—the sense of permanence of a WASPish, rural America—the company's management integrated backward: it bought stands of timber, pulp mills, and expensive printing plants. Its capital thus became frozen in support of a dying image, one that no longer represented the consumers and advertisers who provided the revenues. The mythological structure prevented company management from seeing the significance of Henry Luce's new pictorial journalism (in *Life*, for example); it failed to appreciate the importance of radio, then television, broadcasting. Most of all, it didn't grasp the quickening pace of American life, which ran counter to the sleepy image of a docile country portrayed in the pages of *The Saturday Evening Post*.

Myths: Inclusion and Exclusion

Corporate Life and Stress

It would seem clear that an effective business leader who gains power in a nearly defunct corporation must ferret out the buried ideals in the company's mythology, destroy them as the fixed objects in constituents' **185** psyches, and translate new images and visions into workable business strategies. Lee Iacocca, for example, had to restore product, manufacturing, and selling motifs instead of financial and real estate orientations, which had been reflected in Chrysler's own sense of permanence as the third partner in America's hegemony in the automotive industry. Focusing on finance and milking the business, Chrysler's leadership starved its factories. Iacocca aggressively led the company in reducing its break-even point by closing antiquated plants and upgrading capital equipment in those he intended to keep. By stimulating product engineers and designers to introduce low-priced knockoffs of luxury cars, he gained a renewed following among consumers. Because of his close association with dealers while at Ford and his understanding of what sold cars, Iacocca inspired his organization to do "real work." Indeed, manufacturing executives supported him wholeheartedly, even though he shrank the manufacturing base by closing plants and outsourcing production.

But what price do such outsiders exact on a company? When the corporate "totem" and the underlying mythology are destroyed, what replaces them to maintain cohesion and self-esteem?

Organizations are hierarchies in which power is unevenly distributed. Despite experiments with reforms designed to narrow the gaps between levels of power, inequalities continue and probably always will. An organization's cohesiveness arises out of common identification with the leader as a person, the ideals that person represents, or the mythology that is a legacy of past leadership, as we have seen. Those who are included in the mythology maintain self-esteem through belonging. Institutions such as the church, the military, or a great university whose standing is linked to broad cultural needs and hopes include everyone, regardless of rank and relative power, in their mythology; the structure, moreover, provides a protective, enveloping cocoon to ward off anxiety and feelings of stress.

Because such institutions are linked to universalistic values such as faith, patriotism, or truth, they express cultural hopes that belong to the society as a whole, not to the institution itself. The institutional myths are reflections of broader cultural wishes and values. As members of society, institutional participants have a claim on and a stake in the institutional mythology as well.

Modern economic corporations, however, are instruments of ownership and capital appreciation. Insofar as corporate leadership fails to link company efforts to broader cultural objectives and needs, the myths they sustain are the myths and stories surrounding success itself, the stories of ambition, conquest, and status. Consequently, these myths are by their very nature exclusive, so that lower-level employees cannot participate in them.

186 Thus, it is usually only the power elite that clings stubbornly to totem worship and faithful adherence to the corporate mythology. For those outside the main power structure, there is personal vulnerability from two sides. On one, the perpetuation of the mythology threatens their economic well-being—witness the hundreds of thousands of jobs recently lost in America's industrial heartland, which once appeared invulnerable to foreign competition. On the second side, the mythological structure produces psychological isolation for those excluded from it, which increases the risk of stress illnesses.

The CBC Study

Several years ago, I conducted a study of stress in the Canadian Broadcasting Corporation, a large, quasi-public bureaucracy headquartered in Ottawa (Zaleznik et al., 1977). The study was initiated because of disquieting reports of stress illnesses, including depression, suicide, and alcoholism, among the three thousand professionals in management, staff, and operating positions. (At the CBC, management included hierarchical positions; staff included functions like engineering, law, personnel, and financial; operations involved programming, including the on-air and off-air creative work of the radio and TV networks.)

Earlier, I had worked with CBC top management on revising its formal organization from a highly centralized to a partially decentralized structure. An early CBC mission had been to construct a radio, and eventually television, network across the vast reaches of Canada; this had required large capital expenditures and engineering talent, and centralization appeared the most efficient way to organize. Centralization was reinforced through lines of accountability to government agencies and Parliament, and speaking with one voice appealed to the political instincts of CBC executives as well as to government officials.

New social and political forces in Canada then brought the CBC into the center of an urgent controversy, particularly in the relations between English- and French-speaking Canadians. Commission reports, "white papers," and the press all probed CBC's problems, and the resulting spotlight made management fearful. They centralized further, ordering the operating heads of the English and French networks to Ottawa from their bases of operations in Toronto and Montreal. The mythology surrounding the success in building the physical facilities for nationwide broadcasting was displayed by a "fortress mentality," in which enemies from within and without had to be prevented from undermining the instrument that had perfected the construction of the network. Eventually, the besieged top management was replaced, and the new group introduced partial decentralization, restoring the operating network heads to their former offices. It also initiated the stress study.

Results of the study revealed five major syndromes: (1) emotional distress of a depressive quality; (2) medication use without specific indications, suggesting hypochondriasis; (3) cardiovascular disease; (4) gastrointestinal disturbances; (5) allergy and respiratory symptoms. These stress-related syndromes suggested in the aggregate two main types of response. The first was a sensitizing reaction to stress, in which the individual tended to flood his or her experience with intense emotional reactions such as anxiety and depression. The second type of response was repression, in which the stress-related situation was buried in the psyche, only to reappear in the form of physical symptoms such as respiratory or gastrointestinal symptoms. Statistical analysis showed that younger people, women, operations personnel, and French Canadians tended toward the sensitizing response while older people, males, staff personnel, and English Canadians tended to be repressors.

The most striking finding in this study was the relative absence of stress reactions among managers as compared with staff and operations people. At first glance, this finding made little sense, since conventional wisdom stated that stress is a product of having authority and responsibility. Furthermore, the normal burdens of command were aggravated in this instance because of the media and government attacks. This surprising finding raised a general question about the nature of stress, power, and position in a hierarchy. Are power-holders in a hierarchy psychologically better able to endure the stresses of authority and responsibility, or are they, after all, operating in a less stressful environment compared to individuals at lower levels of power in the hierarchy? The second explanation seems the more credible. Being well positioned in the hierarchy offers an identification with power, whether it can be used or not, and therefore participation in the mythological structure. Such participation provides legitimacy, reassures against external danger, and guards against the feelings of rage and impotence that accompany the apparent arbitrariness of life in general and large organizations in particular. In times of adversity,

187

as in the attacks on CBC, the mythological structure offers protection (often falsely), which helps maintain self-esteem.

Life is experienced differently outside the protection of the power elite and the accompanying mythology. The combination of feeling excluded and the rage that accompanies a conviction that few alternatives exist to improve one's situation is highly frustrating.

Organized Mythology and Isolated Fantasy

Individuals excluded from the group's mythological structure tend to rely on their fantasy life to repair the damage that can occur with isolation. Depending on the many variables, including the availability of talent, the regressive quality of the fantasy itself, and the individual's capacity for using inner conflict in creative work, there are alternatives to falling ill as a result of stress. A strong case can be made that, in part, the mental process of effective leaders is contingent on their tolerance of separation from the group and its mythology. They rely on their fantasy as an instrument for formulating ideas (sometimes called visions) about an organization's future. Their exclusion from the group mythology, whether by personal choice or situational factors, often provides the impetus for fresh examination of familiar information. The resulting objectivity can set the stage for new work and the redefinition of an existing situation.

Nonetheless, when a person lower down in the organization lacks the power to transform a private fantasy into a shared vision, it is likely that the fantasy will not protect the person from stress. The result, as the CBC study suggests and the following dramatic example reveals, is the formation of stress symptoms and impaired ability to perform.

An air traffic controller in his early fifties slipped on the icy metal stairs of a control tower. For some time after the fall, he felt a sharp pain in his lower back. More than experiencing a physical mishap, however, the controller found himself engaged in a psychological accident in which his tendency toward isolated fantasy took a morbid turn toward depression and paranoid reactions.

This controller (call him Robert Graham) took pleasure in the thought that the superbly trained pilots flying large, high-speed aircraft depended upon him to bring their planes and passengers to a safe landing. Pilots would at times go out of their way to compliment him on his performance, providing Graham with some real content to his fantasy that powerful people needed him.

This feeling of being needed contrasted sharply with the solitary quality of the work, the lack of association with his fellow controllers and supervisors, and the awareness that the mythology surrounding commercial aviation, while highlighting the dramatic role played by pilots, excluded the activity of aircraft controllers. This sense of being alone became pointedly real when Graham realized that his supervisor and fellow controllers seemed unaware of his accident. No one paid much attention to him until it became apparent that he could not carry out his duties, at which time his supervisor placed him on sick leave.

Besides a consciousness of being alone, Graham worried about the future. He was afraid he would not be able to keep up with changes in technology and that he would be placed on early retirement. He never had occasion to give voice to these fears until he began to see a psychiatrist for treatment of depression as well as for evaluation in a work-related compensation dispute. He was never able to resume work in the control tower. As a result, what he feared most actually occurred: he lived in a diminished capacity, incapable of taking on a skilled job that measured up to the responsibilities of an air traffic controller.

189

Conclusion

Modern corporate mythology, as we have seen through various examples, leads to a false sense of security that diminishes the intense scrutiny of a company's business environment; it engenders a complacency that dampens imagination and the aggressiveness needed to engage competitive issues long before they become manifest in financial results. Furthermore, the mythology speaks only to the members of the power elite, including those aspiring to it, protecting it from the ravages of stress. Those with lesser status and power are excluded and ironically may be more vulnerable to stress illnesses than those with the responsibility of actually running the organization.

When organizations encounter serious trouble, those included in the mythology find it exceedingly difficult to break out of the stereotypical thinking that belief in the mythology encourages. When problems become sufficiently grave to warrant drastic steps (usually under the threat of outside agendas), new leadership enters the scene. As "outsiders" not under the influence of the prevailing mythology, the new group or individual may be able to approach the business more objectively. New leadership thus has the opportunity to appeal to rationality and to the recognition that clinging to archaic images and ideas, no matter how self-gratifying, leads to disaster and runs counter to the impulses of self-preservation.

REFERENCES

Halberstam, D. 1986. *The Reckoning*. New York: William Morrow.
Zaleznik, A., M. Kets de Vries, and J. Howard. 1977. "Stress Reactions in Organizations: Syndromes, Causes and Consequences." *Behavioral Science*, 22(3), 151–162.

CHAPTER 12

Mentoring and Irrationality:

The Role of Racial Taboos

David A. Thomas

Introduction

Racial Taboos and Irrationality

We can create a partial picture of organizations if we consider them, for a moment, as instruments of rational action. Managers, leaders, and workers collaborate to achieve specific ends with limited means. Using technical logics that link cause and effect in a range of domains (marketing, engineering, production), organizations make decisions on how and when to act. But this is only a partial picture. An organization is also the seat of irrational life. People's unconscious hopes and fears, the dreams and myths they live by, and the history embedded in them—all influence their actions as well.

People experience or suppress the irrational at work when relating to

Reprinted from *Human Resource Management*, vol. 28, number 2 (Summer 1989), pp. 279–290. © 1989 by John Wiley & Sons, Inc. Reprinted by permission of John Wiley & Sons, Inc.

others. Working in and through these relationships, people serve their conscious as well as their unconscious purposes. Researchers have highlighted how the mentor-protégé relationship between members of an organization, or profession, helps the organization reach its goals while facilitating the career and personal development of both parties (Kram, 1985; Clawson, 1980; Phillips, 1982; Dalton and Thompson, 1986). Shaped by broader social and cultural processes, these relationships reflect the ongoing tension between the rational and irrational levels of experience. Thus, for example, mentors and protégés are frequently pulled between two opposing archetypal images of the relationship itself. On the one side, the protégé feels like the child, and the mentor like the parent. On the other side, nourished by the myth of "Mentor," the servant who raised the son of his master Oedipus to manhood, mentors feel obliged to educate the "young" so that the corporation can thrive. In the first case the protégé is the apprentice; in the second the mentor is the servant. The lines between mentor as father or servant and protégé as apprentice or son constantly blur and re-form. Yet this fluidity is experienced largely unconsciously.

As research shows, these relationships have dramatic impacts on a person's career (Roche, 1977; Cox and Nkomo, 1986). By understanding how mentoring's irrational core inhibits certain relationships while facilitating others, we can understand how the irrational and unconscious shape upward mobility in the modern corporation.

In the United States, feelings of racial identity shape unconscious fantasies and fears very powerfully. Just as a superior and subordinate can enact the unconsciously experienced dynamics of a parent and child, whites and blacks can enact the history of race relations, with all its difficulty and promise, in their everyday interaction, in the microdynamics of supervision and mentoring, and in career planning. Good Equal Employment Opportunity (EEO) practices will not eliminate these inner experiences. Indeed, as EEO opens doors to black managers, it engenders the deeper difficulties we face in creating a climate of authentic collaboration among blacks and whites.

Consider a white professional engineer's description of his encounter with a black female subordinate who recently joined his group.

> I was told that Kathy shared my special interests in product design, but I also found that I was staying away from her. I hooked up with all the other new junior people, but not with her. Finally, I approached her to join me on a project. I knew I was attracted to her. When I spoke she responded warmly, but I was also aware of a hesitancy in me, that I wanted to withdraw. It was as if a taboo was operating.

The word "taboo" is suggestive here. Taboos operate on two levels. They forbid action, but they also forbid *reflecting* on what is forbidden.

As an injunction not to notice what is forbidden, a taboo operates out of awareness. That is why people find it difficult to discuss a taboo. It is not that they will perform the forbidden act, but that they will violate the unconsciously experienced injunction to ignore what they are ignoring. The racial taboo described above—the creation of a liaison between a white man and a black woman—links wider cultural processes to organizational reality while operating to suppress this linkage. It thus becomes the source of an experiential underground—a set of experiences often unconsciously enacted and rarely acknowledged which nonetheless shapes the relationships between blacks and whites in significant ways.

Based on a sample of interview results I obtained when studying mentoring relationships between black and white managers in WRL, a large corporation, this chapter suggests that race relations are embedded in taboos that both highlight and suppress the links between race and sex. I begin by examining how these taboos are experienced and then explore the links between these experiences and the process of mentoring. Finally, I suggest some implications for human resource practice.

193

Of course, this chapter violates the very taboos it describes. My own experience suggests that the reader, like the engineer, will want to withdraw and deny the validity or plausibility of the experiences reported here. They may seem too primitive. Indeed, it is their primitiveness that leads us to question their validity. How can such feelings really exist or persist? This is the lesson of psychoanalysis, however. The primitive layer, whether based on sexual feelings or on early experiences of being judged unworthy, continues to shape an adult's unconscious life and ongoing actions. I ask the reader to suspend disbelief as a first step in examining and assessing these taboos rationally. As in psychoanalysis, irrationality must be acknowledged if it is to be overcome.

Sex and Race

Cross-Sex Relationships

Listen to Louise, a black woman manager, describe her experience of race relations at WRL.

> Being seen with white men presents problems. . . . White men are kind of funny around black women and if one knows about history. . . . Actually, I should own [the problem] myself. My being seen with white men, I have a problem with it. You know, being a white man's slut and all the connotations that go with it. So when I'm away on training, I isolate myself after hours. So, I have to own a piece of not feeling extremely comfortable.
>
> I remember all the negative things people used to say about Ann, a black

woman manager, when she was out in the field and moving up. People thought she must have been sleeping her way up. Now those of us who know her realize how full of —— that was.

Louise's reference to "being a white man's slut and all the connotations that go with it" evokes a charged domain of feelings affecting the relationships between blacks and whites. But where do such feelings come from? What are their roots? Scholars of race relations agree that the history of slavery and its chronic aftershocks undergird these feelings. We are still living in the aftermath of a social earthquake—slavery and its sequelae's long-term effects on racial identity, black self-esteem, and white prejudice lie deep within our culture.

While racial dynamics are enacted in many ways, the social psychology of slavery and its later nonslave manifestations, as Grier and Cobbs (1968) and Kovel (1970) point out, typically pit the white man against the black man. At the economic level, of course, the white man owned the black's labor power. But at the intimate and primitive levels of social life, white men dominated because black men could not adequately protect their families, especially black women, from white men's whimsical and most often violent intrusion. In contrast, black men could be lynched simply for speaking to white women. Women became pawns in an unequal struggle that not only undermined the black male's status but distorted the relationship between the men and women of both races. *Thus from slavery's beginnings racial dynamics have been inextricably tied to gender relationships. Indeed, the former, I suggest, are not conceivable without the latter.* This is part of what gives race relationships their irrational character, their primitiveness, and their durability.

Consider, for example, the case that Davis and Watson (1982) relate in a study on black experience in a largely white corporation. A black woman, Joanne, described the pressures and dubious attributions placed on black women who are thought to be involved in career-enhancing relationships with white men. Talking about a black woman who rose up in the hierarchy, she notes:

> You had a lot of black males saying that she was aligning herself with the white boys to help her. Then you had a lot of black men saying that she was aligning herself with the white man against him, saying the white man promoted her and favored her because she could be counted twice on the EEO report. . . . If she hung out with the white boys they accused her of sleeping with white dudes. . . . See, this is history repeating itself.

In short, Joanne is saying that modern-day corporate relationships reproduce the feelings associated with the primitive dynamics of race relations. White men appropriate black women, black women can rise up by going along with this, and black men are angry and suspicious.

194

Similarly, consider the complex case of Bob, a black manager, and his white superior, Mary. They started out as peers in the same division but Mary was quickly promoted, while Bob, highly regarded for his technical skills, was not. Several years later Mary returned as the supervisor of Bob's unit, the two became friends, and Mary worked successfully to get Bob on the fast track.

Mary learned much from her experience. She reported that at committee meetings where promotions were decided, whites could be promoted upon the say-so of their supervisors. By contrast, black candidates faced a tough time. "Unless you sold the black person ahead of time," she noted, "they could get shot down." Reflecting on the struggle she faced in sponsoring Bob, she said that her peers wondered if Bob was "tough enough," ironically punishing him for behaving as blacks are supposed to—not pushy, not uppity.

Bob discussed his own career, and reflecting on his eventual promotion, he said that white men told him that he was considered one of the "good" black guys. There are black guys, he was told, that "vamp" on white women, but he was not one of them. In other words, it was safe to promote him.

195

Nonetheless, while he could be sponsored by a powerful white woman, it was difficult for him to sponsor a subordinate white woman. Thus he reports that later he began helping a white woman who shortly afterward withdrew emotionally from him.

> I can be the mentor and I tried that and did it OK. And it happened to be that the person was a white woman. Someone came to her and said, "You're hanging around with this black man too much; it will damage your career." She came back to tell me what the other one told her. I was the project leader. I am, like, "What can I do?"

Another black male described the dangers black men faced in associating with white females:

> I don't want to be seen too often talking with white females; . . . there is a lot of history that says that black men being somewhat familiar with white women isn't healthy. Maybe that is changing but there is enough history to say that it is something you should have some care around.

Interviewing whites and blacks, I found that none of the white male mentors, including the most enlightened about race relations, seemed aware of, or were willing to discuss, this history of race relations and sexual taboos. Yet this history was salient in the minds of black men and women and, to some degree, white women. This does not mean that the latter were exaggerating. Rather, just as white males once dominated the sexist pigmentocracy of slavery, current organizational and cultural norms support their longstanding tastes and interests. Secure and powerful in ways that women and minorities frequently are not, they can deny the anxieties created by the relationships between blacks and whites. Experiencing it only unconsciously, as a vague sense of uneasiness, they let blacks bear the burden of awareness. The power imbalance is reinforced, as blacks tread lightly, carefully, and whites comfortably go about their business. The powerful can choose what they wish to ignore.

Same-Sex Relationships

As these examples suggest, cross-race/cross-gender relationships pose special difficulties by activating a *triangle* of relationships. A black man mentoring a white female may upset white men. A black female's supportive alliance with a white man can upset black men.

196

Same-sex/cross-race relationships pose different and somewhat less volatile dynamics. For example, Frances, a white woman superior, and Harriet, a black woman subordinate, developed a close mentoring relationship. Frances was Harriet's first female supervisor. The two came to be friends; they socialized together after work, sharing details about one another's private nonwork lives.

Harriet credits Frances with opening up their relationship. As a black woman wary of being unfairly judged, Harriet put herself in a position of never making a mistake. This limited her development. Asking Harriet about this, Frances saw how Harriet's behavior was rooted in the simple reality that blacks' performance was more carefully scrutinized than whites' and their mistakes were more severely penalized. Harriet believed that this conversation was a breakthrough for them. She felt that Frances was the first white person she really trusted.

By contrast, in my study of cross-race couples at WRL, I found that black and white men rarely reported bonding around shared male interests. Men at work form close relationships by participating together in typical male activities after work. They join the same softball team, for example. But while white men could sponsor black men at WRL, they rarely formed close *mentoring* relationships that facilitated such extra-work relationships.

I suggest that female-female cross-race relationships differ radically from their male-male counterparts, because their histories differ. The relationship between Frances and Harriet evokes the earlier history of the frequently warm and congenial relationship between the black woman "house slave" and the white woman mistress (a relationship reproduced well beyond slavery as black women continued to function as "nannies" for white children). The white woman relied on the black woman to protect her children and care for her household. The two thereby developed a way of being with each other that suppressed their racial difference and drew upon the vein of commonality represented in their womanhood.

TABLE 12.1.   Relationships (Ranked by Power to Evoke Taboos)

Rank Order	Relationship	Tabooed Feeling
1	WM superior BF subordinate	White man having unlimited sexual access to black women
1	BM superior WF subordinate	Black man sexually approaching a white woman
2	WM superior BM subordinate	White man "freeing a slave," threatening other white men [a]
3	WF superior BF subordinate	Black woman abandoning her men, counterbalanced by shared experience of womanhood

[a]Wells and Jennings (1983) have described the psychodynamics of this relationship using the paradigm of the scandalous paradox. In this scenario, whites respond to black peers as though they were the illegitimate children of the father—in this instance, white elites who support EEO and black advancement. This relationship is viewed by white subordinates as scandalous and a threat to their inherited privileges and rights.

197

By contrast, black and white men had few opportunities to develop such non-race-based relationships. They remained combatants.

In Sum

My interviews at WRL thus suggest that race relationships are embedded in a complex set of race-gender dynamics. Table 12.1 presents a way of ordering the different pairwise relationships in terms of their complexity, volatility, and the degree to which they evoke taboos.

The Impact on Mentoring and Careers

Mentoring and Identification

Sex and race taboos critically shape the dynamics of cross-race relationships. While linked to the overt process of career development and mobility, mentoring is grounded in the psychodynamics of identification. The mentor sees parts of himself or herself in the subordinate, and the subordinate wants to become like the mentor, to take up his or her voice, manner of dress, way of thinking. The two psychologically identify with each other, bringing their unconscious fantasies of who they are or might be to the relationship. As Kaplan (1984) described it, by identifying with each other, individuals come to know themselves, to discover themselves through their relationships with others.

Racial difference and sex and race taboos can block blacks and whites from feeling close to each other, from identifying with each other. If they emotionally identify with their counterpart, they grow dangerously close to experiencing forbidden feelings and encountering unknown parts of themselves. One white manager talked about these feelings while describing the problem of selecting black managers to mentor.

> The first thing that you have to do is to accept that there is a difference, even though you don't always know what it is. For me a very important part of mentoring is identifying and knowing they'll be good. There has to be something in the person that you have identified. That is difficult in some cases to do with blacks. You have to pick out some dimensions that let you know this person will be good. You also have to realize that there are some things that you will never know. Things that come from growing up black that you may never understand. But if you believe in the person, in some way you have to get around that and work with them.

198

This is a complex statement. The white manager notes that because blacks and whites are different she finds it difficult to find parts or features of blacks that assure her of their goodness. She notes that her difficulty is linked to things "she may never understand." At first blush one might interpret the comment as strictly a racist one and leave it at that. But this manager has worked to overcome her felt inhibitions. I suggest that the statement describes how people unconsciously respond to the unknown, and how racism shapes this response. Just as children disappoint parents, a mentor can never predict for certain how his or her protégé will perform. The mentor overcomes this uncertainty emotionally, by identifying with the protégé, by locating what she trusts in herself and seeing this same characteristic in the protégé. Identification reduces the felt sense of risk and danger. But in the face of racial difference, the sense of what is not known expands, and the resulting anxieties are then unconsciously rationalized with the racist image of the dangerous and inferior black. The core anxiety of mentoring—the dread of what can't be predicted—is filled out by the culture of racism. It is this set of feelings that obscures the white manager's vision of the goodness in blacks.

Cooling Out

Whites and blacks respond frequently to these difficulties by "cooling out" their relationships, by transforming potentially intimate mentoring relationships into more instrumental relationships of sponsorship. Consider the case of Ken and Karen. Ken was a powerful up-and-coming white manager at WRL. Placed on the fast track, he was told that he would shortly become treasurer of the corporation. Well connected to the dominant coalition, he was in fact advised to forgo an immediate promotion because his next would vault him into the power elite.

Karen, a black female, was one of his protégés. Describing her career, she noted that she spent the first four years working through and past her "naive" belief that good work begets recognition. Now she knew that she had to be careful, to stay at a distance from other people and not get hooked into the informal processes of the organization. She valued Ken as a model manager, as fair and competent, but she kept her distance.

Talking about race relations, she noted that at one point she was having some trouble getting good work out of a department that supported her unit. Ken suggested that it might have something to do with the fact that she was black and the other unit head was an older white male. She denied it—there was just a "bunch of old codgers" in that unit—but she confided later in the research interview that she was pleased that Ken could talk about racism openly with her.

Ken described his relationship to Karen in similarly "cool" terms, linking it to the company's strategic needs. He saw that minorities would soon constitute 70 percent of his workforce and that the company needed such people as Karen to become leaders. He was sponsoring Karen, helping her develop to further the organization's leadership needs.

199

Yet while each kept emotional distance from the other, he seeing her as an instrument of the organization's development and she seeing him as a model of the fair manager, in interviewing them I experienced both as vital people, in touch with their power and sexuality. They denied that they were attracted to each other (though what could they tell a black male researcher), but I left the interviews with the feeling that while developing a workable relationship together, they had also depersonalized one another.

Instrumental relationships that provide career support can benefit upwardly mobile managers. Today, many blacks can hope for no more. However, both mentors and protégés lose out when, unable to identify with each other, they fail to connect emotionally. Facing penalties for poor decisions, a white executive will not advocate that a protégé be given risky assignments that can lead to the "top" unless he can see and identify with the protégé's "goodness." This perhaps explains why black high-potential managers in corporations plateau so early (Jones, 1986; Davis and Watson, 1982). By cooling their relationships out, blacks and whites protect themselves from jointly confronting the anxieties and paradoxes of their alliances, but they also limit their impact and significance.

The Limits of EEO

EEO as a Social Defense

Companies introducing and implementing EEO policies can help minority group members have the careers and jobs they deserve. It has been an important first step in overcoming discrimination. But paradoxically EEO can also function as what Hirschhorn (1988) calls a social defense, as a system of procedures that detach people from their experiences so that they won't feel anxious. Situated squarely in the liberal tradition of the "melting pot," EEO is based on the assumption and hope that legislation and rules will make institutions color-blind. But as I have argued, the taboos of race and sex are deeply embedded in feelings and practice, and people consciously hoping to treat one another fairly may nonetheless enact the system of suspicion, mistrust, and devaluation that shapes basic relations between the races in the United States. Ironically, because it posits the goal of a color-blind society, EEO may reinforce the very taboos that stop us from looking at the impact of color on our relationships to each other. Announcing that "here in this company, color doesn't matter" may unconsciously affirm the fantasy that color is unimportant, that its impact need not be confronted.

200

We need to complement the political model of using legislation and rules to reshape behavior with the psychoanalytic model for changing behavior. The latter is based on the assumption that irrationality can be overcome only when it is acknowledged. People must "work through" their feelings and experiences, even if this work is painful and difficult. While EEO has legitimized racism as a problem, we now need to build on this base of experience. We need to help people approach the taboos themselves, by working with them at retreats, workshops, and department meetings where unspoken thoughts can be safely expressed. This is a complex design and facilitation task, and in my experience such encounters work only when black and white people participate in them together. We have only begun to develop a social technology for confronting the racial taboos. But to be true to our pluralist values and to be socially responsible executives, we have no choice.

In Sum

While linking means and ends in rational ways, companies are also the seat of much irrationality. In the United States, racial taboos are at the source of many unspoken feelings and irrational acts. Rooted in the history of slavery, racial feelings are inextricably linked to dynamics of gender relationships. The explosive mix of race and sex makes racism particularly volatile and durable. Research highlights the nature of these taboos, and suggests that cross-sex/cross-race relationships are the most difficult to sustain. Facing the taboos these relationships create, blacks and whites retreat to less intense ways of being together. Protégés are deprived of the mentoring relationship they need to develop and get ahead, and mentors are denied the experience of creativity, of generation, that they need in order to feel able to shape an institution's future and to create a personal legacy.

TABLE 12.2. Interview Pairs

Mentor/Sponsor	Protégé	Number
White Male	Black Female	3
White Female	Black Female	6
White Male	Black Male	9
White Female	Black Male	1
Black Male	White Female	2

EEO has been an important tool in legitimizing the problem of racism, but it is insufficient. Based on the concept of the color-blind institution, it may paradoxically reinforce the power of the original taboo to silence reflection and inhibit thinking. We need to go beyond EEO and develop a social technology that will help blacks and whites more directly confront their history and the present. Only in this way can we create the corporation that truly supports and values pluralism.

201

Appendix

Description of the Research Project

The research result was based upon interviews with senior and junior parties to 22 cross-racial pairs. Three of these relationships took place outside the WRL Corporation. Through these interviews, data were yielded about 18 other cross-racial relationships. The interview study was part of a larger research project that included statistical analysis on survey data obtained for 486 mentoring pairs, 125 of which were cross-racial. Of these, all but 6 involved black protégés and white mentors/sponsors. Table 12.2 gives a breakdown of the focal interview pairs.

NOTE

Acknowledgment: This discussion of taboos has benefited from several conversations with Larry Hirschhorn, who influenced me to use this term rather than a less provocative and, perhaps, less meaningful framing. For an extensive treatment of racial taboos, see Barbara Day, *Sexual Life Between Blacks and Whites* (1974); James Kovel, *White Racism: A Psychohistory* (1970); and Angela Davis, *Women, Race, and Class* (1983).

REFERENCES

Clawson, J. G. 1980. "Mentoring in Managerial Careers." In Brooklyn Derr (ed.), *Work, Family, and Careers.* New York: Praeger.

Cox, T., and S. Nkomo. 1986. "Differential Performance Appraisal Criteria: A Field Study of Black and White Managers." *Group and Organization Studies*, 11(2), 101–119.

Dalton, G., and P. M. Thompson. 1986. *Novations*. Glenville, Ill.: Scott, Foresman.

Davis, A. 1983. *Women, Race, and Class*. New York: Random House.

Davis, G., and G. Watson. 1982. *Black Life in Corporate America*. New York: Random House.

Day, B. 1974. *The Sexual Life Between Blacks and Whites*. Appollon Editions.

Grier, W., and P. Cobbs. 1968. *Black Rage*. New York: Bantam.

Hirschhorn, L. 1988. *The Workplace Within: Psychodynamics of Organizational Life*. Cambridge, Mass.: MIT Press.

Jones, E. W., Jr. 1986. "Black Managers: The Dream Deferred." *Harvard Business Review* (May–June), 84–93.

Kaplan, L. 1984. *Adolescence: A Farewell to Childhood*. New York: Simon and Schuster.

Kovel, J. 1970. *White Racism: A Psychohistory*. New York: Pantheon Press.

Kram, K. 1985. *Mentoring at Work*. Glenville, Ill.: Scott, Foresman.

Phillips, L. L. 1982. *Mentors and Protégés*. New York: Arden House.

Roche, G. R. 1977. "Much Ado about Mentors." *Harvard Business Review* (January), 14–28.

Wells, L., and C. Jennings. 1983. "Black Career Advancement and White Reactions: Remnants of Herrenvolk Democracy and the Scandalous Paradox." In D. Vails-Webber and W. J. Potts (eds.), *NTL Sunrise Seminars*. Arlington, Va.: NTL Institute.

CHAPTER 13

Alexithymia in Organizational Life:

The Organization Man Revisited

Manfred F. R. Kets de Vries

Introduction

More than thirty years have passed since Whyte (1956) wrote his classic work *The Organization Man*. His depiction of what he perceived to be the typical executive very much resembled Sinclair Lewis's satiric but convincing portrait of Babbitt, the bland, totally conformist real estate man from Zenith Corporation, an individual glib and opportunistic in both business and private life. Lewis turned *Babbitt* into a moral tale of how compromising about conformity can become the price required for our business culture. The novel is a prime example of the creation of a personal wasteland, how an individual can lead an empty, thoroughly meaningless existence. Babbitt is a man who

> beheld, and half admitted that he beheld, his way of life as incredibly mechanical. Mechanical business—a brisk selling of badly built houses. Me-

Reprinted from *Human Relations*, vol. 42, number 12, 1989, pp. 1079–1093. Reprinted by permission of Plenum Publishing Corporation, New York. © 1989 Tavistock Institute of Human Relations.

chanical religion—a dry, hard church, shut off from the real life of the streets, inhumanly respectable as a top-hat. Mechanical golf and dinner parties and bridge and conversation . . . mechanical friendships—back-slapping and jocular, never daring to essay the test of quietness. [Lewis, 1922, p. 323]

Whyte's quintessential organization man seems to be quite similar: colorless, dull, and unimaginative. We are faced with a person afraid to make bold decisions, an individual far removed from his opposite, the conquistador of business or the entrepreneur. His description of the organization man also reminds us of Erich Fromm's speculations about the proliferation of a marketing orientation, a form of acting and behaving that he believed to be typical of modern life. Fromm's marketing-oriented person is someone with a shaky feeling of identity, an individual exceedingly superficial and very changeable in his attitudes. For this person, identity seems to be made up of the sum total of the roles he can be expected to play. Thus, "the premise of the marketing orientation is emptiness, the lack of any specific quality which would not be subject to change, since any persistent trait of character might conflict someday with the requirements of the market" (Fromm, 1947, p. 85).

This sense of depersonalization, automation, and emptiness of life comes across very well in Harrington's (1958) ironic presentation of *Life in a Crystal Palace*. In the "crystal palace," a metaphor for a large organization, everything seems to be bland and mechanical. Life is deadening; conversation seems to be merely a "filler," a way of avoiding silence. Everybody automatically and completely accepts and lives according to the organization's policies and procedures. From the author's descriptions, the crystal palace turns into a corporate theater where conformity rules, all the actors are interchangeable, and no one dares to call attention to himself.

In his book *The Gamesman*, Michael Maccoby (1976) presents a more nuanced view of corporate man. He regards the company man as one among a number of types. In his analysis, this individual is less of a caricature; he portrays a person essential to the functioning of the large corporation. This person gives it its strength because of his strong identification with the organization's goals and values. At the same time, however, Maccoby warned against the company man's excessive reactions of dependency, since he tends to feel lost when separated from his organization. To use Maccoby's (1976) words:

Although the company man's work tends to reinforce a responsible attitude to the organization and the project, it may also strengthen a negative syndrome of dependency: submissive surrender to the organization and to authority, sentimental idealization of those in power, a tendency to betray the self in order to gain security, comfort, luxury. [p. 94]

The work of the cultural historian Christopher Lasch echoes this theme of conformity and dependency, which he believes is accentuated by the fact that "the corporation takes on the appearance of a total institution, in which every trace of individual identity disappears" (Lasch, 1984, p. 70).

All these descriptions beg the question as to whether Whyte had identified a specific personality type or was merely trying to satirize organizational life. The appeal of his book and the continuing popularity of its theme do indicate, however, that Whyte must have hit a sensitive chord among businessmen and other people familiar with organizations. It seems that his view of organizational life led to immediate recognition of a pattern that was present in contemporary business culture.

Although he and others dealing with the same theme may sometimes have resorted to stereotypes or oversimplifications, there was something true in what they were saying. Given the kind of impact these authors had, the key question becomes, Why do people in organizational life be- **205** have in such a way? Is there something in organizations that accentuates this behavior pattern? What do organizations do to people? Are certain otherwise dormant personality characteristics more likely to come out into the open in organizations? Or should the question be put differently: Is there a group of people with specific personality characteristics who are attracted to certain types of organizations? Can one compare given organizations to "holding stations" that offer a comfortable but unobtrusive shelter to people with specific predilections?

In answering these questions, Whyte did not have the advantage of using some of the more contemporary conceptualizations of personality. Taking his sociological bent into consideration, he left in-depth psychological speculation to others. But perhaps the time has come to take up where he left off. Given the importance of the behavior patterns described, particularly since such behavior does not usually foster organizational creativity and innovation, the objective of this chapter is to take another look at the organization man and make inferences about his or her existence. In order to arrive at a deeper level of analysis, the organization man's behavior will be explored in the context of a relatively recent clinical construct called *alexithymia*. The study of such a construct offers the opportunity to understand better the development of a specific style of interaction, particularly as it relates to the emotions. As the subsequent discussion will show, there are many interesting parallels between the organization man and the alexithymic disposition. This exploration will also give us the opportunity to make tentative observations as to whether there are certain types of organizations that enhance this mode of behavior and whether there are specific jobs where the behavior is prominent. Such a study is, of course, by its nature speculative. Pursuing this line of investigation may, however, shed light on the reasons for the obstinate survival of the organization man and may also further understanding of the nature of the interface and fit between personality and organization.

The Nature of Alexithymia

In 1963, two French psychoanalysts, Marty and de M'Uzan, identified a style of thought and expression that they named *pensée opératoire*. In studying psychosomatic patients, they found a cognitive and affective style where there was a conspicuous absence of fantasy, little dream recollections, and an unusual, utilitarian way of thinking. They also noticed that in responding to questions, these people would behave in a rather robot-like manner and repeat in great detail past action without enlarging upon their activities. As de M'Uzan (1974) put it: "The patient's language is poor, flat and banal, glued to the present, and only producing facts stated chronologically" (p. 462).

Sifneos (1972, 1973) noticed similar patterns in his psychosomatic patients. He too stressed these individuals' inability to find words to describe emotions, as well as their use of action to express emotion and avoid conflict, their preoccupation with external events rather than fantasy or emotions, and their tendency to describe endlessly the circumstances surrounding an event rather than their feelings. To him goes the credit for having first coined the term *alexithymia*, a word constructed from the Greek meaning "no words for emotions." He and a colleague pursued this line of research and viewed alexithymia as some kind of communication disorder (Nemiah and Sifneos, 1970; Nemiah, 1977, 1978).

Independently, Krystal (1968, 1974, 1982) was coming to similar conclusions while studying severe posttraumatic states. He noted that alexithymic individuals seem to have defects in affective and cognitive functioning and in interpersonal relationships, due to an impoverished intrapsychic life. Elaborating on these differentiating characteristics, Krystal (1979) stated that the people in question "are unable to distinguish between one emotion and another" (p. 17), but, "like the color-blind person, they have become aware of their deficiency and have learned to pick up clues by which they infer what they cannot discern" (p. 18). With respect to their cognitive problems, he mentioned that it almost seems as if these people are superadjusted to reality. He continued by saying, however, that if one gets "past the superficial impression of superb functioning, one discovers a sterility and monotony of ideas and severe impoverishment of their imagination" (Krystal, 1979, p. 19). With respect to their relationships with others, Krystal noticed an impaired capacity for empathy: these people treat others with cool detachment and indifference. The pattern was supported by others, who observed that when dealing with such individuals one is left with a feeling of dullness, boredom, and frustration (Taylor, 1977). Encouraged by these findings, many other researchers and clinicians in the fields of psychiatry, medical psychology, and psychotherapy recalled and recognized similar behavior patterns (Brautigan and Von Rad, 1977).

In this context, it is important to mention the work of one clinician, McDougall, who, cognizant of the high degree of social conformity among alexithymics, used the words "pseudonormality" (1974), "robots" (1980a), and "normopaths" (1984) to describe these people. She argued:

> Instead of some form of psychic management of disturbing affects or unwelcome knowledge or fantasies, the ego may achieve complete destruction of the representations or feelings concerned, so that these are not registered. The result then may be a *super adaptation to external reality*, a robot-like adjustment to inner and outer pressure which short-circuits the world of the imaginary. This "pseudo-normality" is a widespread character trait and may well be a danger sign pointing to the eventuality of psychosomatic symptoms. [McDougall, 1974, p. 444]

207

The origin of this behavior, she speculates, is due to a special kind of parenting whereby the mother tends to use the child as a "drug" (1974, 1980b, 1982a, b). In arguing her case, she presents clinical material demonstrating that from the beginning the mother seems to be out of touch with the child's emotional needs. Many other studies (Krystal, 1979, 1982; Gardos, Schniebolk, Mirin, Wolk, and Rosenthal, 1984) have supported her conjecture that the pathogenesis of alexithymia is created in the first and second years of life. What a number of clinicians suggest is that these mothers (and fathers) solve their own, often narcissistic conflicts through the child, who gets stuck in what may be described as an aborted symbiotic relationship. The child finds him- or herself in a sort of archaic double-bind situation; hence, a state of extreme dependency is artificially prolonged. Separation and autonomous feelings of identity are stifled, and real individuation is prevented. The child is treated like an extension of the mother and is under her constant surveillance; his or her body is handled like someone else's property. Furthermore, the father may even covertly encourage this type of situation in order to be spared a similar "fate," afraid as he may be of the perceived "engulfing" qualities of his wife.

Given such childrearing practice, the mother is not what has sometimes been described as a *mère satisfaisante* (a satisfying mother), but instead becomes a *mère calmante* (a tranquilizing mother). Due to her own problems, the mother does not allow normal identification processes to occur. Consequently, the child never really learns how to feel at ease without being in continual contact with her. He or she does not internalize the *mère satisfaisante*, a necessary process if he or she is going to be able to manage without needing continuous external stimuli (Fain and Kreisher, 1970). The overbearing treatment of the child can probably be looked at as the mother's way of arriving at some form of restitution for assumed defects of her own. Since separation is discouraged, any desire for exploration or any form of initiative is nipped in the bud. Predictably, such treatment has grave consequences for later personality development. Since the mother does not allow for satisfactory transitional space (Winnicott, 1975), she disrupts the process of play, exploration, and symbolization. Moreover, the child does not really experience whatever symbolizations are formed as his or her own mental productions but as something alien coming from the outside. Such a situation can lead to an arrest in affect development (Krystal, 1979, 1982). Differentiation, verbalization, and desomatization of emotions never properly occur, impeding construction of a highly complex matrix of signals essential for daily functioning (as opposed to experiencing emotions as dangerous, potentially uncontrollable forces). These people consequently ignore their bodies' signs and their minds' signals of distress. Symbol formation will be impaired, and a stilted fantasy life may become a reality. Vague somatic sensations will frequently replace dream and fantasy material. Moreover, given their earlier situation of dependency, they may become addictively captive to external stimuli, a lifeline that can structure their world, unable as they are to resort to their own symbolic representations, fantasies, or dreams to work through mental conflict. To use McDougall's (1982b) words, what they "feel will appear in the people [they are] involved with. They are [their] mirror" (p. 88). They attempt *to make substitute objects in the external world do duty for symbolic ones which are absent or damaged in the inner psychic world*" (p. 449). But it is her opinion that such attempts are "doomed to failure" and will lead "to endless repetition and addictive attachment to the outer world and external objects" (p. 449).

Hence, these people are preoccupied with the concrete and the objective; the use of metaphors, allusions, and hidden meanings is strange to them. They tend to negate and deny the existence of emotions (Von Rad, 1983). They somehow seem to be psychological illiterates lacking the capacity for empathy, strangers as they are to reflective self-awareness, and needing to resort to action as a way of dealing with conflicts (Neill and Sandifer, 1982; Lesser and Lesser, 1983; Taylor, 1984). Given their capacity to negate and deny emotions, they are probably not even aware of or experience intrapsychic conflict. Their behavior has a robot-like quality with stiffness of posture and often a lack of facial expressiveness. External details seem to be utilized as a way of filling their inner deadness. Due to the nature of their upbringing, their "true self" (Winnicott, 1975) has never been allowed to emerge.

Some clinicians have differentiated between primary and secondary forms of alexithymia. In the first instance, alexithymia is viewed as a specific character trait caused by possible genetic neurophysiological deficits, that is, a disconnection between the left and right hemispheres due to a commissurotomy, or by early psychic trauma; while in the second instance, sociocultural factors may play a role. There, reference is made to alexithymic reactions that may develop after a specific stressful event or series of events. In this regard, some researchers have looked at rather extreme situations. Examples are the kind of emotional numbing that occurs in the case of concentration camp victims or Vietnam War veterans (Freiberger, 1977; Shipko, Alvarez, and Norello, 1983; Krystal, Giller, and Cicchetti, 1986).

What we can infer from these studies is that alexithymia as communication disorder tends to be relatively widespread. As with most clinical syndromes, estimates of its prevalence among the general population vary, however. For example, one study using undergraduate students as subjects showed that 8.2 percent of the men and 1.8 percent of the women fell within the alexithymic range (Blanchard, Arena, and Pallmeyer, 1981). But this study raises questions about the validity and reliability of the instruments.

209

Whatever the exact percentage of alexithymics in the general population may be, this construct is used to describe individuals with an extreme reality-based cognitive style, an impoverished fantasy life, a paucity of inner emotional experiences, a tendency to engage in stereotypical interpersonal behavior, and a speech pattern characterized by endless, trivial, repetitive details. This last characteristic seems to be the outcome of the need to find some kind of foothold in the external world due to the difficulty these people experience internally in describing what they feel. Whatever feelings they may have tend to be of a vague, diffuse nature. Here, however, is where agreement seems to end. Although psychodynamic inferences have gone a long way toward an explanation, there is still a considerable amount of confusion about the construct's etiology. Is it really a trait? Or is it a situation-specific form of coping behavior? Can it be both trait and state (Von Rad, 1984; Ahrens and Deffner, 1986)? The answers to these questions are not yet clear.

In spite of this confusion, however, what is clear is that the existence of alexithymia is based on a large body of consistent clinical and phenomenological observations. In addition, alexithymia is not an all-or-nothing phenomenon. On the contrary, it appears to be potentially accessible to everyone, admittedly to a varying degree. It seems to be a graded dimension whereby individuals will occupy different positions on a spectrum of cognitive/affective experience and expression (Martin, Phil, and Dobkin, 1984). Moreover, insidiously, these alexithymic inclinations may influence our perceptions and actions. Given what we now know about alexithymic individuals, what is particularly noteworthy for the purposes of this chapter is that, in their behavior, they resemble in an uncanny way the organization man.

The Organization Man's Alexithymic Predisposition

Many years ago, an astute observer of organizational life wrote the following lines about some of its characteristics:

> The dominance of the spirit of formalistic impersonality, "*sine via et studio*," without hatred or passion, and hence without affection or enthusiasm. The dominant norms are concepts of straightforward duty without regard to personal considerations. Everyone is subject to formal equality of treatment, that is, everyone in the same empirical situation. This is the spirit in which the ideal official conducts his office. [Weber, 1947, p. 340]

Reading Max Weber's description of the bureaucrat, we recall the alexithymic's factual, unemotional, and unimaginative way of behaving and acting. We remember the wooden quality implicit in such behavior. Since alexithymics don't know how to manage their emotions, it is easy to perceive how little room they have for feelings. We can actually observe how the people in question will often substitute action, inappropriate as it may be, for feelings. Moreover, we have noted how, when asked how they feel, these people will usually resort to a description of external events. For them, "facts" seem to be what counts. Some people pervert what originally may have been a realistic concern. They have difficulty going beyond this obsession with facts, unable as they are to use their imaginations. They seem to suffer from a deficiency in utilizing feelings and fantasies in their mental functioning. Their behavior appears to be almost overadaptive. But we may discover, that is to say, if we go beyond the first impression of excellent functioning, the sterility of their imaginations and the monotony of their ideas. We can also recall the impression of blandness, dullness, and colorlessness with which we are left when dealing with such people.

Organizational Types

Organizations give alexithymics great opportunities to blend into the organizational culture. These organizational environments legitimize what otherwise may be looked at as strange behavior. As such, they give relief in providing some kind of structure, thus making alexithymic behavior less conspicuous; organizations take on a "containing" function (Bion, 1961). Moreover, given the possibility of the existence of such a phenomenon as secondary alexithymia, it may very well be that certain types of organizations go even further in that they possess the kind of numbing quality that awakens dormant alexithymic tendencies in their employees.

In looking at organizational factors that can contribute to this kind of behavior, we are reminded in particular of two organizational "ideal" types described in earlier research (Kets de Vries and Miller, 1985, 1986, 1988): the "compulsive" and "depressive" organizations. In the former, we find an organization that is bureaucratic and tends to be inwardly focused. A strict hierarchy exists in which an individual manager's status derives directly from a specific position. The leadership tends to dominate the organization from top to bottom, insisting that others conform to tightly prescribed rules and procedures. Slavish adherence to programmed, standardized, routine practices is the norm. There is strategic reliance on a narrow, established theme to the exclusion of other factors. Rigid formal codes, ritualized evaluation processes, and an attitude of risk aversion makes any form of change an extremely difficult proposition.

The "depressive" organization is similar in many ways but is in worse shape. This type of organization drifts with no sense of direction and is often confined to antiquated "mature" markets. Various protectionistic practices are the only reason it still survives. Extreme conservatism, a very vague set of goals and strategies, and an absence of plans are the rule. Structurally, these organizations are bureaucratic, ritualistic, and inflexible. There is a leadership vacuum, a lack of motivation and initiative, and an attitude of passivity and negativity. Communications are poor and so is scanning, as there is ignorance of market trends. The organizational climate is impersonal, "decidophobia" being the rule, leading to a great resistance to change.

From the description of these two types of organizations, we can see how well they fit with the alexithymic disposition. They provide an ideal holding environment that makes alexithymics less conspicuous. At the same time, we should not forget the effect of the organization on the individual, with its potential to bring out otherwise dormant alexithymic characteristics. Although other types of organizations may have similar effects, none has that kind of numbing quality that we find in the "compulsive" and "depressive" organizations.

Individual Styles

The Detached CEO. Going from an organizational to an individual orientation, we can occasionally find top executives who experience great difficulty in dealing with emotions. To protect themselves from emotional involvement these people may use a detached style. McDougall (1982b) has already equated alexithymic symptoms "to a form of schizoid withdrawal from others and to the maintenance of a devitalized inner state of which the individual is unaware" (p. 88). This form of emotional isolation can, however, have serious organizational repercussions since such behavior may frustrate the dependency needs of the other executives, leading to feelings of bewilderment and aggressiveness (Kets de Vries and Miller, 1985, 1986, 1988). A highly politicized organizational culture may develop a playground for second-tier "gamesmen" (Maccoby, 1976). Warring and uncooperative fiefdoms may be the consequences. If so, self-imposed barriers to the free flow of information will prevail. With such an organizational culture, it is no wonder that there is insufficient scanning of the external environment; the focus of the organization is more internal. A vacillating, inconsistent, muddling-through type of strategy can usually be observed, its orientation depending on which clique managed to get the ear of the senior executive.

In this case, we can see how alexithymic behavior at the top, given the dynamics of power, can have serious organizational consequences. We don't have to go all the way to the top, however, to find this type of behavior. There are certain kinds of jobs that suit the alexithymic disposition very well. Here, two groups of people come to mind, both of which show a type of behavior also observed in the context of the schizoid condition (Kets de Vries, 1980).

212

The Systems Person. These people will disguise their interpersonal difficulties by resorting to jobs that are thing-oriented. Abstractions, tasks, ideas, and inanimate objects become of overriding importance. Feelings are superfluous here; what really counts is "the system." Their contacts with others are depersonalized and mechanical. Attachment to procedures and rules and regulations becomes their way of coping with the sterility of their inner world. The present information revolution is a great facilitator in making such behavior less conspicuous. The increasing importance of the human/computer interface becomes a marvelous disguise for some of the people in question. The systems person operates in an automaton-like way, hanging on to fixed routines or zealously advocating abstractions and thereby abolishing relationships with real people. His or her pace is directed, and stimulus is provided by the terminal of his or her computer. Such people seem to be perfectly programmed. Unfortunately, with their often mindless and rigid pursuit of routines, curiosity and initiative are missing. Hence, they may not possess a sufficient adaptive capacity to cope with environmental changes, a deficiency that can have devastating consequences for the organization.

The Social Sensor. The behavior of these people has a chameleon-like quality. They are the role players par excellence, taking on new roles when it suits them. They are very astute in picking up signals from the outside world and adjust their behavior accordingly. The only structure they know seems to come from the external environment. They are the "as if" personalities described as having "a highly plastic readiness to pick up signals from the outer world and to mold oneself and one's behavior accordingly" (Deutsch, 1965, p. 265). They resemble the marketing-oriented people referred to by Erich Fromm (1947). They are also like the color-blind persons described by Krystal (1979, 1982), those who have learned how to cover up their deficiencies in affectual reactions. And they fit very well in service-oriented industries where "prescribed" emotions frequently become the norm. But in spite of all their efforts and notwithstanding their superficial adjustment, a sense of conviction is lacking in their actions. Although the first impression is one of complete normality and they seem to be superadaptive, under the veneer one quickly discovers a sense of desperate shallowness and lack of warmth. Changeability in their attitudes and their talent for mimicry seem to be their only permanent qualities. Their glibness in behavior makes for a notion of pseudosincerity and pseudoauthenticity. Their superadaptability and pseudocompliance seem to take place with only one goal in mind, that is, to avoid having to deal with feelings. What seems like adaptiveness is really insensitivity to the feelings and reactions of the people around them. The mask of extroversion becomes a disguise for the emptiness of their "inner theater." Given the deadness of their inner world, creativity and insight will be found wanting.

213

Searching for Solutions

Although the alexithymic predisposition, be it primary or secondary, is something that a number of executives possess or at least are susceptible to, albeit to varying degrees, this does not mean we cannot do something about it. Granted, we have seen how some individuals perpetuate the situation by finding jobs that shelter them from circumstances that may demand affective responses, and we have observed how some people manage to pursue rather stunted lifestyles. We have seen how such behavior, when it involves top managers, can sometimes influence the overall organization dramatically. We have also noted how organizations may take advantage of alexithymic predispositions and, through particular structural and strategic arrangements, even accentuate such a situation in their organizational cultures through the suppression or exact prescription of emotion (Hochschild, 1983). We have seen how the information and service revolution with all its accompaniments has very much facilitated this behavior.

In our assessment of alexithymic behavior we have observed that, in general, organizations do not appreciate it when people do own up to their emotions. In large bureaucratic organizations, affect is avoided; "greyness" in dress, behavior, and actions appears to be the norm; and conformity is the prevailing pattern. Even sexuality seems to be eradicated (Burrell, 1984). All in all, the executive and "the man in the grey flannel suit" are apparently almost synonymous. Expression of emotion is feared to disrupt organizational processes, or emotion is carefully managed with all the associated strains due to the suppression of one's "true self" (Winnicott, 1975). The climb to the executive suite is not enhanced by eccentricity in behavior. Executives have to "fit," and that does not necessarily make for the best and the brightest. However, we should also take note that in this context, innovation and creativity in organizations do not come from alexithymic-oriented behavior. For creativity in organizations we need bold moves, leaps of imagination, passion, and vision.

To break the vicious circle of emotionlessness is not going to be easy. Unfortunately, there are no quick fixes to the problem. This does not mean, however, that nothing can be done about it, that alexithymic behavior patterns in organizations are inevitable. But if change is desired, if there is a wish to enliven organizational life, it will need a sustained effort.

214

When we look at "ideal types," meaning in this instance the "heroes" of the business world, we notice that the ones who tend to be admired most are those who engage in bold action. It is leaders such as Iacocca, Jobs, and Ross Perot, people with "fire in their belly," who are chosen as examples of how to run corporations. And in light of their behavior and actions these people are no strangers to emotion.

What this tells us is that executives do not have to be alexithymic to succeed. They do not necessarily have to give in to potential alexithymic tendencies in their make-up. The negative sides of the organization man and the stifling effects of organizational life can be avoided. But in order to be able to do so, both the manager and the organization have a responsibility. The manager has to take the initiative and establish preventive steps. Here, Whyte went even further and argued for a combative attitude on the part of the organization man.

> The organization man is not in the grip of vast social forces about which it is impossible for him to do anything; the options are there, and with wisdom and foresight he can turn the future away from the dehumanized collective that so haunts our thoughts. . . . He must fight The Organization. Not stupidly or selfishly, for the defects of individual self-regard are no more to be venerated than the defects of cooperation. But fight he must, for the demands for his surrender are constant and powerful; and the more he has come to like the life of organization the more difficult does he find it to resist these demands, or even to recognize them. It is wretched dispiriting advice to hold before him the dream that ideally there need be no conflict between him and society. There always is; there always must be. [Whyte, 1956, p. 404]

We don't have to go that far and preach revolution. However, to create more effective organizations, an effort must be made to help executives own up to their emotions and practice their capacity for reflective self-observation. The tendency of many executives merely to give in to "flight into action" (Klein, 1935) without the balance of reflection has to be carefully monitored. Executives have to discover or rediscover the ability to "play," learn how to use humor and how to engage in flights of fancy. It is from such characteristics that vision and adaptability derive. Executives should be able to confront their feelings and not remain prisoners of a fictitious balance for which they are partially responsible. They should not hide their true selves, but show authenticity in action. They should try to overcome infantile fixations and aims. To do so, imaginative experience and fantasy production must be encouraged, even if, paradoxically, this has to be done in a directed way. Not only therapists but also organizational leaders can play an important role fostering such practices. More important, organizational leadership can set the example that the expression of emotion is an acceptable practice by showing it themselves. They also should encourage a diversity in emotional expression and not just stick to prescribed routines. Of course, to make this work within the organization, a climate of trust becomes a necessity. Executives should come to realize that the expression of emotion in a business context does **215** not have negative career implications, that there is room for critical give and take and space for imagination.

Other signals can be given by the organization through structural arrangements that encourage risk-taking, experimentation, and participation. In order to foster such behavior, there will also be a need for imagination in human resource practices with respect to hiring, training, and development, which will in turn avoid creating organizations populated by "clones." Encouraging a positive attitude toward change should become a central concern. For the purposes of establishing a culture of change, slack in the system will be needed to allow for continuous adaptation and development. Naturally, not only should structures be hospitable to change and adaptation, but so should individuals. To be able to do so, however, further exploratory work will be needed to understand better the nature and prevalence of alexithymia in organizations. A greater knowledge of this behavior pattern may be helpful to arrive at a more complete equilibration between individual style and organizational infra- and suprastructure. And in balancing these forces, we could keep in mind the words of Yeats, who once said: "By logic and reason we die hourly; by imagination we live!"

REFERENCES

Ahrens, S., and G. Deffner. 1986. "Empirical Study of Alexithymia: Methodology and Results." *American Journal of Psychiatry*, 40 (3), 430–447.

Bion, S. G. 1961. *Experiences in Groups*. London: Tavistock.

Blanchard, E. B., J. G. Arena, T. P. Pallmeyer. 1981. "Psychosomatic Properties of a Scale to Measure Alexithymia." *Psychotherapy and Psychosomatics*, 35, 64–71.

Brautigan, B., and M. Von Rad. 1977. *Toward a Theory of Psychosomatic Disorders*. Basel: Karger.

Burrell, G. 1984. "Sex and Organizational Analysis." *Organization Studies*, 5(2), 97–118.

Deutsch, H. 1965. *Neuroses and Character Types*. New York: International Universities Press.

Fain, M., and L. Kreisher. 1970. "Discussion sur la genèse des fonctions représentatives." *Revue Française de Psychanalyse*, 34, 285–306.

Freiberger, H. 1977. "Supportive Psychotherapeutic Techniques in Primary and Secondary Alexithymia." *Psychotherapy and Psychosomatics*, 20, 337–342.

Fromm, E. 1947. *Man for Himself: An Inquiry into the Psychiatry of Ethics*. New York: Fawcett.

Gardos, G., S. Schniebolk, S. M. Mirin, P. Wolk, and K. L. Rosenthal. 1984. "Alexithymia: Toward Validation and Measurement." *Comprehensive Psychiatry*, 25(3), 278–282.

Harrington, A. 1958. *Life in a Crystal Palace*. New York: Alfred A. Knopf.

Hochschild, A. R. 1983. *The Managed Heart*. Berkeley: University of California Press.

Kets de Vries, M. F. R. 1980. *Organizational Paradoxes: Clinical Approaches to Management*. London: Tavistock.

Kets de Vries, M. F. R., and D. Miller. 1985. *The Neurotic Organization*. San Francisco: Jossey-Bass.

———. 1986. "Personality, Culture and Organization." *Academy of Management Review*, 11(2), 266–279.

———. 1988. *Unstable at the Top: Inside the Neurotic Organization*. New York: New American Library.

Klein, M. 1935. "A Contribution to the Psychogenesis of Manic-Depressive States." *International Journal of Psycho-Analysis*, 16.

———. 1964. "A Contribution to the Psychogenesis of Manic-Depressive States." In *Contributions to Psychoanalysis, 1921–1945*. International Psycho-Analytic Library, No. 34. New York: McGraw-Hill.

Krystal, H. 1968. *Massive Psychic Trauma*. New York: International Universities Press.

———. 1974. "The Genetic Development of Affects and Affect Regression." *Annual of Psychoanalysis* (Part 2), 98–126.

———. 1979. "Alexithymia and Psychotherapy." *American Journal of Psychotherapy*, 33, 17–31.

———. 1982. "Alexithymia and the Effectiveness of Psychoanalytic Treatment." *International Journal of Psychoanalytic Psychotherapy*, 9, 353–378.

Krystal, J. H., E. L. Giller, and V. Cicchetti. 1986. "Assessment of Alexithymia in Post-Traumatic Stress Disorder and Somatic Illness: Introduction of a Reliable Measure." *Psychosomatic Medicine*, 48(½), 84–94.

Lasch, C. 1984. *The Minimal Self—Psychic Survival in Troubled Times*. New York: W.W. Norton.

Lesser, I. M., and B. Z. Lesser. 1983. "Alexithymia: Examining the Development of a Psychological Concept." *American Journal of Psychiatry*, 140(10), 1305–1308.

Lewis, S. *Babbitt*. 1922. New York: P. F. Collier and Son.

Maccoby, M. 1976. *The Gamesman*. New York: Simon and Schuster.

Martin, J. B., R. O. Phil, and P. Dobkin. 1984. "Schalling-Sifneos Personality Scale: Findings and Recommendations." *Psychotherapy and Psychosomatics*, 41, 145–152.

Marty, P., and M. de M'Uzan. 1963. "La pensée opératoire." *Revue Française de Psychanalyse*, 27, 1345–1354.

McDougall, J. 1974. "The Psychosoma and the Psychoanalytic Process." *International Review of Psychoanalysis*, 1, 437–459.

———. 1980a. "The Anti-Analysant in Analysis." In S. Lebovici and D. Widlöcher (eds.), *Psychoanalysis in France*. New York: International Universities Press.

———. 1980b. *Plea for a Measure of Abnormality*. New York: International Universities Press.

————. 1982a. "Alexithymia, Psychosomatics, and Psychosis." *International Journal of Psychoanalytic Psychotherapy*, 9, 379–388.

————. 1982b. "Alexithymia: A Psychoanalytic Viewpoint." *Psychotherapy and Psychosomatics*, 38, 81–90.

————. 1984. "The Dis-affected Patient: Reflections on Affect Pathology." *Psychoanalytic Quarterly*, 53, 386–409.

de M'Uzan, J. 1974. "Analytical Process and the Notion of the Past." *International Review of Psychoanalysis*, 1, 461–466.

Neill, J. R., and M. G. Sandifer. 1982. "The Clinical Approach to Alexithymia: A Review." *Psychosomatics*, 23, 1223–1231.

Nemiah, J. C. 1977. "Alexithymia: Theoretical Considerations." *Psychotherapy and Psychosomatics*, 28, 199–206.

————. 1978. "Alexithymia and Psychosomatic Illness." *Journal of Continuing Education in Psychiatry*, 39, 25–27.

Nemiah, J. C., and E. Sifneos. 1970. "Affect and Fantasy in Patients with Psychosomatic Disorders." In O. Hill (ed.), *Modern Trends in Psychosomatic Medicine* (Vol. 2). London: Butterworths.

Shipko, S. W., W. A. Alvarez, and N. Norrello. 1983. "Towards a Teleological Model of Alexithymia: Alexithymia and Post-Traumatic Stress Disorder." *Psychotherapy and Psychosomatics*, 39, 122–126.

Sifneos, P. E. 1972. *Short-Term Psychotherapy and Emotional Crisis*. Cambridge, Mass.: Harvard University Press.

————. 1973. "The Prevalence of Alexithymic Characteristics in Psychosomatic Patients." *Psychotherapy and Psychosomatics*, 22, 255–262.

Taylor, G. J. 1977. "Alexithymia and the Counter-Transference." *Psychotherapy and Psychosomatics*, 28, 141–147.

————. 1984. "Alexithymia: Concept, Measurement and Implications for Treatment." *American Journal of Psychiatry*, 141(6), 725–732.

Von Rad, M. 1983. *Alexithymie, Empirische Untersuchen zur Diagnostik und Therpaie Psychosomatische Kranker*. Berlin: Springer Verlag.

————. 1984. "Alexithymia and Symptom Formation." *Psychotherapy and Psychosomatics*, 42, 80–89.

Weber, M. 1947. *The Theory of Social and Economic Organization*. Translated by A. M. Henderson and T. Parsons. New York: Oxford University Press.

Whyte, W. H. 1956. *The Organization Man*. New York: Simon and Schuster.

Winnicott, D. W. 1975. *Through Pediatrics to Psycho-Analysis*. London: Hogarth Press and the Institute of Psycho-Analysis.

217

CHAPTER 14

Bureaucracy as Externalized Self-System: A View from the Psychological Interior

Michael A. Diamond

Bureaucracy has been described externally as the product of modern civilization (Weber, 1968a). Much subsequent work has delved into detail from this external perspective—a sociological one. This chapter attempts to illustrate what bureaucracy looks like from the inside out, from a psychodynamic perspective, by applying Harry Stack Sullivan's interpersonal theory of psychiatry to an analysis of bureaucratic behavior.

The psychodynamic perspective uncovers the fact that bureacracy in modern culture is the result of psychological defenses in operation. It is an unintentional, but nevertheless actual, externalized self-system. Tendencies for bureaucratization of human relations in the workplace are the result of externalized interpersonal defense mechanisms.[1] This chapter suggests to what extent bureaucratized human relations and formal orga-

Reprinted from *Administration & Society*, vol. 16, no. 2 (August 1984), 195–214. © 1984 Sage Publications, Inc. Reprinted by permission of Sage Publications, Inc.

nizational structures are products of the psyche and thereby perpetuated by people. Further, this chapter intends to direct future empirical research toward the topics of interpersonal and organizational resistance to change and psychological reliance on bureaucratic styles of management.

In the following section, I describe briefly the bureaucratic model, maintaining, as did German sociologist Max Weber, that the theory of bureaucracy represents an ideal against which we measure and contrast existing social structures. Here I borrow from the pioneering works of Weber so that we may share the same image of bureaucracy. Subsequently, I introduce Sullivan's interpersonal psychiatry and those concepts germane to our discussion of the bureaucratic experience. After this brief presentation of Sullivan's work, I analyze the connection between bureaucracy and self-system operations from a psychodynamic perspective, drawing on several psychoanalytic applications of organization theory.

220

Constructing the Bureaucratic Image

According to Weber, bureaucratic structures consist of the following: (1) a hierarchy of supersubordinate authority relationships, (2) administrative rules to guide organizational tasks, (3) decision-making procedures according to technical and legal rules, (4) administrative behavior based on the maintenance of files and records, and (5) administration as a vocation in which the private lives of public officials are considered separate from the office occupied, reinforcing a prevailing norm of impersonality of interpersonal relationships (Weber, 1948, pp. 196–198).

Formal characteristics of bureaucracy tend to neutralize the otherwise personal, emotional, irrational, and often political behavior of its human inmates. As Weber himself understood, bureaucracy offers the civil servant job security and compensation along with a high degree of certainty of expectations and performance in return for the relinquishment of independence and autonomy of action. To meet the human needs of predictability and certainty, bureaucracy emphasizes control and efficiency of operations in rationally defined, instrumental, means-ends administration.

Social scientists like Robert Presthus, Erich Fromm, Harold Lasswell, Michael Maccoby, and recently, Douglas LaBier suggest that these organizational characteristics foster certain personality types "whose skill and behavior reflect the demands of organizational society" (Presthus, 1978, p. 5). My purpose is to suggest not only that such organizational characteristics promote certain personality types, but more fundamentally, that people perpetuate these bureaucratic forms on the basis of interpersonal security needs. Next I present Sullivan's theory of personality and self-system. Later I discuss self-system tendencies manifested in bureaucratic constructs of organizing human relations. I suggest a logical connection between structured security needs and their defensive operations of the self-system and bureaucratic behavior. Bureaucracy, as a mental construct, expresses reified defense mechanisms against anxiety.

Personality and Self-System:
Countervailing Need Structures

Self-systems are motivational forces of psychic energy within the personality concentrating on the maintenance of interpersonal security and the avoidance of anxiety. More simply, self-systems are learned defensive activities against anxiety—anxiety caused by the loss of security or self-esteem. For Sullivan, self-systems are cultivated, somewhat unwittingly, by one's constant experience with threats of anxiety.[2] Anxiety is first experienced by way of linkage with the mother during infancy. Unfortunately, at the time of our earliest experiences with anxiety during infancy, we lack the defensive structures of a self-system to resist any onslaught of uncanny, bad feelings.

221

As the object relations theorists of psychoanalysis have explained: given the early state of fusion between mother and infant, the anxiety of the mother is incorporated into the world of the infant, where no distinction or boundaries between self and other (ego functions) yet exist. Consequently, the infant internalizes both good and bad feelings during the preverbal, empathic relationship with the caretaker-mother. These intense feelings represent internalized "objects" affecting one's developing sense of self or ego and further set the stage for later development of the self-system's security operations that crystallize during the juvenile years from five to nine. Early "object" relations with parents form internalized images of self-worth and greatly affect the degree of self-system defense activities against the anxiety caused by loss of security and low self-esteem. Self-systems indicate our generalized, mostly covert, needs for recognition, response, security, and self-esteem.

Human behavior in bureaucracy is an expression of self-system needs. In particular, security needs are a component of human instinct; the extent or degree to which they drive the personality to action depends upon the satisfaction of recognition, response, security, and self-esteem acquired from the organization of interpersonal experience in the environment. The degree to which security operations of the human self-system narrow and distort cognitive functions is relative to the level of anxiety or perceived anxiety that the individual experiences as a direct threat to the self—a lowering of security and self-esteem produced by the environment. Self-system activities of the human personality are a result of the human organism's encounter with culture. Bureaucracy is a human product of the self-system. Hierarchical and impersonal, it encourages defensive behavior and self-protectiveness that use self-system components of personality for maintenance of security and avoidance of anxiety. Here, human behavior (which is motivated by the need for security) is not merely expressed, but reinforced by the structure of bureaucracy.

According to Sullivan, "security operations" of the self-system encompass many forms of defensive psychic configurations (such as selective inattention and parataxic distortions) that often distort and confine one's reality in the interests of avoiding anxiety. Self-systems function to censor potential experiences, information, and knowledge that might stimulate anxiety and loss of security. A threatening (potentially anxiety-ridden) environment, perceived by the person or group of people, will activate security operations of self-systems, resulting in some distortion of reality and cognition. That is, self-systems may serve a protective function for the person by narrowing one's cognitive scope on reality and limiting one's actions to the familiar and routine. However, these security operations against anxiety protect the person from unsettling change and disorientation at the price of not recognizing necessary change and healthy adaptive response, and jeopardizing our ability to learn from experience in order to take action to change.

An example of such massive social denial in the interests of security needs is the case of the Jews of the Warsaw ghetto during Germany's occupation of Poland in World War II. Jewish resistance to the Nazis was delayed by fantasies, illusions, and distortions of reality—a form of massive selective inattention. Until the final outburst of resistance, many Jews attempted to live their lives as usual, relying on familiar routines and rituals. Intuitive judgments and common sense were suspended for security needs and a wish to return to the status quo. Denial and separation from a threatening reality were functions of active security operations of the group self-system.

An organizational example of social denial in the interests of security needs (what Sullivan might refer to as a case of selective inattention) is management's failure, in the American automobile industry, to respond adequately to Japan's challenge in the international marketplace. Clearly, political, economic, cultural, and technological factors offer a partial explanation for Japan's competitive edge. But these factors do not offer an adequate explanation of why (given reliable statistical and economic indicators of market demands) executives and managers of major American automobile companies resisted necessary changes in the form of retooling, redesigning, and reevaluating current product designs. One must consider the combination of psychological and organizational indicators that distorts reasonable decision making and the organization's overall ability to learn from, and respond to, challenges (or threats) apparent in their task environment. This indicates the interaction between security operations of corporate managers and executives under stress with the characteristically bureaucratic structure.

The manner in which individuals receive, process, and interpret information has great significance for the study of organizational behavior and administrative decision making. Sullivan's insights into the distorting effects anxiety imposes on cognitive processes suggest that previous interpersonal experience and cultural environment influence present attitudes toward self, others, and the organization. For Sullivan, both positive and negative changes in the personality's self-system can occur at different phases in a person's life based upon different experiences with interpersonal relationships. That is, self-system activities can diminish with more secure and less anxiety-provoking experiences with others. A healthy, emotionally supportive juvenile and adolescent set of interpersonal experiences can counteract personality warps derived from earlier experiences during childhood. These counter experiences reduce the need for security operations, enhancing a person's ability to process information, knowledge, and most important, novel experiences. Chrzanowski writes:

223

> The mediation of experience and the way the experience shapes information about oneself and others is a central consideration of interpersonal formulations. In that respect, we are dealing with the input of information, the processing of information, and the storing of information. Developmentally it is the ability to conceptualize, generalize, and personalize information that makes up the structure of cognitive phenomena. [1977, p. 45]

Past and present experiences with anxiety distort information-gathering and decision-making activities. Collective, as well as interpersonal, experiences of key organization members such as senior executives and high-level managers shape the kinds of information processes that form administrative action.

The effects of anxiety, security operations, and selective inattention constrict the capacity for processing and storing information. Sullivan explains:

> Selective inattention is, more than any other of the inappropriate and inadequate performances of life, the classic means by which we do not profit from experience which falls within the area of our particular handicap. We don't have the experience from which we might profit—that is, although it occurs, we never notice what it must mean; in fact, we never notice that a good deal of it has occurred at all. [1953b, p. 319]

Active security operations stimulated by a threatening or overprotective environment produce a cognitive inability to learn from experience and past mistakes—what some psychoanalysts might refer to as "repetition-compulsion" (incapacity to "unlearn" bad habits). Selective inattention uses not only defense mechanisms of denial, but rationalization, ritualism, and routinization as well.

Bureaucracy tends to be the ideal environmental context for these obsessional activities of selective inattention. For example, a compulsive reliance on "files and records" for task activities often ignores technological, manpower, socioeconomic, and political changes in the organization's environment. An abundance of committee meetings often reflect ritualistic behavior rather than substantive accomplishments.

Sullivan discovered that security operations of the self-system, such as selective inattention, distort human needs that originally were warped in the personality by the experience of anxiety. Selective inattention is a psychological process (defensive in character) that intentionally ignores specific information in the interests of protecting the self from the recurrence of anxiety-fraught situations. Therefore, the self-system acts to protect the self from severe changes in personality due to anxiety-producing circumstances, while at the same moment limiting information processing that can enhance self-awareness and competence. This inner contradiction illuminates the competing human motives for security needs and growth needs.

224

The defensive activity of "parataxic distortion," known in Freudian terminology as "transference," is another security operation of the self-system formulated in Sullivan's interpersonal psychiatry. In the classical psychoanalytic sense, "transference" is the displacement of internalized objects (images) of projection.

The term "transference" originated from the therapeutic exchange between analyst and analysand. The process involves the transference of internalized feelings from the patient's earlier experiences with significant others, onto the therapist. In analysis, transference functions as an emotional channel for the communication of unresolved feelings, private motives, and internalized images of self, in addition to operating as a method for interpreting distorted elements of the self-system.

For Sullivan, the psychiatrist acts as a "participant-observer," offering an alternative reality to previous interpersonal relationships by countering the parataxic distortion of the patient's self-system. Stimulated by meaningful interpersonal attachment and interdependency reminiscent of earlier parental and authority figures, parataxic distortions further enhance the self-system's ability to frustrate both learning and reality testing. Chrzanowski explains:

> As a result of this distorting process we find the person's thinking to contain many stereotyped conceptualizations about himself and others with an excessive readiness toward experiences of disparagement and derogation pertaining to one's own and the other person's feeling of personal worth. Furthermore,

parataxic distortions include a reaction to the requirements of the ongoing situation. [1977, p. 81]

Sullivan's theory of personality and self-system uncovers the essence of psychic conflict. This continual antagonism, which many organization theorists neglect, between security needs and personal growth needs for cognitive and emotional development is fundamental to interpersonal competence and organizational effectiveness (Argyris, 1962). Paradoxically, while self-systems of the personality protect people from high levels of anxiety, their operations often thwart crucial human needs for growth, development, and learning (Sullivan, 1953a). In the interests of interpersonal security, self-system defenses keep the person away from the unknown, uncertain, and unpredictable. These psychological defenses tread a successful path in one's experience of avoiding anxiety and loss of security. Based on previous experiences with anxiety and insecurity, the individual's defenses are often overdetermined and result in actions of highly rationalized, routine, and sometimes ritualistic interpersonal behavior and narrow-mindedness (Rokeach, 1975). Self-systems are characteristically defensive operations geared toward both adaptability and maintenance of security. These psychic processes tend to be rigid and inflexible.

225

From a psychodynamic point of view, bureaucratization of managerial and personnel activities in the workplace represents the institutionalization of interpersonal defensive operations, otherwise known in Sullivanian psychiatry as self-systems of human personality. When viewed from the perspective of interpersonal psychiatry and contemporary psychoanalysis, the tendencies of modern social systems toward bureaucratization, as characterized by Weber's model of the "ideal type," express self-system operations for security and avoidance of anxiety (security needs) more than any other human motivational needs.

Stubborn resistance to environmental (socioeconomic and political), technical, and personal demands for change in organizational design, objectives, and personnel policies (characteristic of management's dependence on traditional bureaucratic styles of organizing and planning) represent overactive self-system operations. Further, massive denial of the impending state (in many public organizations, the presently occurring state) of organizational decline suggests a dependency on bureaucracy, resulting in an inability for management to test accurately the reality of organizational environments (Whetten, 1980). An application of Sullivan's interpersonal theory to contemporary organizational behavior, particularly in times of unusual stress due to cutbacks, retrenchment, and overall decline, illuminates the extent of our emotional investment in, and overdependencies on, bureaucratic structures. Moreover, Sullivan's theory of self-system and personality illustrates that resistance to change is psychological at its roots and that political attempts at change often ignore the "psychological anchors" of attachment to prevailing forms. In the following section, I explain this extraordinary "cathexis" of the individual on bureaucracy.

Psychoanalytic Applications to Organization Theory

Contemporary applications of psychoanalytic theory to the study of organizational behavior owe their intellectual debt and gratitude to the originator of psychoanalysis, Sigmund Freud, and particularly his later works like *Group Psychology and the Analysis of the Ego*. In this work, Freud explains the individual's emotional investment in the group and its leader. In general, he suggests that the individual is willing to give up his or her distinctiveness and uniqueness for group membership in return for love relationships, a sense of belongingness, and identity. Freud views group membership, along with the leader's influence over individual members (what Freud calls the combination of "hypnosis" and "suggestion" derived from the person's degree of emotional attachment to the object of the leader), as preferable to, and less anxiety-provoking than, loneliness and isolation. Through a process of identification, Freud believes the ego further developed itself with the "properties of the object" (meaning the group leader) by "introjecting" the object (leader as ego ideal) into itself (Freud, 1922, p. 41). In the emotional attachment to the leader, the individual narcissistically identifies with the ideals of group membership and its leader, thereby incorporating the image of the object-leader into his or her own personal aspirations and expectations.

Freud distinguishes these private motives for group membership from more extreme and dangerously dependent acts of followership. He suggests that the crucial question is "whether the object is put in the place of the ego or the ego ideal" (Freud, 1922, p. 46). On "fascination" or "bondage," he writes: "It (the self or ego) is impoverished, it has surrendered itself to the object of its own most important constituent" (Freud, 1922, p. 45). In human bondage, the person surrenders independence, autonomy, and judgment to the external authority in the object of the leader. This surrendering of freedom is characteristic of the original, extraordinary dependency of the infant on the mother. This form of surrender and attachment during adulthood is psychologically regressive but serves the limited human motives of security and belonging.

According to Freud, anxiety in the child represents his fear of being left alone (Freud, 1922, p. 51). In group psychology, panic occurs when the individual is abandoned by the group. Libidinal attachment to the group and its authority represents, therefore, the psychological functioning of defenses against anxiety, the drive for security, self-esteem, and a sense of belonging by identification with the group and its leader. Freud suggests that the demand for justice and equal treatment in groups illustrates a "reaction-formation" to the initial envy with which the elder child receives the younger one, his point being that crucial to the survival of the group is that all feel equally loved by the leader (Freud, 1922, p. 52).

In the tradition of British psychoanalyst Klein, Jaques explains "how much institutions are used by their individual members for defense against anxiety, and in particular against recurrence of the early paranoid and depressive anxieties" (Jaques, 1955, p. 277). For Jaques, "one of the primary cohesive elements binding individuals into institutionalized human association is that of defense against psychotic anxiety" (Jaques, 1955, p. 278).

Following Freud's discussion of the processes of identification used by the person in his formation of an emotional attachment ("cathexis") to the group and its leader, Jaques, drawing predominantly from Klein, describes the primary and secondary intrapsychic processes used in the individual's association with the institution. He suggests a sequence from primary processes (in which the child identifies with the parental figure and introjects the image into the ego ideal) to secondary unconscious processes (in which the adult reinforces his defenses against anxiety by identifying with the group and projecting security needs onto the institutional authority). These "social defenses," according to Jaques, "bear a reciprocal relationship with the internal defense mechanisms."

227

> For instance, the schizoid and manic defenses against anxiety and guilt both involve splitting and projection mechanisms, and through projection, a link with the outside world. When external objects are shared with others and used in common for purposes of projection, fantasy social relationships may be established through projective identification with the common object. These fantasy relationships are further elaborated by introjection, and the two-way character of social relationships is mediated by virtue of the two-way play of projective and introjective identification. [Jaques, 1955, p. 281]

Consequently, "socially structured defense mechanisms" operate in formal institutions where previously "introjected" good or bad objects are split off and thereby projected onto externalized objects, so that bad internal images may be projected onto particular members of the institution.

In Sullivanian psychiatry, this unconscious phenomenon represents the activity of security operations producing parataxic distortions. Fantasy replaces one's ability cognitively to test reality to a great extent. Attachment to the institution, peers, and authority are enhanced by the degree of one's need for defensive reinforcements against anxiety and loss of security. Fellow members and superiors in the organization may often symbolize aspects of self that need to be rejected and, thereby, are projected by the individual onto the external world. Since internalized bad images stimulate anxiety and insecurity, the person tends to external-ize such images by means of projection. This projective-identification is often experienced as hostile and sadistic, seen correctly by the object per-son as a distorted vision of reality. Yet, from a psychological perspective, projective-identification, or what Sullivan calls "parataxic distortions," functions to protect the individual from paranoid and depressive anxiety. Moreover, the attachment of the individual to the institution is not nec-essarily destructive or sadistic but often serves an integrative purpose, in which the replacement of an ego ideal by an object (often a superior or executive in the hierarchy) ensures emotional investment and loyalty to the organization. People are often willing to give up some autonomy and independence for a sense of purpose.

228

Psychoanalytic applications of organization theory indicate how people unconsciously use institutions as a defense against anxiety. These theories and their clinical applications in case studies, such as Menzies's "A Case-Study in the Functioning of Social Systems as a Defense Against Anxiety: A Report on a Study of the Nursing Service of a General Hospital," con-tribute significantly to our understanding of unconscious motivational forces operating at the work-group level inside formal institutions (1960).

Further, psychoanalysis of human relations improves our ability to recognize the difficulty inherent in strategies of organizational change. Organization theorists and interventionists must comprehend the under-lying psychological processes and their inherent anxieties in order to cope with inevitable "resistance to change" (Zaleznik and Kets de Vries, 1975; Levinson, 1981). Jaques comments: "It may well be because of the effects on the unconscious defense systems of individuals against psy-chotic anxiety that social change is resisted—and in particular, imposed social change" (1955, p. 297). Few contemporary psychoanalysts under-stand human tendencies to resist change better than Harry Stack Sullivan. His interpersonal theory of psychiatry elucidates defense processes in his notion of the self-system of personality in which security needs often dominate all other human needs, including those for change and growth.

Self-System and Bureaucracy

Culture of Dependency on Bureaucracy

I agree with other organization theorists (Denhardt, 1981; Hummel, 1977) who purport that we live and work in a culture of dependence on bureaucracy. This cultural dependence adds to the cathexis between bureacracy and self-system which I have thus far described—a strong ca-thexis that is the result of cultural transference in which defensiveness is supported by modern social systems and, in turn, activated by these external structures. In a recent treatise on organization theory, Denhardt elaborates on the theme of cultural dependency on bureaucracy: "The result of this socialization process is the widespread assumption of a particular viewpoint, a sort of organizational ethic, one which supports the extension of an organizational society and offers itself as a way of life for persons in our society" (1981, p. 5). Denhardt sees an organizational ethic that prevails in our everyday lives at the workplace and elsewhere—an ethic that emphasizes structure and order over conflict and change.

In his essay "The Culture Trait of Hierarchy in Middle Class Children," Wilcox found that by high school age, most children from a white, suburban, middle-class background who attend public schools will "strongly exhibit the trait" of hierarchy. Wilcox found that "the most important period for acculturation in relation to the trait is prior to age 11 and possibly age 9" (1968, p. 229).

These findings complement Sullivan's clinical observations that self-system operations for defense against anxiety mature in the juvenile era during the child's earliest experiences with formal educational institutions, or what I refer to as their first experiences with bureaucratic authority relations and institutional forms of social behavior.[3]

In *The Bureaucratic Experience*, Hummel views the outcome of society's cultural collision with bureaucracy as the end of culture as we know it and those values and issues of human concern we hold dear. He writes:

> The cultural conflict between bureaucracy and society is between system needs [i.e., self-system defenses] and human needs [other needs]. In society, culture is the pattern of norms and behaviors that have proved adaptive in keeping society and its members alive in the past. These patterns are frozen into standards to keep society and its members alive in the present and future. In bureaucracy, whose creators prided themselves on the independence of this form of organization from the actual people who fill its offices, the purpose of culture is to keep the bureaucracy alive whatever that does to the human beings who are bureaucrats. [1977, p. 56]

In summary, Hummel, following Habermas and Weber, contends that the result of the individual's dependency on bureaucracy is displacement of social norms like love and hate, freedom and oppression, and justice and violence by institutional norms of precision, stability, control, and efficiency. Consequently, our culture of dependence on bureaucracy appears to have lost its conscience and system of values, becoming a social system without culture.

These conclusions, suggesting a culture of dependence on bureaucracy, support my perspective that bureaucracy is an externalized self-system that reinforces security needs for structure, order, and certainty above all other human needs. An organizational society, then, reinforces and encourages defensive aspects of human personalities and social systems in which stressful and changing environments only enhance human tendencies to perpetuate bureaucratic form.

For Sullivan, the demands of modern society for uniform behavior and a shared system of values inspire psychological defenses that function to protect and secure the self. He writes: "The origin of the self-system can be said to rest on the irrational character of culture or, more specifically, society" (1953b, p. 168). After all, self-system structures of personality are formed in response to anxiety initially experienced in the preverbal, empathic relationship between mother and infant. Defense mechanisms of the self-system originate in the infant's fear of annihilation in reaction to uncanny emotions. Self-system activities of the personality direct a person's efforts toward primary needs for security. In the case of active security operations, the self-system drives personal motives for belonging in the direction of structure and order, in which the outcome of behavior is consistent and predictable, not anxiety-provoking.

Commenting on the social-psychological and cultural contributions of the environment to the necessary development of a self-system of defense mechanisms, Sullivan remarks:

> Were it not for the fact that a great many prescribed ways of doing things have to be lived up to, in order that one shall maintain workable, profitable, satisfactory relations with his fellows; or, were the prescriptions for the types of behavior in carrying on relations with one's fellows perfectly rational— then, for all I know, there would not be evolved, in the course of becoming a person, anything like the sort of self-system that we always encounter. [1953b, p. 168]

Psychological defensiveness and the cultivation of a self-system perform adaptive as well as protective functions for the individual. Sullivan seems to say that the construction of a self-system within the personality is a necessary psychodynamic reaction to an irrational world of interpersonal relationships, such that the person exerts a good deal of his or her psychic energy learning and constructing patterns of behavior to maintain at least minimal security from anxiety and loss of self-esteem. Yet construction of this self-fortress does not conclude with a person's arrival into adulthood (whether chronologically or developmentally). Nor do defenses limit their activity to the intrapsychic and interpersonal. Self-system activities extend into the part of our physical environment that we construct for the human species—the human organization.

Psyche of Dependency on Bureaucracy

Bureaucratic Rules and Self-System. Self-systems materialize in bureaucratically designed organizations where so-called rationally organized actions reinforce formal rules, regulations, and norms of impersonality that function as interpersonal defense structures. For example, is it necessary to take responsibility for one's actions when those actions merely follow prescribed behavior? And isn't it true that inflexible compliance with rules and regulations protects the bureaucrat from personal involvement in his or her task and decision-making process and thereby functions defensively?

Formal rules and regulations often defend the bureaucrat from personal responsibility by disconnecting him or her from the intent of human action. This frustrates the public's demand for accountability, because members need only respond to the demands of particular tasks as specified in the official job description. Traditional managerial philosophies based upon a common reward-punishment orientation to motivation encourage functionaries strictly to follow patterns of behavior prescribed in their job descriptions. Subordinates comply with rules in order to avoid anxiety about superordinate disapproval. Further strict adherence to official rules and regulations enhances impersonality, protecting the functionary from emotional involvement with a client's circumstances as well as responsibility for the consequences of his or her decisions.

231

Of course, many productive and substantially independent organizational members learn how to accomplish tasks inside bureaucracies with minimal rule constraints. They find that with experience they can work around cumbersome regulations. These bureaucrats realize that task functions of administrative behavior often operate quite differently in reality than as prescribed in the official job description. On the other hand, at moments of external organizational stress or internal tensions, bureaucratic functionaries find that strict reliance on rules and regulations are a secure and minimally anxiety-provoking method of task accomplishment. Moreover, functionaries with active security operations (that is, those who are basically insecure and have low self-esteem) tend to rely on bureaucratic rules and regulations. In general, bureaucracy's emphasis on compliance with rules, regulations, and procedures supports active security operations that often thwart effectiveness and encourage resistance to change. This match between bureaucracy and self-system only adds to the functionary's tendency to use social systems as a defense and to deny personal responsibility for his or her actions and their consequences.

Hierarchy, Oligarchy, and Self-System. Hierarchy of authority relations is not an invention of the modern Western world. It is as old as civilization itself. Anxiety predates bureaucracy. For the individual, it first occurs during infancy when the baby has no self-system apparatus to avoid uncanny emotions. Anxiety and its accompanying security operations function in all dependency-oriented relationships, such as master-slave relationships, parent-child relationships, and manager-functionary relationships. Security operations of the self-system work to sustain the underling's emotional attachment to his or her superior. Anxiety is avoided as long as the dependent does not wander (psychologically and physically) from the boundaries of the structured interpersonal relationship. Bureaucracy, as a more highly structured and uniquely impersonal form of interpersonal activity, represents a peculiar form of a "merger relationship," in which the functionary performs a service but is not a separate human being. The combination of obedience to hierarchical authority; impersonal norms of administrative behavior; compliance with bureaucratic rules, regulations, and procedures; and the person's emotional attachment to bureaucratic structure acts to avoid anxiety and maintain security, while thwarting human potential for growth and individuality.

Bureaucracy represents the ultimate social tool of domination. Its hierarchical design of a top-to-bottom chain of command unintentionally enhances a primitive human tendency toward dependency and "containment."[4] Through a hierarchy of authority, management (superordinacy) functions as the "containers" while bureaucratic functionaries (subordinacy) perform as the "contained." Management experiences both hierarchical positions of superordinacy and subordinacy. Managers must depend upon subordinate loyalty and deference to their authority, and in turn, they must display such characteristics to their superiors. Throughout traditional organizational hierarchies, interpersonal security and self-esteem depend on the approval of a superior, as well as the satisfactory performance and conformity of a subordinate. Interdependencies permeate bureaucratic social systems.

Inevitable conflicts and anxiety, rooted in earlier stages of development, are stimulated by the hierarchy of authority, particularly when superior-subordinate ties are based on suppressed emotional needs grounded in desires for parental approval and rewards of love and attention. The emotional aspects of rewards are anxiety-reducing, whereas fears of punishment, often experienced as the mother's removal of love or the father's physical retribution on the child, are anxiety-provoking, fostering defensiveness and security operations. Hierarchy is predicated on a reward-punishment system of motivation, in which anxiety is a central function in the covert activities of subordinates and in the unintentional manipulation by management.

Psychological dependencies on bureaucratic structures that foster "inhibiting" authority relationships serve as a defense against anxiety. Avoidance of anxiety and maintenance of security are powerfully motivating forces in organizations like bureaucracies and are designed to accommodate such needs, beyond all others. As the famous Milgram experiments indicated, anxiety is generated when people are forced to reject authority (Milgram, 1974). And, as Sullivan's clinical investigations and theory of psychiatry suggest, security needs dominate other psychic processes. In bureaucratic society, security operations embody the authoritarian structure of hierarchy, which means that these psychological processes of defense against anxiety are present in the superior-subordinate relationships that maintain the power to control rewards and punishments. Can one expect hierarchy to produce results that minimize security operations in people? Or does hierarchy logically support and reinforce them, if not constitute an externalized version of them?

Hierarchy and oligarchy encourage security operations. When power and authority are monopolized by a few elites in pyramidal (oligarchical) organizations, leaders are vulnerable to delusional and psychopathological behavior. Interpersonal security needs acquire primary significance in the motivation of personnel, often at the price of surrendering cognition grounded in reality. Bureaucracy is a construct of the psyche: it acquires a reality of its own only by the individual's reliance on its structures for protection and security against anxiety. In extreme situations, bureaucracy consumes individual initiative and will. As a highly structured mode of interpersonal behavior, bureaucracy is most ideally reliable for organizational members in times of stress as a defense against potential loss of security; it is a structured environment where role conformity and self-protectiveness may become the dominant pattern of subordinate behavior.

233

Conclusion

My application of Sullivan's interpersonal theory of psychiatry to the study of bureaucracy may appear as a justification for the presence of bureaucratic form because that social system serves legitimate psychological needs for security. However, my purpose is to illuminate, by using Sullivan's theory of social psychiatry, how bureaucratic structures reinforce and support security operations and defensiveness among functionaries and represent what I call an externalized self-system. My point is that bureaucracy magnifies the structural manifestation of embedded defensive operations of the person. Traditional characteristics of bureaucracy like hierarchy of authority, functional specialization, and impersonality (along with the functional as well as dysfunctional consequences of those structures) share with Sullivan's conception of a self-system a common purpose of defending people from anxiety provoked by uncertainty of conflict and change. Sullivan's psychiatry vividly demonstrates a central human conflict, often underestimated by organizational humanists, between human needs for development and growth and interpersonal security defenses from the anxieties inherent in growth. As the covert result of active security operations, bureaucracies resist necessary conflict and change, constraining the growth and development of both management and the organization as a whole.

Modern management, in both public and private business enterprises, is experiencing greater external stress and less job security than ever witnessed over the last four decades of American society. Environmental threats to organizational dynamics and interpersonal relations between senior executives, managers, and functionaries permeate the climates of many contemporary giant and powerful enterprises in business and government. Given economic and political uncertainties, organizational members fall back on familiar and often psychologically regressive behavior patterns. Denial of the personal and organizational realities of decline persists in many institutions, where management makes decisions on the basis of a growth economy (Whetten, 1980). At the interpersonal level, members under stress depend upon what Bion calls "basic assumptions" of emotionality.[5] Security activities rise and the functionaries' reliance on bureaucratic forms of control and patterns for routine and rationalized behavior are enhanced. Defensive modes of operation at the interpersonal and institutional levels become more overt and commonplace. Individual bureaucrats become more defensive, turning psychic energies inward in an attempt to thwart insecurities and anxieties caused by a lowering of self-esteem and sense of self-worth.

Normal sublimation as a productive, adaptive style for everyday work activities is displaced by active resistance and denial of organizational realities in which the necessity for structural and behavioral change seems imminent. Healthy, human affect derived from satisfying work experience through affiliation with fellow employees and organizational goals is sacrificed for the primary human need to maintain minimal interpersonal security. Security needs, more than ever, outweigh growth needs as the basis for human motivation in contemporary organizational climates during decline, retrenchment, and cutbacks.

Stressful institutional environments only reinforce a member's proclivity to engage in what Sullivan calls security operations, in which distortion, fantasy, and a neurotic reliance on bureaucratic (impersonal, noncollaborative, nonintimate, security-oriented, routine) behavior is reinforced. Aggression, contained by hierarchy's top-to-bottom chain of command and bureaucracy's inherent repression of emotions, is turned inward upon work-group members and individual functionaries. Finally, traditional bureaucratic stereotypes enforced by politicians, media, and the public become self-fulfilling prophecies for many workers, reinforcing the bureaucrat's low self-image and his tendency to turn blame into feelings of guilt. This inevitably enhances levels of anxiety and cognitive distortion, diminishing effectiveness and productivity, along with some organizations' chances for survival.

NOTES

Acknowledgment: The author is indebted to James M. Glass and Ralph P. Hummel for their comments, criticism, and support in the writing of this manuscript.

1. Bureaucracy, like any social institution, is a human product. It represents characteristics of the human species' needs. Externalization is the human activity of constructing the objective reality known as bureaucracy. Here we view that peculiar modern institution as a manifestation of man's security needs operating from the motivational forces of the self-system of the human personality. For a further explanation of the concept "externalization," see Berger and Luckmann's *The Social Construction of Reality* (1967).

2. According to Sullivan, "anxiety is a tension in opposition to the tension of needs and to action appropriate to their relief" (1953b, p. 44). In contrast to fear, anxiety is not the consequence of a clearly definable causal object or event. Its very experience blocks from awareness the origins of the anxiety and distorts the cognitive field of observation. Anxiety is experienced in terror, as a direct threat to the living human organism. As Heidegger describes, anxiety symbolizes "nothingness," "the complete negation of what is" (1975, p. 246). Unsettling feelings of powerlessness and helplessness and a disconnectedness from reality further describe this disturbing psychodynamic phenomenon.

3. Bureaucratic activity is a pseudosocial ritual in which people are involved with one another but nothing personal transpires. Activity is characterized by a devotion to games in which actors devise strategies and game plans for getting ahead and for simply maintaining their position. Personalities are unintentionally transformed in order to fit the game plan, increase the probability of success, and enhance the internal security operations. Consequently, the self-system is highly attuned to its competitors, and pretentious and defensive interpersonal relations are commonplace. Bureaucratic activity is competitive game playing that often materializes in juvenile activities such as ostracism, stereotyping, and disparagement. Hierarchy encourages these forms of juvenile competition and, in some instances, demands this behavior of midlevel bureaucrats striving for upward mobility in higher levels of management. Bureaucratic society is a manifestation of juvenile society where certain bureaucrats are held in high esteem and may feel ostracized when they are not considered for status positions by management. This is comparable to the child's feeling in school society that some juveniles, usually segregated from others, are held in higher esteem by teachers, principals, and other authority figures. The juvenile who is excluded from such status groups in the school society is emotionally wounded and feels ostracized, lowering his or her self-esteem and enhancing anxiety. Bureaucracy often awakens anxieties when functionaries appear victimized because the system does not recognize the human qualities of compassion and empathy but instead values control, precision, and impersonality.

4. See W. R. Bion's *Elements of Psycho-analysis* (1963), in which he discusses in great detail the "dynamic relationship between container and contained."

5. See Bion's work (1970) on group dynamics in which "fight-flight," "dependency," and "pairing" are observed as basic assumption patterns of emotionality among group members under stress and anxiety.

235

REFERENCES

Argyris, C. 1962. *Interpersonal Competence and Organizational Effectiveness*. Homewood, Ill.: Irwin-Dorsey.

Berger, P. L., and T. Luckmann. 1967. *The Social Construction of Reality*. New York: Doubleday.

Bion, W. R. 1963. *Elements of Psycho-Analysis*. New York: Basic Books.

———. 1970. *Attention and Interpretation*. New York: Basic Books.

Chrzanowski, G. 1977. *Interpersonal Approach to Psychoanalysis: Contemporary Views of Harry Stack Sullivan*. New York: Gardner Press.

Denhardt, R. B. 1981. *In the Shadow of Organization*. Lawrence: Regents Press of Kansas.

Erikson, E. H. 1968. *Identity: Youth and Crisis*. New York: W. W. Norton.

Freud, S. 1922. *Group Psychology and the Analysis of the Ego*. Translated by James Strachey. New York: W. W. Norton.

Fromm, E. 1941. *Escape from Freedom*. New York: Holt, Rinehart, and Winston.

Heidegger, M. 1975. "What Is Metaphysics?" In Walter Kaufman (ed.), *Existentialism from Dostoevsky to Sartre*. New York: New American Library.

Hummel, R. 1977. *The Bureaucratic Experience*. New York: St. Martin's Press.

Jaques, E. 1955. "Social Systems as a Defense Against Persecutory and Depressive Anxiety." In M. Klein, P. Heimann, and R. E. Money-Kyrle (eds.), *New Directions in Psychoanalysis*. London: Tavistock.

Kernberg, O. 1979. "Regression in Organizational Leadership." *Psychiatry*, 42, 24–39.

Kets de Vries, M. F. R. 1979. "Managers Can Drive Their Subordinates Mad." *Harvard Business Review*, 57 (July–August), 125–134.

Kohut, H. 1971. *The Analysis of the Self*. New York: International Universities Press.

LaBier, D. 1983. "Emotional Disturbances in the Federal Bureaucracy." *Administration and Society*, 14 (4), 403–448.

Lasswell, H. 1948. *Power and Personality*. New York: W. W. Norton.

———. 1977. *Psychopathology and Politics*. Chicago: University of Chicago Press.

Laurent, A. 1978. "Managerial Subordinacy: A Neglected Aspect of Organizational Hierarchies." *Academy of Management Review*, 3 (April), 220–230.

Levinson, H. 1981. *Executive*. Cambridge, Mass.: Harvard University Press.

Maccoby, M. 1976. *The Gamesman*. New York: Simon and Schuster.

Menzies, I. 1960. "A Case-Study in the Functioning of Social Systems as a Defense Against Anxiety: A Report on a Study of the Nursing Service of a General Hospital." *Human Relations*, 13, 95–121.

Merton, R. K. 1968. *Social Theory and Social Structure*. New York: Free Press.

Milgram, S. 1974. *Obedience to Authority: An Experimental View*. New York: Harper and Row.

Mullahy, P. 1970. *Psychoanalysis and Interpersonal Psychiatry*. New York: Science House.

Neilsen, E. H., and J. Gypen. 1979. "The Subordinate's Predicaments." *Harvard Business Review*, 57 (September–October), 133–143.

Presthus, R. 1978. *The Organizational Society*. New York: St. Martin's Press.

Rokeach, M. 1975. "Narrow-Mindedness and Personality." *Journal of Personality*, 20, 234–251.

Sperling, O. 1950. "Psychoanalytic Aspects of Bureaucracy." *Psychoanalytic Quarterly*, 19, 88–100.

Sullivan, H. S. 1950. "The Illusion of Personal Individuality." *Psychiatry*, 13, 317–332.

———. 1953a. *Conceptions of Modern Psychiatry*. New York: W. W. Norton.

———. 1953b. *The Interpersonal Theory of Psychiatry*. New York: W. W. Norton.

———. 1964. *The Fusion of Psychiatry and Social Science*. New York: W. W. Norton.

Thompson, J. D. 1967. *Organizations in Action*. New York: McGraw-Hill.

Weber, M. 1948. *From Max Weber: Essays in Sociology*. Edited and translated by H. H. Gerth and C. W. Mills. London: Oxford University Press.

———. 1968a. *Economy and Society: An Outline of Interpretive Sociology*. New York: Bedminster Press.

———. 1968b. *On Charisma and Institution Building*. Edited by S. W. Eisenstadt. Chicago: University of Chicago Press.

Whetten, D. A. 1980. "Organizational Decline: A Neglected Topic in Organizational Science." *Academy of Management Review*, 5, 577–588.

Wilcox, H. 1968. "The Culture Trait of Hierarchy in Middle Class Children." *Public Administration Review*, 28 (May), 222–232.

Zaleznik, A., and M. F. R. Kets de Vries. 1975. *Power and the Corporate Mind*. Boston: Houghton Mifflin.

CHAPTER 15

On the Psychodynamics of

Organizational Totalitarianism

Howard S. Schwartz

Understandably, discussions of totalitarianism tend to focus upon its more dramatic manifestations. Unfortunately, this often leads us to miss aspects of totalitarianism that pervade our own times and culture and that may be, if not equally destructive, at least sufficiently destructive to require study and criticism. An exception is the work of Earl Shorris (1981) on totalitarian aspects of corporate life.

Shorris defines *totalitarianism* as the process of defining people's happiness for them. The element that makes this process noxious is that the definer of happiness is not the person whose happiness is being defined. This has the effect of taking the individual's sense of determining the direction of his or her life away from that individual and ceding it to another, whereas it is the very sense of giving direction to our lives, even if only in thought, that constitutes our moral autonomy. For Shorris, who in this respect echoes George Herbert Mead's (1934) distinction between the *I* and the *me*, the human being stands apart from any symbol. It is this standing-apartness that constitutes one's self-consciousness that is the source of one's specific identity. To cause a person to collapse into a symbol one has projected for him or her is to cause the self-consciousness to become not the essence of that person's identity, but something alien to it—to separate the person from him- or herself.

This is the fundamental psychodynamic of totalitarianism. It alienates people from themselves and gives them over to others. Whatever victories may ensue must be pyrrhic. Whatever happiness is to be attained here is not the happiness of the individual. Indeed, it is not happiness at all. It is the drama of happiness attaching to a role that the person performs in a play that is written and directed by others.

We can gain insight into the underlying psychodynamics of this process by exploring the connection between Shorris's view and the Freudian theory of narcissism and the ego ideal.

Narcissism and the Ego Ideal

238

For Freud (1957) the infant starts off in the congenial state of being at the center of a loving world. It is thus a perfect combination of agency and communion, subjectivity and objectivity, activity and passivity, freedom and determinateness, yang and yin. Freud refers to this happy synthesis as "primary narcissism."

But the world is, alas, not a loving place, and none of us is the center of it. No one in it loves us quite as much as we need to be loved. And if, as life goes on, others are to love us at all, we must love them in return—and give up, in a word, the centrality that the love of others was an instrument for preserving. Further, even if I gain the love of a few individuals, what good does it do me? My real problem is with the world. And they cannot protect me from it any more than I can protect them. For the world can do very well without me. It did without me before I was and it will do without me when I am not. In the end, by virtue of the laws of biology if nothing else, I get rubbed out. To be sure, I can make some contribution to the world. Perhaps, in some sense, that will live after me. But what is it that lives after me? Obviously, whatever it is, it is not me. The world is precisely the arrangement that, among other things, this shall happen. Why should I love that? If I don't, what ground is there for my making any contribution to the world at all?

The idea that the world was not made with us in mind, that the only place we can have in it is small and temporary, underlies what Melanie Klein (1975) called the "depressive position." You can understand why. Much of the psychology of social institutions is organized against this position.

For Klein, the depression of the depressive position is often defended against by adopting what she calls the "manic defense," or a regression to an earlier stage of development called the "paranoid-schizoid position." The characteristic psychology here is determined by what she calls "splitting," which is a lack of integration of the good aspects of the world with the bad aspects and a denial of the ultimate reality of the bad aspects. In one way or another, we attribute the cause of our anxiety to a person or a place or a time or a group or a social arrangement or a part of ourselves and direct our aggression at this "bad" stuff. We hold before us the image of a perfect "good" world that will be our world when the bad stuff is gotten rid of or gotten away from.

This good world represents for us the possibility of a return to narcissism, to a world in which annihilation is not a problem, a world in which it is perfectly all right to do whatever we want to do, a world that has us as its reason for being, a world free of anxiety. Stories of the goodness of the good world and stories of the roots of our anxiety constitute mythology and help structure culture. A main function of culture, that is to say, is to give content and direction, to render sensible, our longings to return to narcissism and to avoid the anxiety arising from our mortality (Becker, 1971, 1973).

239

In Freudian terms, the representation that we make to ourselves of the good world is called the "ego ideal." This is what we are driven toward by our anxiety over our finitude, by our rejection of whatever it is about ourselves that is vulnerable and limited. Because this is our spontaneous self, it is always the case that the motivation toward the ego ideal involves the rejection (in Freudian terms, the repression) of our spontaneity, our "real self" (Horney, 1950). Thus, we experience the pursuit of the ego ideal as an imperative—as an attempt to be what we ought to be, not a natural expression of what we are. The recognition that we are not what we are supposed to be, that we are playing a role rather than being the role we are playing, is the experience of shame (Goffman, 1959). Another consequence is that we never get to be the ego ideal. The ego ideal represents us as we believe we would be if we could get rid of what causes our anxiety. But what causes our anxiety is what is most specifically ourselves. While we are alive, we can never get rid of it—it is one's own individual life.

As Freud (1955) pointed out, the ego ideal may be formed in any of a number of ways. Of particular interest in this chapter is the case in which an abstraction, a leading idea, has taken the place of a leader, and in which that abstraction is the idea of the organization itself. In this case, we may recognize the committed organizational participant as a person whose ego ideal is the organization.[1] Thus, for the committed organizational participant, the organization represents a means for the return to narcissism.

To talk about the organization as ego ideal is to refer not to the actual organization but to the committed person's idea of the organization, which may have little relation to the person's experience with the actual organization. It is what the committed organizational participant holds out as what the organization is supposed to be and would be except for the effect of "bad" aspects of the world, and what he or she accepts as an obligation to help bring about. This is clearly an ideal organization. Thus, I refer to this concept, that of the organization's serving the function of the ego ideal, as the *organization ideal*. How does the organization ideal serve as an ego ideal, and what are the consequences?

The Ego Ideal and the Organization Ideal

In the first place, the organization ideal represents power. Denhardt (1981) has noted how deeply the concept of control is built into our concept of the organization. In psychoanalytic terms, the organization ideal serves as a reaction formation that covers over and represses the anxiety-evoking idea of our finitude, vulnerability, and mortality (Schwartz, 1982, 1985; Diamond, 1984).

240

Second, the organization ideal is a scenario of love as well and offers the possibility of a return to centrality in a loving world. For, by taking the organization as ego ideal, the individual assumes the possibility of a boundary-dispelling relationship to others who have done likewise. Both love and centrality are possible in this scenario, because each of the individuals who have taken the organization as their ego ideal assumes that the others have also redefined themselves as the organization and therefore as essentially the same and having the same interest. Conflict is defined away, therefore, and along with it all social anxiety within the organization. Indeed, what we have here is a perfect analog for Freud's reference to the tale of Narcissus, who falls in love with his own image in a pond. Here the other organizational participants would ideally provide a mirror for the focal participant and reflect that participant's love for her- or himself.

Third, a related point ties the intrapsychic processes involved to the normative structure of the organization. We have seen that, by defining themselves in terms of the organization, individuals put themselves into an interesting relationship with others who have done the same: on the one hand, this is a relationship of idealized love that would not interfere with narcissism; on the other hand, it is a relationship of mutual responsibility because it is up to each to uphold the organization ideal for all the others. It becomes not only a matter of the fulfillment of mutual personal principle but the direct object of moral sanction—the threat of the loss of love—by ideally loved others. This gives a moral force to the maintenance of the definition of oneself and one's relations as the organization ideal.

Fourth, and perhaps most comprehensively, defining oneself as the organization removes from consideration a problem that in a way contributed most powerfully to the anxiety the participant was trying to allay. As noted before, the self-conscious self, the spontaneous self, Mead's

(1934) *I*, though it is on the one hand what is most intimately myself, is also the cause of my greatest ontological trouble. For it can never be fully represented by a symbol (Mead's *me*) and therefore cannot become part of the enacted world, but always stands aside from my enactments and says of them, "That is not me, that is not me." Defining myself as the organization ideal solves this problem for me. Having defined myself in terms of the organization as an ethical standard, I have a basis upon which I can reject my spontaneous self-consciousness as an obstacle to my self and to my obligations. It becomes an impulse for me to negate: a source of shame and guilt. What I cannot deny phenomenologically, I can repudiate morally. To be sure, I can do that only by rejecting that part of me that is most uniquely myself. But after all, it was precisely the fact that I have a spontaneous self that got me into trouble in the first place.

To illustrate, consider an interview that Studs Terkel (1974) conducted with a man named Wheeler Stanley, who was then the youngest general **241** supervisor in a Ford assembly plant. From an impoverished background, Stanley had come, through Ford, to a position of status in the world and felt that he was in line for more. His ambitions lay within the company hierarchy, and his conscious concerns were company concerns. His ego ideal was the organization ideal. But listen to the way this conversation evolved:

> I've got a great feeling for Ford because it's been good to me. . . . My son, he's only six years old and I've taken him through the plant. . . . And that's all he talks about: "I'm going to work for Ford too." And I say, "Oh, no you ain't." And my wife will shut me up and she'll say, "Why not?" Then I think to myself, "Why not? It's been good to me." [p. 185]

Stanley here expressed an underlying resentment at Ford, which was not acceptable to his moral consciousness. He reported an occasion when the veneer slipped and the thought was blurted out. But then it was repudiated as unworthy, and the veneer of the company man was put back in place. "[Ford] has been good to me," replaced and covered over the apparently spontaneous opposite thought: "Ford has been bad to me."

Fifth, the repudiation of the spontaneous self leaves open a possibility of a redefinition of the self that is wholly in accordance with the organization ideal. This is a redefinition of the "wants" of the individual. In terms of the organization ideal, the participant undertakes to "want" to do what the organization needs doing. Thus, the polarity of subject and object, activity and passivity, is projected to be overcome.

The picture of the organization as organization ideal will be familiar to all teachers of organizational behavior. This is an organization in which everyone knows what he or she is doing, in which there is no conflict or coercion, in which communication is open and direct, in which people want to do what needs to be done, in which every member is solely concerned with and works diligently to promote the common good. The picture is of an organization that has never existed and never will. But somehow it is of the utmost importance to students to be able to believe in it.

Indeed, the picture of the organization as ego ideal is familiar and important not only to the naive observer, but to the sophisticated one as well. The idea of the model organization as the integration of individual spontaneity and organizational necessity is, after all, in one form or another at the heart of many normative theories of organization, and the attainment of organization ideal is a large part of the promise made by practitioners of "organizational development."

Often, as with Argyris (1957), organizational development efforts are aimed at encouraging what Maslow (1970) called *self-actualization* through work. But notice here that an important shift takes place away from Maslow's concept.[2] Instead of saying that self-actualization means "Be healthy and then you may trust your impulses" (p. 179), these thinkers seem to believe it means, "Want what the organization wants you to want, and then you may do what you want."

To this point, we have considered the nature of the organization ideal and its relation to the individual who adopts it as his or her ego ideal. But though the organizational processes so characterized may resemble totalitarianism, they also resemble social processes that are, arguably, not only more benign but often even positive, such as idealistic movements for social change. Indeed, these processes involve the psychodynamic underpinnings of social organization generally, at least to the extent that people put their faith in it. If I have noted that it involves repression and decentering of the self, I have said no more than Freud in *Civilization and Its Discontents* (1961). And if the impossibility of attaining the ego ideal leads almost inevitably to disillusionment, it is at least arguable that disillusionment is a necessary element of adult development and growth (Levinson, 1978). In order to show how the processes I have described lead to totalitarianism, it will be necessary to show how they tend to degenerate in the context of organizational power.

Hierarchy and Ontological Differentiation

Because the organization ideal represents the return to narcissism and because the return to narcissism can never be achieved, there must be some way of accounting for the failure of the return to narcissism while still remaining true to the idea of the organization ideal.

For the committed organizational participant, there are two available reasons why narcissism has not returned—why I still feel threatened, why everybody doesn't love me, why I am not doing what I want, and so on. One possibility involves scapegoating. Here, the anxiety is attributed to "bad" forces, external or internal, that are threatening the organization. Once the forces can be given an identity, it is possible to struggle against them. The community of strugglers can be conceived as wholly good, because all the anxiety can be attributed to the enemy. Under the circumstances, a quite satisfying degree of localized collective narcissism can be achieved. This, apparently, represents the dynamic of the cohesiveness of many in-groups that feel themselves arrayed against out-groups. We can easily see in it the root of the loyalty, cohesiveness, and high morale of work organizations that can identify some external threat or of parts of work organizations that can attribute the organization's problems to other parts of the same organization.

Scapegoating is certainly a tool used by totalitarian work organizations to increase their control. Thus, the president of a major auto manufacturing company referred to the Japanese as "the enemy" in an address to Oakland University students. He made it manifest that this climate of warfare was very much a part of the cultural process underlying his organization's "quality of working life" program. Certainly the feeling of threat from an enemy increases the level of anxiety and therefore the need to believe that the organization is the organization ideal. But the feeling of being threatened by an outside enemy does not, by itself, create the kind of internal split, the alienation, the separation from the self, that totalitarianism represents. In order to account for that, another dynamic must be considered.

This other dynamic involves what I shall call the process of *ontological differentiation*. Here the attribution of the cause of anxiety is made to the self and experienced as shame—shame for oneself and for the parts of the organization with which one is associated. Because the organization is understood as the organization ideal, and because one and one's associates fall short of this ideal, these have evidently not been fully integrated into the organization. One experiences shame as a result of contrasting oneself and one's associates to others who are, one believes, what they are supposed to be—who are more integrated with the organization ideal and presumably do not have the deficiency in their identity that one is ashamed of. This contrast is ontological differentiation.

In the classic bureaucratic organization, ontological differentiation takes the structural form of vertical differentiation, or hierarchy. As Arendt (1966) and Shorris (1981) note, what I am calling ontological differentiation does not always correspond precisely with the organizational pyramid. Arendt, for example, compares the totalitarian organization to an onion, in which one goes deeper and deeper, rather than higher and higher.[3] Thus, the Nazi party, for example, contained ideological fanatics at all levels of the state apparatus, trusted to wield power even over their nominal superiors through their capacity for denunciation. Nonetheless, as Shorris notes, the pyramid and the onion intersect at the point that is both highest and deepest. In traditional organizational terms, this is the top of the organization. For the purposes of this discussion, the dimensions of vertical differentiation and depth will be taken to be combined in the organization's hierarchy.

In the traditional view, hierarchy serves a variety of managerial functions, such as coordination, control, and the like. Although there is certainly some truth to this view, it cannot provide fully for a phenomenology of hierarchy—for the simple reason that hierarchy represents not only a differentiation of function and task, but a moral differentiation as well (Parsons, 1954). Thus, the organizational ladder is conceived as a sort of "great chain of being." It represents, in a word, a structured adaptation to the idea that organizational participation does not amount to a return to narcissism, while retaining the idea of the organization as organization ideal, and therefore permitting the idea of the return to narcissism as a possibility.

Thus, it is easy to suppose that more status in the organization's hierarchy will represent a greater degree of attainment of the organization ideal and therefore progress in the return to narcissism.[4] On the one hand, the organization's actions will be more the result of my actions, and its deliberations will include my thoughts. On the other hand, by definition, my actions and thoughts will be the appropriate actions and thoughts with regard to the organization. The problem is that commitment to the belief that progress in the hierarchy will mean progress in the attainment of the organization ideal for me involves commitment to the belief that it represents such progress for others as well.

Ontological differentiation is the primary vehicle through which organizational and specifically corporate life becomes totalitarian. For at this point it becomes possible for some to use their ontological stature and the power that goes with it to narcissistically impose their fantasy of their own perfection upon others as the organization ideal—or, in Shorris's definition of totalitarianism, for some to define the happiness of others.

The point is that the top of the organization is not merely an abstract position, but has a population and a history of action. *In organizational totalitarianism the organization, as defined by its leadership's understanding of their own actions, is proclaimed to be the organization ideal; and the organization's power is used to impose this as the ego ideal for the organization's participants.*

Thus, locating the return to narcissism at the head of the organization means more than establishing a direction toward the ego ideal. It involves establishing certain definite others, with their own way of looking at the world and at themselves and with their own history of actions, as already ideal. It involves, in other words, acquiescing to the perfection of some specific others as one's own moral obligation, collectively enforceable by all others who have done so and with whom one defines oneself as ideally in community. It legitimizes the coercion by the powerful that causes the less powerful to act out a drama whose theme is the perfection of the powerful. And it does so in such a way that the powerful can feel self-righteous about this coercion—as if they were performing a service or committing a sacrifice.

Totalitarianism and Ontological Differentiation

The human consequences of ontological differentiation can be explored in any of a number of ways. One way is through consideration of the ways in which people's defenses work. It has become a commonplace of cognitive psychology that persons see the world in ways that are systematically biased. Weiner et al. (1971), for example, note a self-enhancing bias that consists of seeing oneself responsible for positive outcomes and others responsible for negative outcomes. The self-enhancement that this bias promotes is the attributional correlate of narcissism.

    245

Now, consider the vicissitudes of this bias in the structure I have described. Here, because the head of the organization serves as the specification of the organization ideal and hence as the definer of reality, we may expect that the reality so defined will have the leader's self-enhancing bias built into it. In terms of maintaining the stability of the organization ideal, this is necessary, but consider the consequences for the subordinate. The subordinate has to see the world in a way that enhances not his or her own self-image, but the self-image of the leader.

The self-enhancing bias that operates within the subordinate must be abandoned and overruled in favor of the self-enhancing bias of the leader. But whereas the self-enhancing bias of the leader arises naturally and almost automatically in the mind of the leader, for the subordinate to approximate the leader's self-enhancing bias must be a tortuous, contrived, painful, and self-destructive process. And yet the organization ideal demands just that. It demands, in a word, that in the name of the common good, the individual must not only deny his or her own natural tendencies toward self-enhancement and even self-protection, but morally condemn them. Moreover, informal pressure on the part of other participants and even legitimized formal coercion on the part of authorities may be used to enforce this self-abasement. This, it seems to me, is the source of the slavishness and passivity Shorris, for example, finds so common in totalitarianism.[5]

A related feature of totalitarian life is uncertainty regarding the appropriate. If the definition of the appropriate is based retrospectively on the actions and self-definitions of the leader, the subordinate must be in constant uncertainty as to what actions will correspond to the leader's whims. If the rationale of the leader's whims is not comprehended, the result must be not only uncertainty with regard to appropriate action, but uncertainty over one's own moral worth. This is because one's own perceptions, instincts, and analyses cannot be relied upon as grounds for moral judgment and because actions that turn out later to be deviations from the leader's position are condemnable. This is liable to be all the more so to the extent that the subordinate maintains the organization ideal and therefore cannot blame what he or she sees as inadequacies on the organization, but rather has to accept him- or herself as the source of the blame. The result of this must be a more or less permanent state of shamefulness.

The alternative here is cynicism. Remember that the leader is defined as the ideal, rather than having that capacity in reality. The wisdom of the leader's actions and thoughts are limited in just the same way that the rest of ours are. Accordingly, rationality cannot be used as a guide to action on the part of the subordinate. Rather, the particular irrationality that the leader manifests must be the criterion. But a person's specific irrationality, we may suppose, is an outgrowth of that particular person's personality. Although it may come naturally to him or her, it must seem to others, if they understand it at all, as some sort of systematic quirkiness. Understanding this quirkiness, the subordinate may well be able to anticipate the leader's judgments and use this knowledge as a way of "playing the game." The problem is that this can be achieved only through giving up idealization of the organization ideal while, at the same time, one's self-presentation conforms to it. This is cynicism.

Another feature of totalitarianism is the isolation of people from one another. This isolation is related to a similar dynamic. The organization ideal is held in place not only by the subordinate's own need to do what he or she feels ought to be done, but by sanctions issuing from ideally loved others. This means that deviations from them threaten the meaning structures of others whose love is needed to maintain one's own meaning structure.

There is something not only unnatural but positively impossible about becoming someone else. But this is obligatory. The result is that the person one really is not only is unacceptable to oneself, but is unacceptable in social life, which is in turn composed of persons who are each unacceptable in social life for the same reasons. The result is that social interaction takes place not between persons, but between performances. Roles utter words at other roles. And if at any time any one of them were to say, as each of them somehow knows, "This is a bunch of nonsense," that person would become a pariah because he or she would bring out in all these people the anxiety that motivated the performance in the first place and maintained it at all times. Thus, each of these persons must live in more or less complete isolation and be terribly lonely.

An example may be useful to illustrate some of these processes. Some colleagues were doing consulting work for a corporation that was getting ready to open a new plant in our area. A distinguished professor, call him D, well known for his organizational development work, was to give a presentation to the "design team," made up of middle managers recruited from the rest of the corporation, to help them in designing a compensation system for the new plant. I wangled an invitation.

The presentation turned out to be mostly a summary of D's widely published work, spiced with anecdotes about the utopian bliss in the factories he had "installed." As the day went on, I shifted my interest from D's presentation to the response of the design team. I eavesdropped on their informal conversations and watched their body language. Particularly suggestive was the way they responded when it appeared that their leader was going to ask them a question. They looked for all the world like unprepared schoolchildren trying to make themselves inconspicuous so the teacher would not notice them.

It became increasingly clear to me that this was the first time the members of the design team had ever been exposed to systematic thinking about compensation systems. Aside from various idiosyncratic attitudes toward certain aspects of what D was saying, none of them had any thoughts on the matter at all. Moreover, they appeared to know that they were in over their heads. Behind a certain bluster in their facade, I thought I could detect shamefulness and panic. Evidently, this state was not a unique response to this particular subject. A colleague who had been sitting in on the meetings where they "designed" other "behavioral systems" reported that, despite tremendous time investment, very little headway was ever made. From my colleague's account, it appeared that the meetings were consumed by attempts to assign blame for their lack of progress.

These team members had apparently been recruited into what they thought was a fast-track position in a new direction the corporation was taking. Elements of the corporate personnel and training staffs, led by a guru who was officially a "consultant," had managed to persuade the corporate hierarchy to give them wide-ranging control over the design of the new plant, which would employ a new culture, based upon a team concept. So, naturally, a team was recruited to do the design work, with the guru acting as "facilitator." Something magical was supposed to happen when a number of people got together in a room. Each was supposed to contribute him- or herself, and the synergism of their cooperation would add up to a whole that was greater than the parts.

As it turned out, it was not themselves that they were contributing at all. What they had to do, instead, once they were committed, was to figure out what the guru thought the selves were that they were supposed to be, perform those selves, and hope for the best. Their future was out of their own hands and in the hands of the guru. The best the group could do (the hidden agenda, really) was simply to take D's package and adopt it. But they would not be able to admit that they were doing this, because they were supposed to be the "design team" and to fit D's "recommendations" into their own conceptual framework. For the same reason, they couldn't even admit that the "facilitator" was in fact running the show. For the show that the guru was running was one in which they were autonomous, self-determining agents.

The point is that it was the guru's fantasy that was being enacted here. We can imagine that he saw himself as the shepherd loved by his flock, the Lone Ranger who makes factories and travels on, the Taoist sage who moves others without moving himself, perhaps even the revolutionary in the pin-striped suit.

There is no place in any of these for the design team members as the persons that they were. Their function was to be absorbed into the guru's fantasy. Even the promise of the fast track, by which they were enticed, must have been felt as shameful in the fantasy they undertook to enact. No self-serving fantasy can fit into an organization designed around somebody else's narcissism. To be sure, one could come back and say that no narcissistic fantasy has a place in an organization—even the guru's. But that would be naive. For what we mean when we conceive of a perfect organization is an organization ideal; and an organization ideal is a narcissistic fantasy. The only question is who ultimately gets to be the narcissist.

In this case none of them got to be the narcissist. Not even the guru. The company did not build the plant. All of the design team members were laid off. I don't know where the guru is. He is probably pursuing his dream someplace else. And he has another line in his résumé.

Finally, perhaps the most poignant loss suffered by participants in organizations of this sort is the loss of the sense of worth and human connectedness that could otherwise come from work. For organizations of this sort do not exist to do useful work. They do work in order to exist. And because their existence is the fiction of their organizational ideal, we may say that everything that goes on within them finds its meaning in connection with maintaining this fiction.

One of my students invited me after class one night to have a drink. One drink turned to many, and I soon was involved in a very sad story of the mortification of a soul that bore upon many of the points I have described here. He was employed by a large corporation in a unit whose function had almost ceased to exist. Yet his supervisor spent all his time trying to expand his empire by hiring more people. What my student did all day, when he did anything at all, was to play up to the vanity of his supervisor and tell him and others how important the supervisor and the department were. He had to do this because he hated it there and wanted a transfer, which required the blessing of the supervisor. The heart of the dilemma turned out to be that the more he was successful at building up the supervisor's image, the more the supervisor refused to permit him to transfer, because the department was, according to the drama, already short on personnel. I asked him why he hated this so much, what he would do if he could do whatever he wanted to at work. He said: "I'm an engineer. All I want to do is build cars."

Concluding Reflection

This last observation, that totalitarianism may deprive organizational participants of the opportunity to do useful work, suggests that there is a practical dimension to this issue. It appears that, in the totalitarian organization, productive work comes to be less important than the maintenance of narcissistic fantasy. This cannot help but have an impact on the productivity of the entire enterprise. For totalitarianism represents a turning away from reality. And organizations need to deal with real environments, even if this means only that they need to deal with narcissism projects that are not represented by the organization's own organization ideal. Such turning away from reality must have serious consequences for the organization's effectiveness.

249

NOTES

Acknowledgment: Thanks to the Southern Management Association and the *Journal of Management* for permission to reprint this article, which appeared in 13:1 (1987): 41–54. This article also appeared in Schwarz's book *Narcissistic Process and Corporate Decay: The Theory of the Organization Ideal* (N.Y.: New York University Press, 1990).

1. Putting the matter more precisely, I might say that psychological involvement in the organization is a result of taking it as an ego ideal and that commitment is the case in which the organization is the individual's *exclusive* ego ideal. Since I am concerned to discuss the psychology and consequences of taking the organization as the ego ideal, it seems appropriate to concentrate on the "ideal case" of commitment. Nonetheless, much of what will be said here applies to cases of less exclusive psychological involvement as well. Some of the totalitarian processes described in this chapter serve strongly to strengthen the importance of the organization as ego ideal by rendering other involvements untenable.

2. I have elsewhere (1983) developed a psychodynamic interpretation of Maslow's hierarchy.

3. Note the connection between this depth dimension and Schein's (1980) concept of organizational centrality.

4. For a further discussion of the psychodynamics of hierarchy, see Schwartz (1987).

5. What has been said with regard to cognitive bias could have been said as well in terms of the theory of retrospective sense-making (Weick, 1969). Here a distinction would be noted between the leader, whose retrospective justifications would be taken as valid, and followers, who would have to adapt to the retrospective sense of the leader while being subject to having the sense of their own actions determined for them by the leader. Alternatively,

the differentiation could have been drawn in terms of Argyris and Schön's (1974) distinction between espoused theories and theories-in-use. In this case, the espoused theories of the leader would have to be taken by followers as being the leader's theory-in-use, while the followers' theory-in-use would always be available to be held up by the leader as differing from the acceptable espoused theories—espoused theories that, as has been noted, must be publicly declared as guiding the behavior of the leader.

REFERENCES

Arendt, H. 1966. *The Origins of Totalitarianism.* New York: Harcourt, Brace and World.

Argyris, C. 1957. *Personality and Organization: The Conflict between the System and the Individual.* New York: Harper and Row.

Argyris, C., and D. A. Schön. 1974. *Theory in Practice.* San Francisco: Jossey-Bass.

Becker, E. 1971. *The Birth and Death of Meaning.* 2d ed. New York: Free Press.

———. 1973. *The Denial of Death.* New York: Free Press.

Denhardt, R. D. 1981. *In the Shadow of Organization.* Lawrence: Regents Press of Kansas.

Diamond, M. 1984. "Bureaucracy as Externalized Self-System: A View from the Psychological Interior." *Adminstration and Society*, 16(2), 195–214.

Freud, S. 1955. *Group Psychology and the Analysis of the Ego.* The Standard Edition of the Complete Psychological Works of Sigmund Freud, volume 18. London: Hogarth Press.

———. 1957. *On Narcissism: An Introduction.* The Standard Edition of the Complete Psychological Works of Sigmund Freud, Volume 14. London: Hogarth Press.

———. 1961. *Civilization and Its Discontents.* The Standard Edition of the Complete Psychological Works of Sigmund Freud, Volume 21. London: Hogarth Press.

Goffman, E. 1959. *The Presentation of Self in Everyday Life.* New York: Doubleday, Anchor.

Horney, K. 1950. *Neurosis and Human Growth.* New York: W. W. Norton.

Klein, M. 1975. "A Contribution to the Psychogenesis of Manic-Depressive States." In *Love, Guilt, and Reparation, and Other Works, 1921-1945.* London: Hogarth Press.

Levinson, D. J. 1978. *The Seasons of a Man's Life.* New York: Knopf.

Maslow, A. H. 1970. *Motivation and Personality.* 2d ed. New York: Harper and Row.

Mead, G. H. 1934. *Mind, Self, and Society.* Chicago: University of Chicago Press.

Parsons, T. 1954. "An Analytical Approach to the Theory of Social Stratification." In *Essays in Sociological Theory*, rev. ed. New York: Free Press.

Schein, E. H. 1980. *Organizational Psychology.* 3d ed. Englewood Cliffs, N.J.: Prentice-Hall.

Schwartz, H. S. 1982. "Job Involvement as Obsession Compulsion." *Academy of Management Review*, 7(3), 429–432.

———. 1983. "Maslow and the Hierarchical Enactment of Organizational Reality." *Human Relations*, 36(10), 933–956.

———. 1985. "The Usefulness of Myth and the Myth of Usefulness: A Dilemma for the Applied Organizational Scientist." *Journal of Management*, 11(1), 31–42.

———. 1987. "Rousseau's Discourse on Inequality Revisited: Psychology of Work at the Public Esteem Stage of Maslow's Hierarchy." *International Journal of Management*, 4(2), 180–193.

Shorris, E. 1981. *The Oppressed Middle: Politics of Middle Management/Scenes from Corporate Life.* Garden City, N.Y.: Doubleday, Anchor.

Terkel, S. 1974. *Working.* New York: Pantheon.

Weick, K. E. 1969. *The Social Psychology of Organizing.* Reading, Mass.: Addison-Wesley.

Weiner, B., I. Frieze, A. Kulka, L. Reed, S. Rest, and R. M. Rosenbaum. 1971. *Perceiving the Causes of Success and Failure.* Morristown, N.J.: General Learning Press.

About the Contributors and Index

ABOUT THE CONTRIBUTORS

Carole K. Barnett is an organizational studies Ph.D. candidate in the University of Michigan's Organizational Psychology Program.

Howell S. Baum teaches organizational behavior, planning, theory, and social planning at the University of Maryland's Institute for Urban Studies. He is a founding member of the International Society for the Psychoanalytic Study of Organizations (ISPSO).

Michael A. Diamond is professor of public administration and chair in the College of Business and Public Administration at the University of Missouri, Columbia. He is a founding member and the current president of the International Society for the Psychoanalytic Study of Organizations (ISPSO).

Steven P. Feldman is an associate professor of management at the Weatherhead School of Management at Case Western Reserve University. He received his Ph.D. in social systems sciences from the Wharton School of Business, University of Pennsylvania, in 1983.

Thomas N. Gilmore is a vice-president of the Center for Applied Research, a private consulting firm in Philadelphia, and adjunct associate professor of health care management at the Wharton School, University of Pennsylvania. He is a founding member of the International Society for the Psychoanalytic Study of Organizations (ISPSO). He is a faculty member in the Program in Organizational Consultation and Development at the William Alanson White Institute.

Laurence J. Gould is professor of psychology and director of the Psychological Center in the clinical psychology doctoral program at the City University of New York. He is a founding member of the International Society for the Psychoanalytic Study of Organizations (ISPSO), a principal in the firm of Gould Krantz White, Inc., a practicing psychoanalyst, and the director of the Program in Organizational Consultation and Development at the William Alanson White Institute.

Larry Hirschhorn is a principal with the Center for Applied Research, a private consulting firm in Philadelphia. He is a founding member of the International Society for the Psychoanalytic Study of Organizations (ISPSO) and is on the faculty of the Program in Organizational Consultation and Development at the William Alanson White Institute.

Manfred F. R. Kets de Vries is the Raoul de Vitry d'Avaucourt Chair of Human Resource Management at the European Institute of Business Administration (INSEAD) in Fountainebleau, France. He has been certified by the Canadian Psychoanalytic Society as a practicing psychoanalyst and is a founding member of the International Society for the Psychoanalytic Study of Organizations (ISPSO).

James Krantz is a principal in Gould Krantz White, Inc., an organizational consultation firm in New York. He taught organizational behavior at the School of Organization and Management at Yale University. He is a founding member of the International Society for the Psychoanalytic Study of Organizations (ISPSO) and is a faculty member in the Program in Organizational Consultation and Development at the William Alanson White Institute.

Laurent Lapierre is professor of management and leadership at the Ecole des Hautes Etudes Commerciales de Montreal. He is a founding member of the International Society for the Psychoanalytic Study of Organizations (ISPSO) and currently serves on the Steering Committee.

Howard S. Schwartz is associate professor of organizational behavior at Oakland University, Rochester, Michigan. He is a founding member of the International Society for the Psychoanalytic Study of Organizations (ISPSO).

Glenn Swogger, Jr., M.D., is senior psychiatric consultant and director of consultation services at the Menninger Management Institute. He is also the chairman of Kaw Valley State Bank, Topeka, Kansas.

David A. Thomas is associate professor of organizational behavior at the Harvard Business School. He is a member of the Academy of Management and the National Training Laboratories.

Eric L. Trist is a founding member and past chairman of the Tavistock Institute of Human Relations. He is emeritus professor in the Social Systems Sciences Department, the Wharton School, University of Pennsylvania.

Donald R. Young is a human resource professional in the petroleum industry and has developed programs in support of employee health and well-being, including organizational consultation, substance abuse, and a wide range of employee assistance plans. He was a founding member of the Marriage and Family Consultation Center in Houston, Texas, and has practiced marriage and family therapy at the Menninger Institute and at the University of Pennsylvania.

255

Abraham Zaleznik is the Konowsuke Matsushita Emeritus Professor of Leadership at Harvard University's Graduate School of Business Administration. He is certified by the American Psychoanalytic Association as a clinical psychoanalyst.

INDEX

263